Rapid WordPress Websites

A visual step-by-step guide to building Wordpress websites fast!

Dr. Andy Williams

http://ezseonews.com

Released 2nd May 2014

"I work in the education department at one of the top academic institutions in the U.S. and if I could hire Dr. Williams to write all of my online training, I wouldn't hesitate." *Laura*

appearance → Theme options -
home page
Featured Content

Contents

What people are saying about this book:

"Complete, quick, and to the point. Just what most people need. Good information. No filler. Great price. A well thought out book by Dr. Andy Williams" **Zoie Brytin**

"This guide or more accurately a manual is an excellent training guide by a teacher that I have been learning from for many years. It is well written and laid out and will help you learn Wordpress without stress. Highly recommended." **Dale Reardon**

"By following the steps in the book, you'll easily have your wordpress site up & running in no time and, as Andy knows his stuff, you can be confident it will be set up well." **SBUK**

"Great content from a great author! Highly recommended!" **David H**

"I have read articles which say just set up a wordpress blog and I haven't the faintest idea but this book is very simply and carefully written so no steps are left out. Andy is an expert who seems to be able to explain things in a way which helps the non-expert. A rare talent. It gave me confidence to have a go." **Chris Wade**

"I think everyone thinking of building a wordpress website should read this guide first. I've been using wordpress for several years and I am amazed at how much I didn't know about wordpress. The guide takes you through the whole process of getting web hosting, buying a domain name, designing your website to help with Seach Engine Optimisation and everyting else you need to know about posts versus pages, widgets,plugins and lots more.Dr Andy has a very pleasant writing style which concentrates on what to do and why to do it, without making lots of unnecessary remarks just to fill out a few more pages. And the bonus is that readers get access to his website which he built alongside writing the book and he plans to provide a lot more relevant information there in the future." **John D Bridson**

"The step by step approach is excellent and the added bonus of the rapidwpsites website is incredibly useful not only for those building their first WP website but also for people like me who want to learn more." **Carole**

"Doing anything for the first time can be daunting. Putting up your first WordPress site is no different - especially for the software challenged. Luckily this book offers an easy-to-follow step-by-step process covering all that is needed to overcome any lack of previous experience. With this guide in hand, a new site can realistically be in place in a matter of hours." **John Gergye**

"With this product, it was as if he read my mind (or was watching over my shoulder). " Alan **Northcott**

“The first thing I want to say about "Rapid Wordpress Websites" is that you should download it immediately because you need look no further for information about building your first Wordpress website.” **Norman Morrison**

“Dr. Andy walks you through the Wordpress setup process, step by step. He explains the why's of the steps you are taking, what to do, how to do it, and why you should do it. "Rapid Wordpress Websites" is a great instructional refresher guide for even the Pro.” **E. W. Aldridge, Sr**

“Anyone who gets this book and follows the steps will be able to have their own website up and running in no time. I hadn't installed a WP blog in years and had forgotten how to do it. Dr. Andy's book made the process simple and painless.” **J. Tanner**

“I have been struggling with my Wordpress Website - not anymore. This is a must read for beginners and I bet even some long time user will find information in Andy's book. I now realize how little I knew about Wordpress, the great thing about this book is it walks you by the hand to get your site going and getting down to business. This is one of those books that you will refer to time and time again. So keep it handy!” **Suzanne Dean**

DISCLAIMER AND TERMS OF USE AGREEMENT

The author and publisher of this eBook and the accompanying materials have used their best efforts in preparing this eBook. The author and publisher make no representation or warranties with respect to the accuracy, applicability, fitness, or completeness of the contents of this eBook. The information contained in this eBook is strictly for educational purposes. Therefore, if you wish to apply ideas contained in this eBook, you are taking full responsibility for your actions.

The author and publisher disclaim any warranties (express or implied), merchantability, or fitness for any particular purpose. The author and publisher shall in no event be held liable to any party for any direct, indirect, punitive, special, incidental or other consequential damages arising directly or indirectly from any use of this material, which is provided "as is", and without warranties.

The author and publisher do not warrant the performance, effectiveness or applicability of any sites listed or linked to in this eBook.

All links are for information purposes only and are not warranted for content, accuracy or any other implied or explicit purpose.

The author and publisher of this book are not in any way associated with Google.

Introduction

Firstly, thank you for buying my book. I hope it's exactly what you've been looking for, and that in a few short hours, you'll sitting in front of your computer looking at your very own website!

The aim of this book is to teach anybody (yes anybody, even complete non-techie beginners) to create a website by working through the book, chapter by chapter.

I have written other books on Wordpress, but this one is special. The emphasis is on teaching you on a need-to-know basis, and not trying to cover everything that Wordpress can do (my Wordpress for Beginners book does that (B009ZVO3H6), and is over 300 pages in length with almost as many screenshots).

As we work through the book, I will be building a website which you will be able to visit and refer to. This website will be a real site, that I created just for this book, but will also contain really useful information for all students of Wordpress. There will be tutorials, articles on plugins and themes and much more. Think of it not only as an example website, but as an extension of this book and a resource for learning more about this fabulous tool.

The Demo Website

You can find the website that I build in this book at:

http://rapidwpsites.com

Wordpress.com v Wordpress.org

The first thing that confuses many Wordpress students is that there are actually two types of Wordpress. These are found on two separate websites.

If you visit Wordpress.com, you can sign up to create a Wordpress site for free. Wordpress.com hosts your site on their servers, meaning you do not need to buy a domain, or hosting. The version of Wordpress you get there is more limited, as Wordpress.com control what you can and cannot do on your own site. For example, you won't be able to customize Wordpress in the way you want, because you cannot just install any theme or plugin you want. You also won't be using your own domain name. Your website address will be something like:

myhealthsite.wordpress.com

Another downside is that you do not own the domain and Wordpress.com could theoretically close your site down if they think you are abusing their terms of service.

Wordpress.org, on the other hand, is a site where you can download the Wordpress software for yourself, to install on a server of your choice, and customize it however you wish. This allows you to create a website that you own, and you can do whatever you want on it. You also get to choose your own domain name, like:

myhealthsite.com

Doesn't that look better? Be aware though that domain names are on a strictly first come, first served basis. You obviously cannot choose a domain name that someone else already owns.

In this book, we are using the Wordpress from Wordpress.org, buying a domain name, and building the site on our own web host.

Let's get started...

Domains, Registrars & Hosting

Your domain name is important to you. It will be your website address where you can send your friends & family to view your site. It is the website address that Google and other search engines will send people to. Therefore choosing a domain name is really important, and you want to get it right the first time, since you cannot get a refund on a purchased domain name if you find you made a spelling mistake, or changed your mind about the name.

Two types of domain name

There are two main types of domain name. The first category, which I suggest you avoid, is often referred to as "Exact Match Domain", or EMD for short.

An EMD is a domain name that exactly matches a phrase you want to rank for in Google. For example, if you decide you wanted to be #1 in Google when anyone searched for "Healthy Coconut Oil", then and EMD would be something like:

- Healthycoconutoil.com
- Healthy-coconut-oil.com
- Healthcocounutoil.org

See how the exact phrase makes up the domain name?

This used to work really well in Google, and in the past we could easily rank sites for phrases by choosing an EMD for the phrase we were interested in. However, in the last couple of years, things have changed, and EMDs can actually cause you problems, including getting your site penalized in Google, or even banned if you are not careful.

I therefore suggest you choose my second category of domain name - a brandable name.

This type of domain name is one that is memorable and could be used as branding. Think of Google itself. This is a brand name we all recognize, but what would have happened if they had chosen "best search engine" as an EMD? Bestsearchengine.com does not have the same ring to it, does it?

I recommend you sit down and think about your domain name carefully. Avoid choosing a name simply because it contains a phrase you want to rank for. Instead think of a memorable name. Imagine being out and about and you see a friend. You want to send them over to look at your new web site, but you don't have a pencil to write the name down. The domain you choose should be memorable enough that your friend can remember it once you tell them.

TLDs

TLD stands for Top Level Domain, and simply refers to the extension given to your domain. Possible TLDs include .com, .org, .net, .co.uk, .de etc. There are new TLDs coming out on a regular basis, and it can all be confusing for beginners.

Some TLDs are country specific, e.g. .co.uk is used for websites targeting the UK.

My advice on choosing which TLD to use is simple.

If you only want to target one country with your site, choose the TLD for that country:

.es for Spain

.co.uk for the UK

.de for Germany

If on the other hand, your site has global appeal, choose a .com.

How much is it all going to cost?

Since we need to buy a domain and hosting, you may already be wondering how much this is going to cost. Let me break it down for you:

You need to buy a domain name which will cost around $9.99 per year. You buy domain names from "domain registrars" (see below).

You need to get web hosting, and that costs from around $3.99 per month. You buy web hosting from a "web host" (see below).

These are your only required costs, though obviously you can decide to buy a premium Wordpress theme, and maybe some commercial plugins. However, these are not required, and you can build a great looking, feature-packed site without any additional costs.

So, overall then, your total cost for a self-hosted website will be around $58 per year. That's not bad, especially if you are making money with your website.

What is a Domain Registrar?

A domain registrar is a company that you buy your domain name from. Good registrars will make sure your domain auto-renews at the end of the year, can keep your site "anonymous", lock your domain so it cannot be transferred to another individual without your approval, and a lot of other administrative stuff.

What is a Web host?

A web host is a company that will rent you some computer space to host your website. Web hosts are responsible for making sure your site is up and running 24/7, and loading as fast as possible so your website visitors do not need to wait around for your site to load. All websites can go down at times (as I am sure you have seen), but good web hosts will have your website up and running 99.9% of the time.

All-in-one registrar and web host?

Most web hosts will also offer to be your domain registrar. In other words, they look after everything for you. The advantage of this is that everything is in one place, and you are only dealing with one company.

The disadvantage of this is that if you have problems with your site, e.g. it seems to be down a lot, or very slow loading, and you want to find a different web host to move your site to, it can take a week or more to move the site. It can take a lot longer if the web host wants to make the move more "difficult" for you, and I have heard a lot of horror stories.

The thing about web hosts is that they might be great today, but suck tomorrow. I have seen a number of great hosts go downhill quickly. Being able to move your site quickly is vital to keep your site up and running and your visitors happy.

I therefore recommend you do not use your web host as registrar.

Before you start thinking that a separate registrar and host is more complicated, it really isn't.

I will show you how to painlessly and easily set up your domain so that that you are using a separate domain registrar and hosting company. Then, if you ever need to move from one web host to another, the process is very simple, and your site can be moved within hours, with zero downtime.

My Recommended Web Host and Registrar

As you might guess from the information above, I do change my web hosts occasionally. What I recommend today may not be what I recommend in a year's time. Therefore, to make sure you are using the absolute best services that I know of (the ones I personally use), I recommend you visit my page here to check:

http://rapidwpsites.com/hosting

I will keep it updated if there are any changes.

At the time of writing this book, my chosen registrar is Namecheap and my chosen Web host is StableHost. I will show you how to set a site up using those two services.

NOTE: If you visit the page above and find that my chosen host has changed (it is unlikely my chosen registrar will change), I will include a full tutorial on that page showing you how to set this all up.

OK; visit this page:

http://rapidwpsites.com/hosting

Click on the link for my recommended Registrar and sign up for a free account. Once you have that account set up, come back here and we will continue.

Buying the domain at the registrar

Over at the registrar (Namecheap), we want to buy a new domain.

From the Domains menu at the top, select **Registration**:

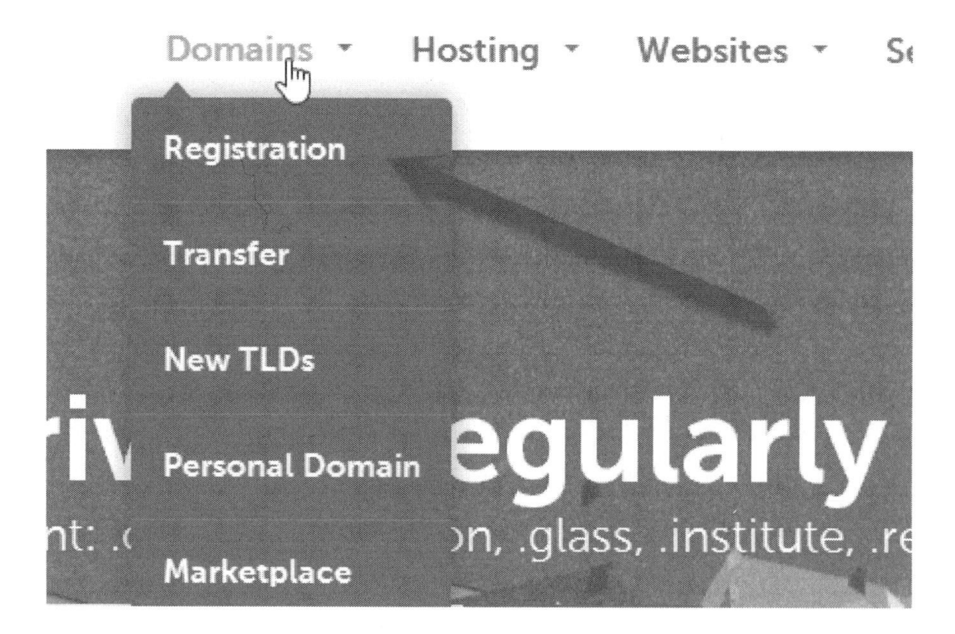

You can then type in your chosen domain name (with TLD) and click the search button to see if it is available.

My chosen domain is available:

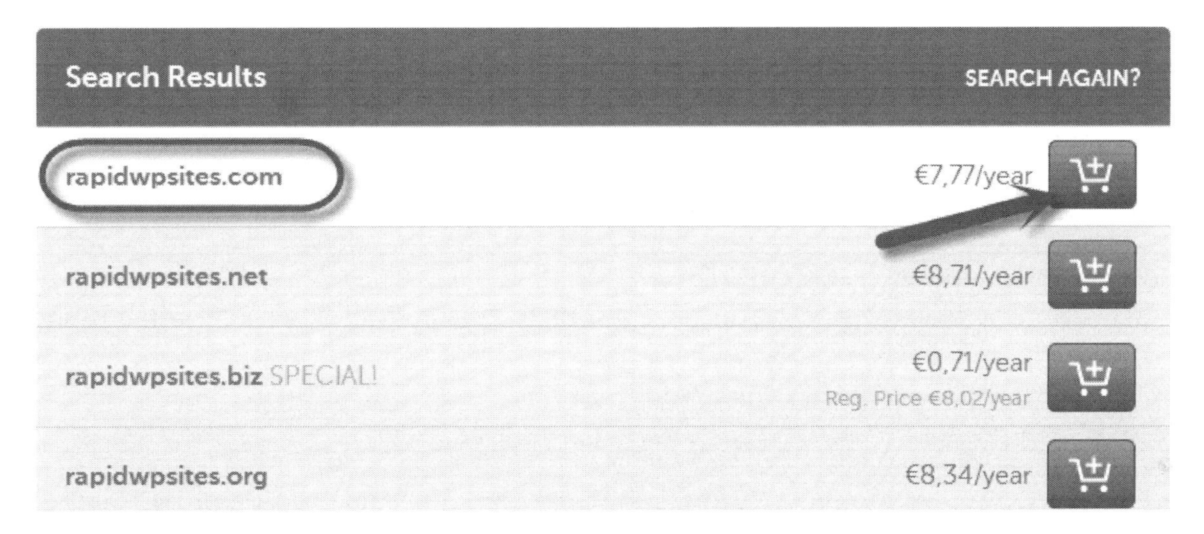

Click the shopping trolley button to buy the domain.

The domain will be added to your cart. View the cart and make sure your domain is correct (check the spelling), and then buy it.

At the checkout, make sure you check the button to **Enable Autorenew** for the domain.

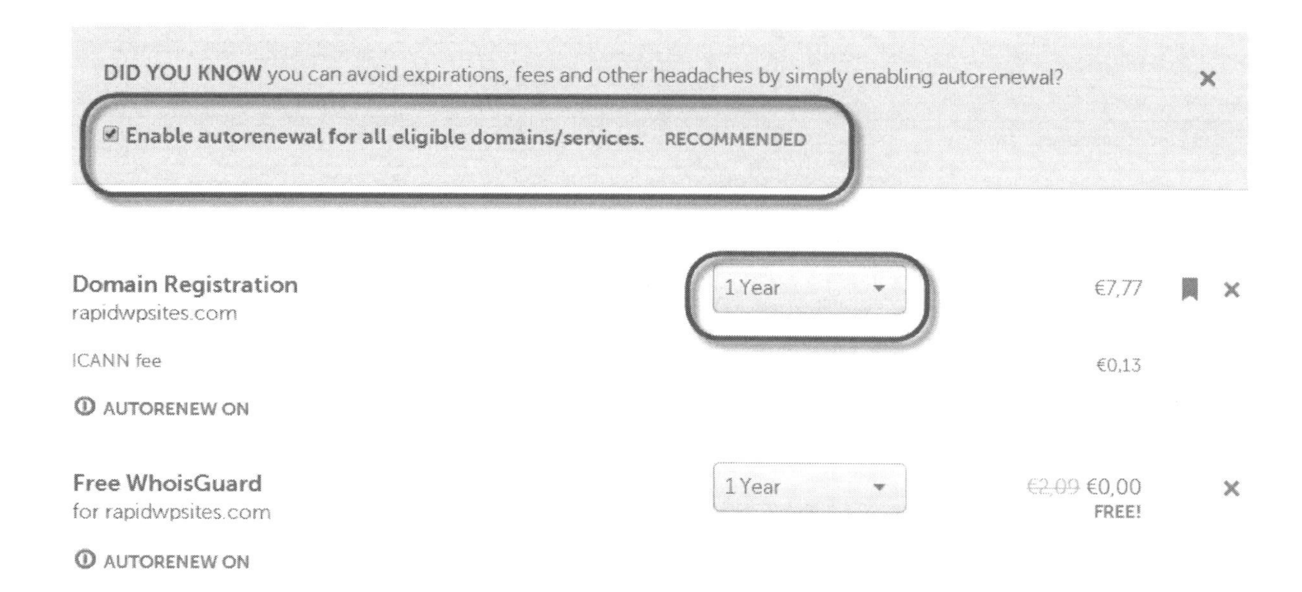

This will ensure that the registrar will automatically renew your domain name each year (until you cancel). Failure to do this will result in your domain being released when the year is up, and someone else will be able to buy it.

When you buy your domain, you can buy it for longer than one year to begin with if you want. As long as you have autorenew enabled, I see no reason to buy for longer than one year.

Also, you may be offered free WhoisGuard. This service is only free for the first year.

WhoisGuard protects your name, address, phone number and other contact details from the Whois.net database. Anyone can search this database online (at http://whois.net) to find contact details for the owner of a website. If you want the privacy, this is a good option to include.

When you are happy with your selection, click the confirm order button to buy your domain.

If you got the WhoisGuard as well, there will be a link asking you to activate it on the domain. Just follow the instructions there.

OK; that's the registrar done. Let's head over to the web hosting company.

Visit this page again, and click through to the recommended web host:

http://rapidwpsites.com/hosting

If my recommendation is still StableHost, check for a discount code I've included on that page which will give you a 40% discount on hosting (I cannot guarantee how long this will be available).

Buying Web hosting

On the web host page, you can sign up for hosting here:

I recommend you just use the Shared Stable Basic hosting to begin with. If your site becomes very popular, or you decide to build other sites, you can always upgrade to a more comprehensive plan when you need to.

Web hosts often give incentives for paying for hosting up front. For example, if you only want to pay for 6 months, it might cost you $3.95 per month. However if you pay for 24 months up front, it'll only cost you $3.62 per month.

Buy hosting for whatever period you are comfortable with. If a discount code was available on my web page, use that for a 40% discount on your first payment. This discount code should be an incentive to buy for a longer period, since you only save the 40% on what you are paying when you order right now. You won't get the discount when the payment is up for renewal.

Once you click on the order button, you'll be taken to this screen:

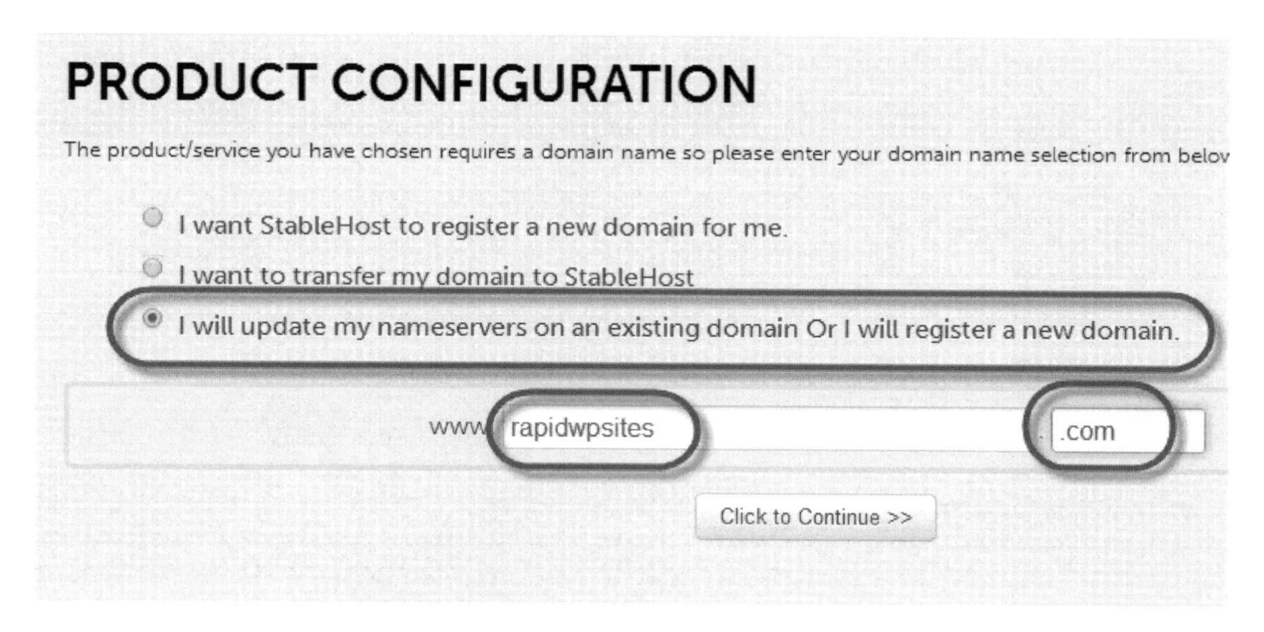

Make sure you check the third option. We have our domain on Namecheap and will be updating the nameservers for that domain.

In the boxes below, enter your domain name (the one you bought at Namecheap) and TLD. This will be only used to set up your web space on the web host. You will NOT have to pay again for the domain, as you already own it on Namecheap.

On the next screen, select the billing cycle you want, remembering those prices are per month:

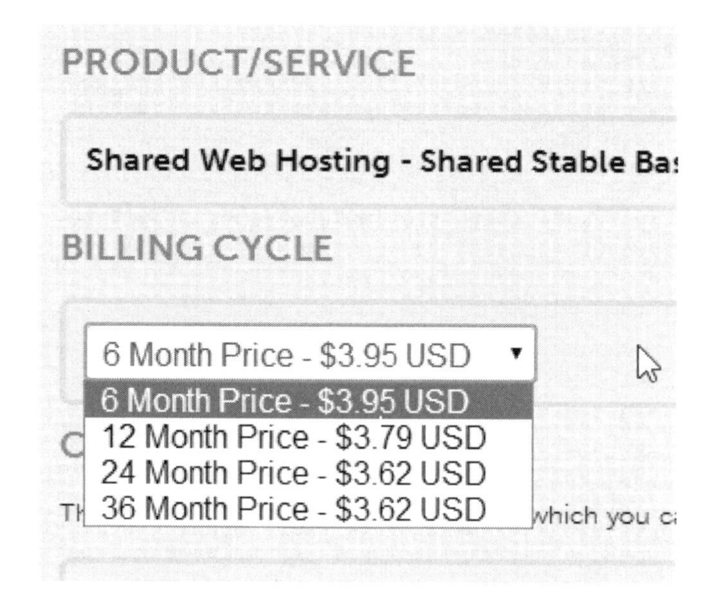

For "hosting location":

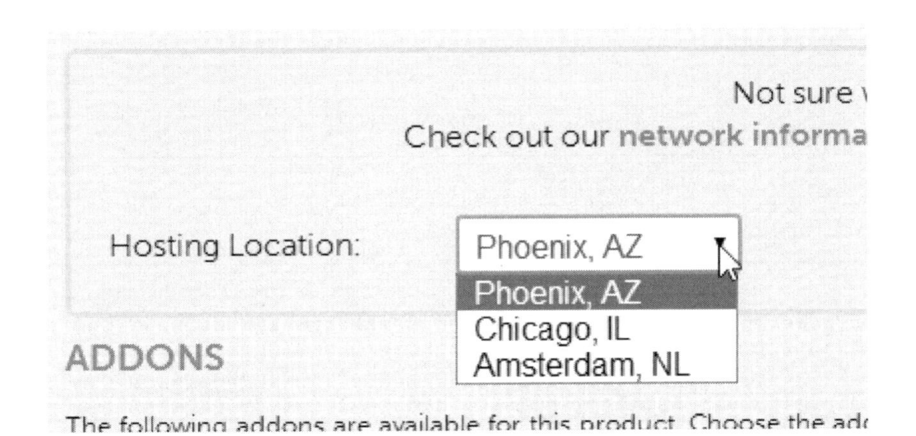

If you are based in Europe, and so is most of your target audience, you might want to choose Amsterdam. This will make the site faster for those people visiting from Europe. If your target audience is the US (or global audience), you should choose either Chicago or Phoenix.

There is a link on this screen where you can see network information for these servers:

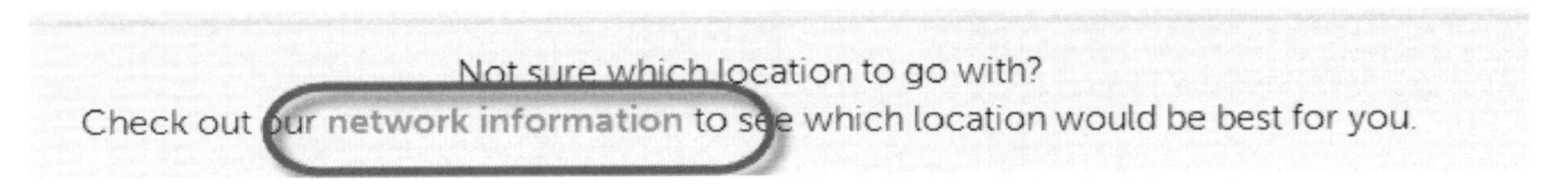

Not sure which location to go with?
Check out our network information to see which location would be best for you.

Click that link and run the speed tests to see which one is faster for you. Then choose the fastest.

At the bottom of the screen, you'll see a checkbox for SSH Access. You do not need this.

Click the Add to Cart button.

You will now be taken to the order summary page, and the opportunity to enter that promotional code from my web page (if available):

ORDER SUMMARY

Description	Price
Shared Web Hosting - **Shared Stable Basic** (rapidwpsites.com) » Hosting Location: Phoenix, AZ [Edit Configuration] [Remove]	$130.35 USD
Subtotal:	$130.35 USD
40% One Time Discount:	$52.14 USD
Total Due Today:	$78.21 USD
Total Recurring:	$130.35 USD Triennially

Promotional Code ezseonews - 40% One Time Discount
Don't use Promotional Code

Empty Cart | Continue Shopping | Checkout

The above screenshot shows that the promotional code would save me over $52 on this hosting package.

Instead of costing $130.35, it's just $78.21!

Go through to the checkout and pay for your hosting.

It may take a few hours for your hosting to be set up. Once it is, the host will email you will login details for your cPanel (which you'll need for setting up Wordpress). You will also have login details for your "Client Login", and it's in there you can get support if you need it.

The other thing you'll get in your welcome email is the Server information. This is what you are looking for:

Server Information
Server Name: en01.stablehost.com
If you are using an existing domain with your new hosting a
below.
Nameserver 1: ns1.stablehost.com (199.192.218.10)
Nameserver 2: ns2.stablehost.com (199.192.219.10)

There are two Nameservers. If you are using the same host as me, they'll be the same as in the screenshot above.

We will need these in the next step.

Connecting the Registrar and host

Login to your registrar (Namecheap).

From the menu at the top left (where you username is).

.. select **Manage Domains.**

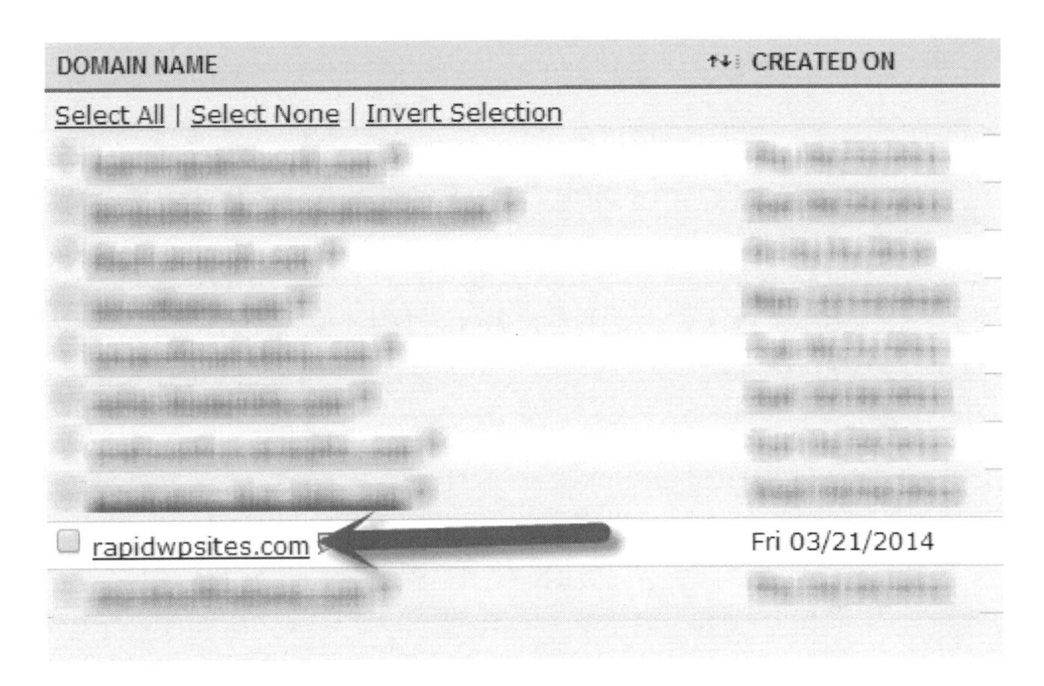

You will see your domain listed. Click on it.

Now in the menu on the left:

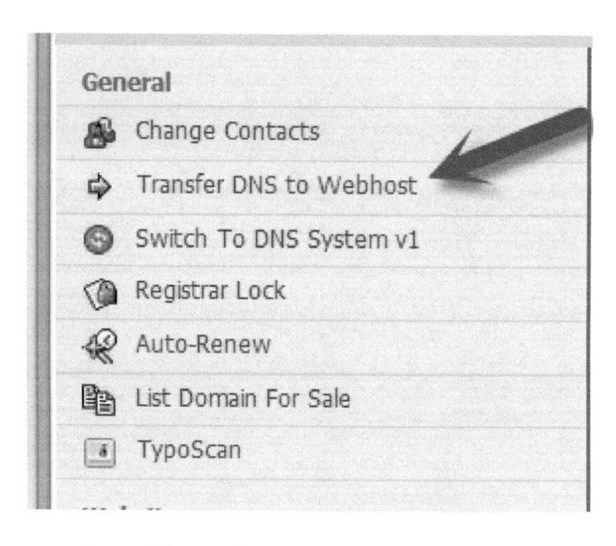

.. select **Transfer DNS to Webhost.**

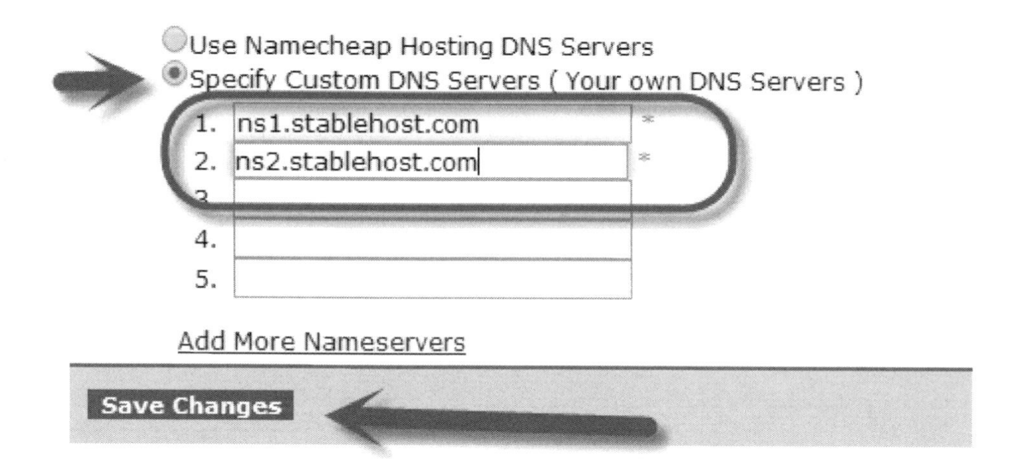

Make sure the **Specify Custom DNS Servers** is checked, and then enter the two nameservers (that we located in the previous section) in boxes 1 & 2. Finally click the **Save Changes** button.

That's it. The registrar and the web host will now work together. Not that difficult, was it?

Now we can go and install Wordpress on the domain.

Installing Wordpress

For this, you need to login to the cPanel of your hosting. The URL, username and password were all in that welcome email the host sent to you.

Once you are logged in, scroll down to the **Software/Services** section, and click on **Softaculous**.

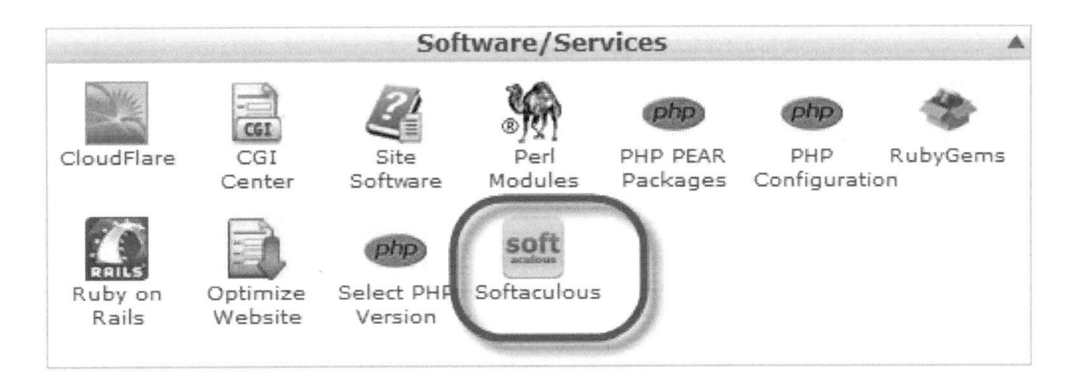

On the next screen, you'll see a box containing the Wordpress logo. Move your mouse over it, and an **Install** button will appear:

Click the **Install** button.

At the top of the next screen, you'll see this:

Software Setup

Choose Protocol
If your site has SSL, then please choose the HTTPS protocol.
http://

Choose Domain
Please choose the domain to install the software.
rapidwpsites.com

In Directory
The directory is relative to your domain and **should not exist**. e.g. To install at http://mydomain/dir/ just type **dir**. To install only in http://mydomain/ leave this empty.

Database Name
Type the name of the database to be created for the installation
wpRWPS

In the "**Choose Domain**" box, select your domain.

In the "**In Directory**" box, delete the pre-filled value, leaving this empty.

Under "**Database Name**", you can leave this as the default value. I personally change it a little, so I know which database in my account belongs to which website, but that is because I have a number of sites in my hosting package.

Next we have these settings:

Database Settings

Table Prefix
wp_

Site Settings

Site Name
Rapid WP Sites

Site Description
urces and help with Wordpress

Enable Multisite (WPMU)
This feature will Enable Multisite option for your WordPress blog.
Your server must support Apache mod_rewrite to use this feature.

You can leave the table prefix as it is. I always change mine, just to make it more difficult for hackers that might be trying to hack my site. wp_ is the default value, and hackers know this. If you want, change it to a different 2 or 3 letters, followed by an underscore.

Enter a name & description for your site. You can change these later, so don't worry too much about it.

Leave Enable Multisite (WPMU) unchecked.

Next we have the Admin account settings:

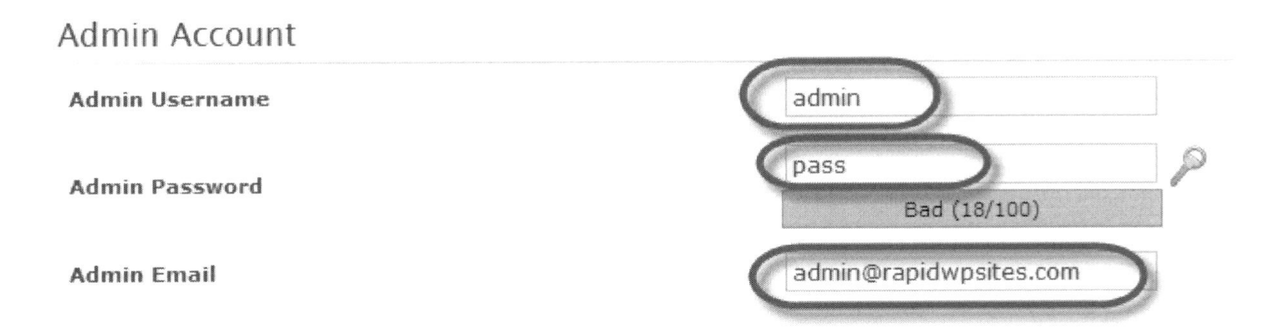

Don't use admin as your username. Again, this is the default and makes it easier for hackers. Change your admin username to something else. Also add a strong password. This username and password combination will be used to login to your Wordpress Dashboard, so make a note of what you enter here. The "Admin email" box will set the admin email in your Wordpress dashboard, and this will be used to notify you of events, like people leaving comments. This can be changed later.

By default, the language will be set to English, but change this if you need to.

Select Plugins

Limit Login Attempts
If selected Limit Login Attempts plugin will be installed and activated with your installation.
Click here to visit plugin site.

Advanced Options

Disable Update Notifications
If checked you will not receive an email notification for updates available for this installation.

Auto Upgrade
If checked, this installation will be automatically upgraded to the latest version when a new version is available.

Automated backups
Softaculous will take automated backups via CRON as per the frequency you select

Once a month

Backup Rotation
If the backup rotation limit is reached Softaculous will delete the oldest backup for this installation and create a new backup. The backups will utilize your space so choose the backup rotation as per the space available on your server

4

Install

Email installation details to :

Check the box next to “**Limit Login Attempts**”. This is another layer of protection against hackers.

Under the “**Advanced Options**”, select “**Once a Month**” for automated backups (or more frequently if you will be adding content on a daily basis).

The “Backup Rotation” is the number of backups the host will keep for you. Once that number of backups has been created, the oldest will be deleted to make room for the new backup. On a monthly backup schedule, 4 is about right. If you are backing up more frequently, choose a larger number of backups.

Finally, enter your email address at the bottom before clicking the install button. You Wordpress login details will be emailed to you at this address when Wordpress is installed.

OK, once the installation has finished, you’ll be shown something like this:

Congratulations, the software was installed successfully

WordPress has been successfully installed at :
http://rapidwpsites.com
Administrative URL : http://rapidwpsites.com/wp-admin/

We hope the installation process was easy.

NOTE: Softaculous is just an automatic software installer and does not prov
visit the software vendor's web site for support!

Regards,

The first link will load your website (currently a skeleton site created by Wordpress). Here is mine:

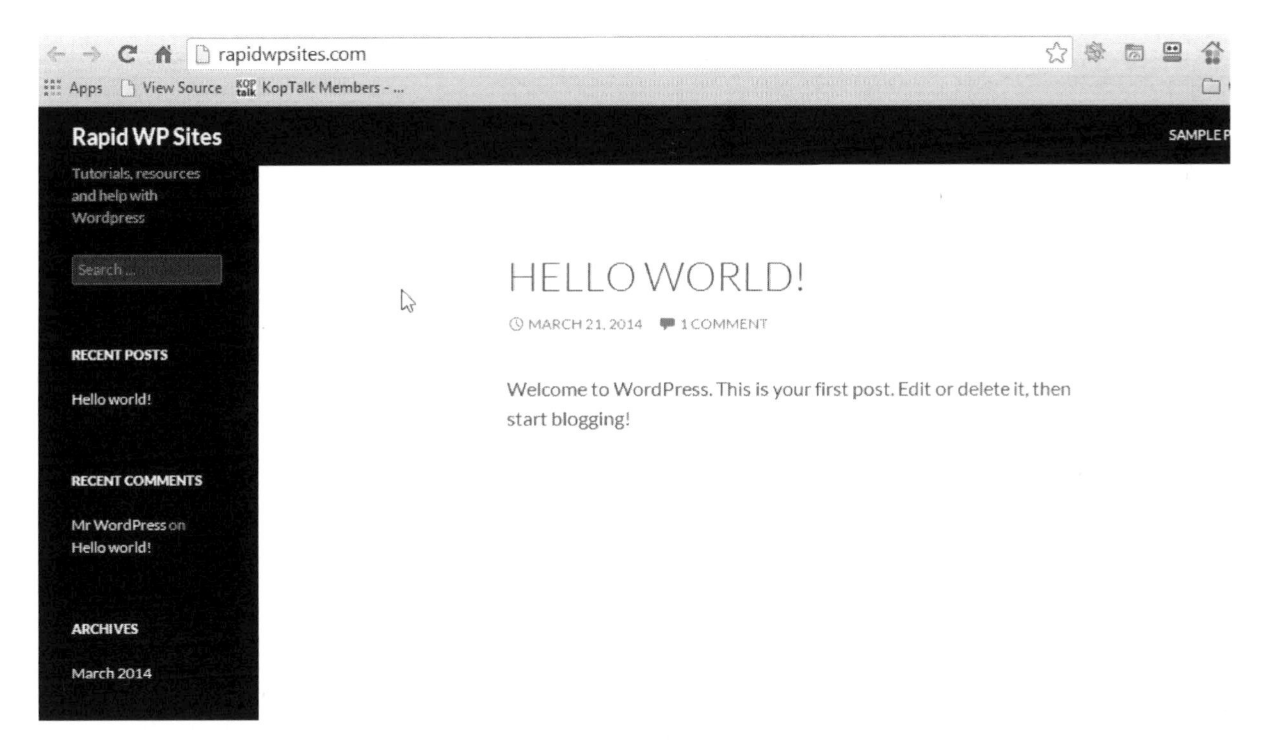

Yours will probably look very similar.

The second URL listed is the Administrative URL. You can click that link to login to the Wordpress Dashboard for your site. The username and password are those that you used when filling in the Admin Details a few minutes ago.

OK, let's login to the Dashboard.

Login and Logout of your Wordpress Dashboard

The Wordpress Dashboard is where you go to add content and customize the look of your site. Think of it as the control center for your website. We will be going in there a lot as we build the RapidWPSites.com website.

You can access the Dashboard login (Administrative URL) by adding **/wp-admin/** to the end of your domain URL. In my case, it's:

http://rapidwpsites.com/wp-admin/

This is what the login page looks like:

Enter your Admin username and Admin password. I recommend you check the **Remember Me** box, so that it remembers your login details next time.

Now click the **Log In** button.

You will be taken inside the dashboard. Here is mine:

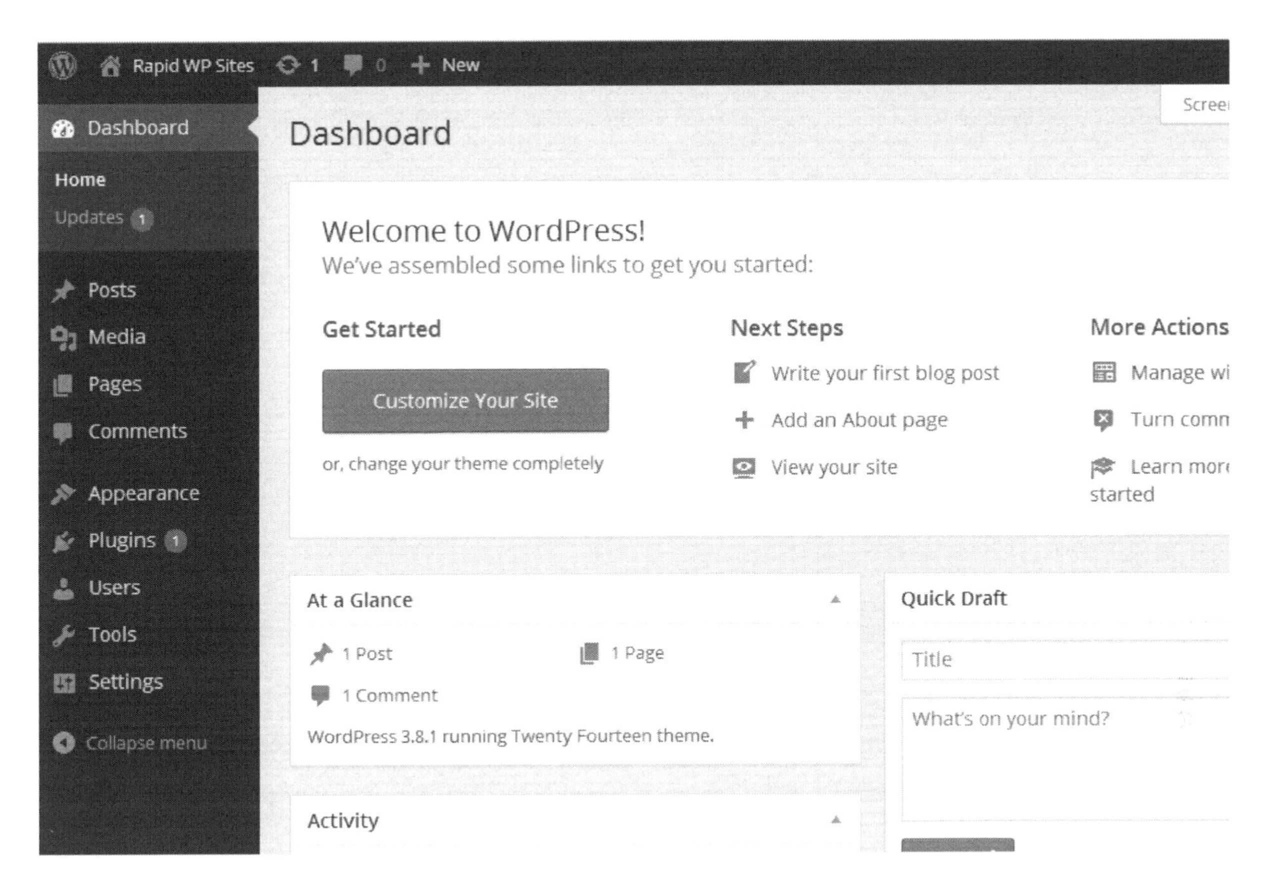

OK, this is where the fun starts.

Looking at the demo page, post and comment

.. and deleting them

When you install Wordpress, you will get some demo content installed by default. This includes:

- A post
- A page
- A comment

OK, so you might be wondering. What is a post, what is a page, and how are they different. Well, we will discuss that later. For now, let's just take a quick look at them, and then we can delete them.

If you visit your site in your web browser, you'll see a "Hello World" post. Under the title, you'll also see a "1" next to COMMENT:

HELLO WORLD!
MARCH 21, 2014
1 COMMENT
EDIT
Welcome to WordPress. This is your first post. Edit or delete it, then start blogging!

A note about the homepage

When you visit your site by typing the domain URL into a browser, you will visit the site's Homepage. This is a special page. By default, Wordpress will show your most recent 10 posts on the homepage (there is only one on your homepage right now, because there is only one post on your site - the "Hello World" post).

The homepage can display the full post(s), or what is called excerpts. What it shows depends on the Wordpress theme you are using and how you set it up. While the latest posts appear on the Homepage, you should also know that they also each appear on their own "post page". If you click the "Hello World!" title shown in the screenshot above, you will be taken to the "post's page". This page only contains the single post, as well as any comments on the post, and a “Leave a Reply” comment box for visitors to leave a comment.

Here is the “Hello World!” post page:

HELLO WORLD!

MARCH 21, 2014 ANDY 1 COMMENT EDIT

Welcome to WordPress. This is your first post. Edit or delete it, then start blogging!

ONE THOUGHT ON "HELLO WORLD!"

Mr WordPress

MARCH 21, 2014 AT 12:36 PM EDIT

Hi, this is a comment.
To delete a comment, just log in and view the post's comments. There you will have the option to edit or delete them.

REPLY

LEAVE A REPLY

Logged in as Andy. Log out?

Comment

We can customize the homepage so that instead of showing the last 10 posts, we display a "static" page (a page that will always look the same and contain the same information). This allows us to create a homepage that gives us a little more creative freedom in guiding our visitors around our site. We'll look at the options for the homepage later, once we have some content on the site.

OK, look at your homepage again.

On the left sidebar, you'll see that "Hello World!" is listed under **Recent Post**.

There is also a section in that sidebar called **Recent Comments**, with one entry:

When Wordpress was installed, it added this "Hello World!" post and the comment (on that post) as a kind of demo for you. It also added a "Page" which is called **Sample Page** and can be seen top right in your web browser:

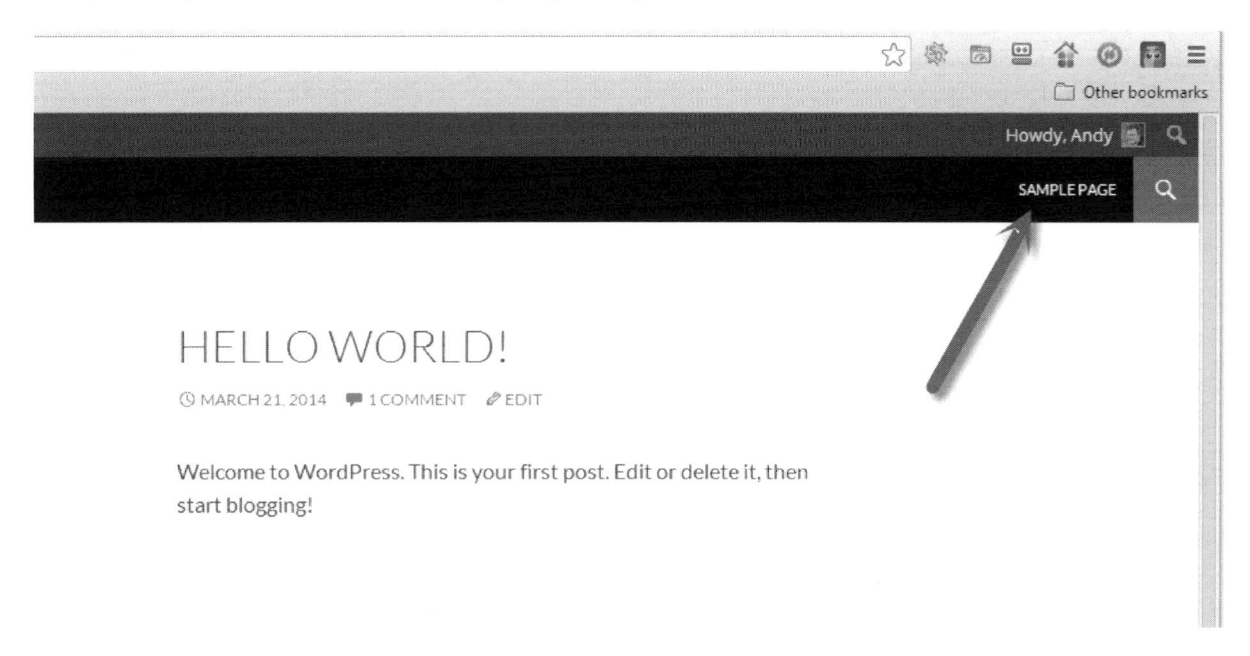

Let's login to the Dashboard and we can see where these things are.

On logging in, you'll have a menu down the left:

You can see the menu items for "Posts", "Pages" and "Comments".

Click on the Posts menu item and you'll be taken to a screen listing all posts on the site.

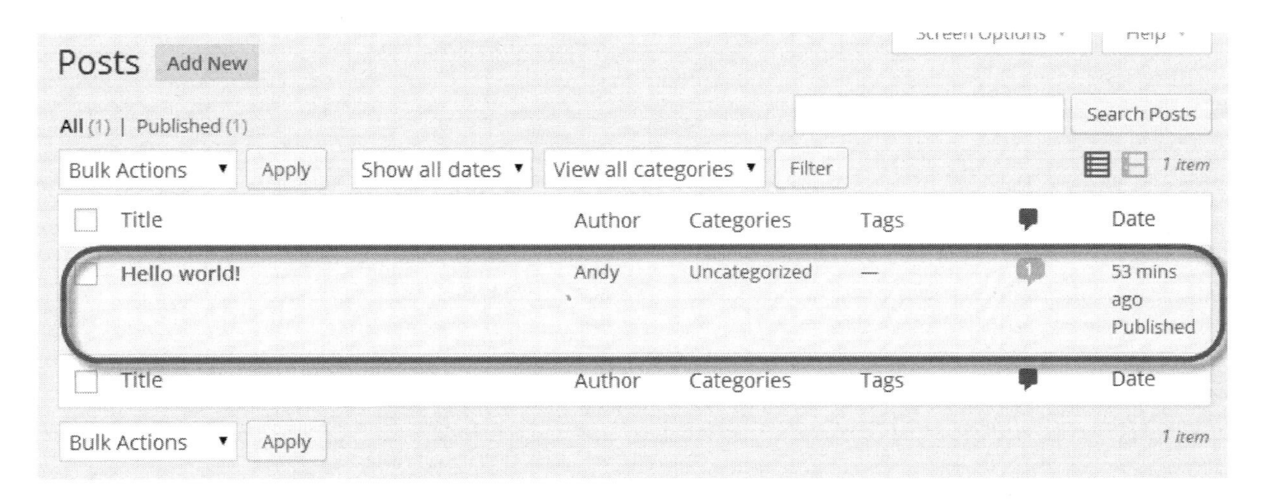

At the moment, there's only one - the "Hello World" post. No surprise there as we haven't added any yet.

OK, click on the "Comments" menu in the left sidebar.

This is a similar looking screen to the last one. This time, all of the comments on the site are listed. At the moment, there is just the one that Wordpress installed. At the top right of the comment entry, you can see what post the comment was made on. In this case it says "Hello World!"

That is actually a link to the post. Click it and you'll be taken to the post edit screen, with that post open for editing:

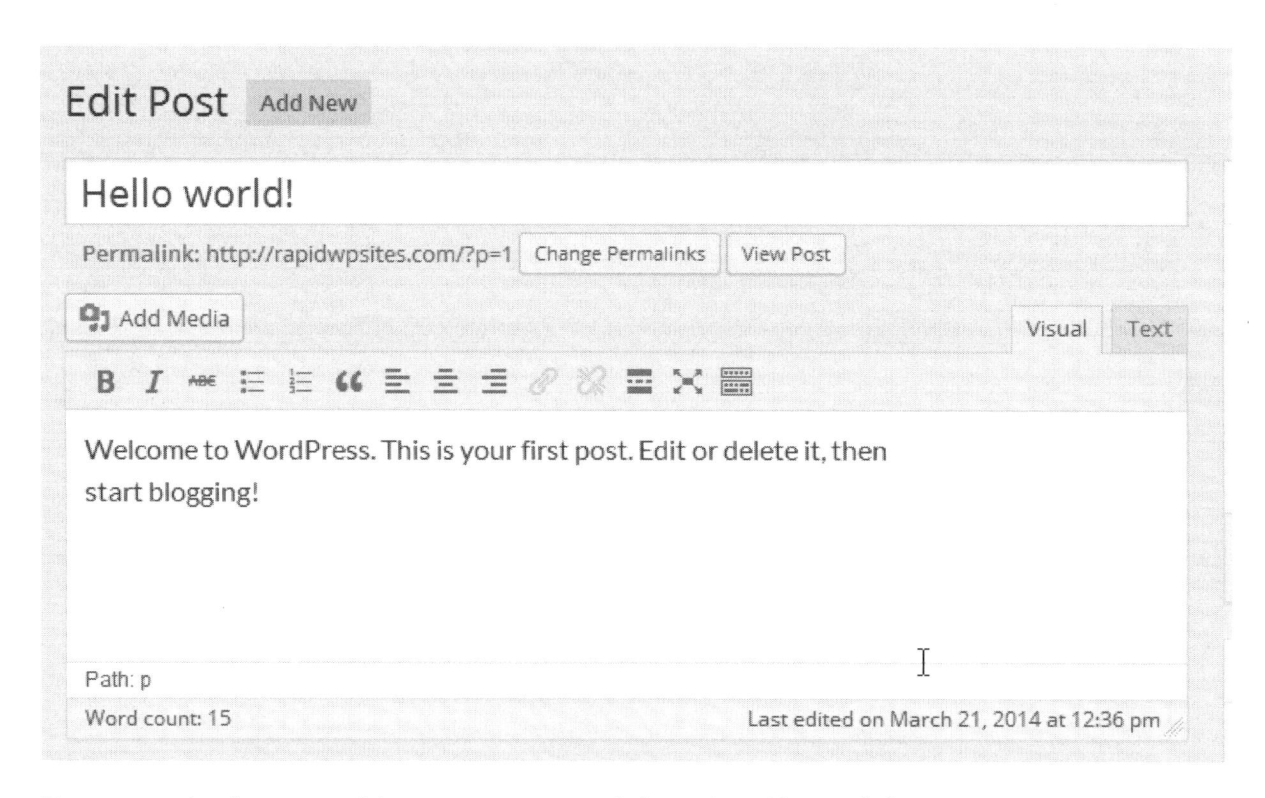

Since we don't want this post, we can delete it. If we delete a post, any comments associated with the post are also deleted.

Note, you may want to keep the demo post, comment and page a while longer, as we will revisit them in this book.

To delete a post, click the Post menu in the left sidebar again to display all of the posts.

You will go back to that list of posts on the site.

You can delete the post by either:

- Moving your mouse over the title of the post, and selecting **Trash** from the menu that appears.

  Notice that you also have an option to **Edit** the post.
- Check the box next to the post you want to delete and select **Move to Trash** from the drop down box.

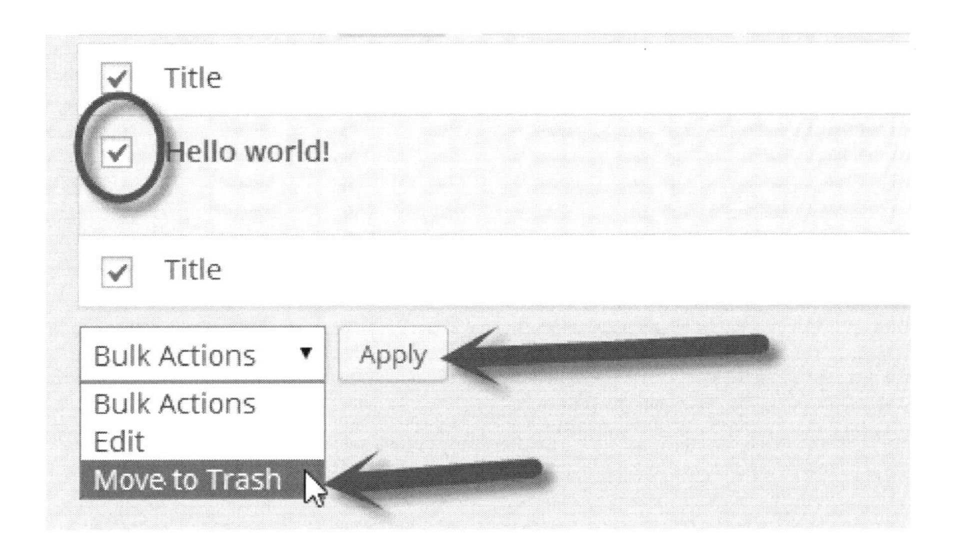

Then click the **Apply** button.

This latter option is useful if you want to delete several posts. A similar system works in the comments section. You can delete comments one by one, or select several comments and send them all to the Trash in one go. We'll see that later.

If you want to delete the "Hello World" post now, do it!

Once sent to **Trash**, you'll notice that there is now an entry in the trash:

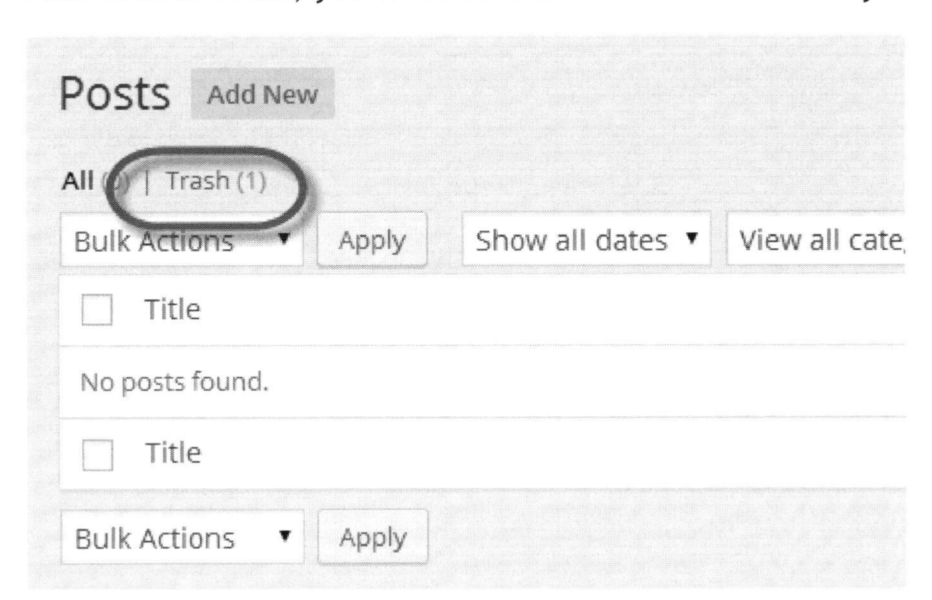

Clicking that Trash link will show you all of the posts in the trash, and if you decide you made a mistake, and want a post back, you can restore it (move your mouse over the title and select **restore** from the menu that appears.

After deleting it, go back to the comments screen. Notice the comment has now gone, since comments are attached to POSTS. If you delete the post, you delete the comments that were attached to that post.

OK, now let's look at the Page that Wordpress installed. Click the Pages menu item in the left sidebar.

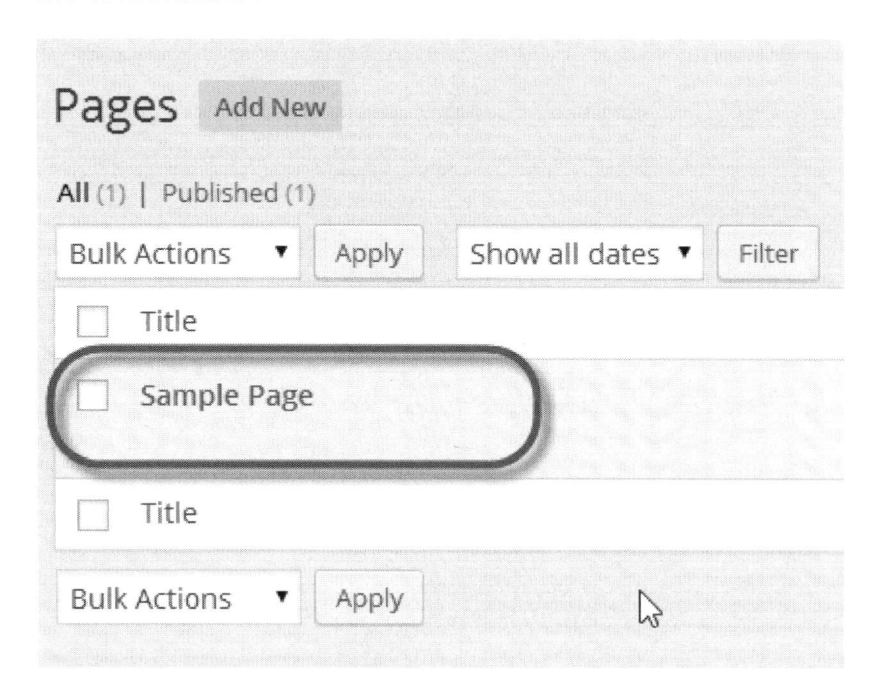

It's a familiar looking screen, isn't it? It's very similar to the screen for posts and for comments.

Click the **Sample Page** title to open the page in the Page editor.

You'll see that the main editor window is identical to the one for posts, though other options on the screen are different. We'll look at those later.

OK, delete the Page. Go to the "Pages" screen using the sidebar menu, and delete it in the same way you deleted the "Hello World!" post.

Once everything is deleted, if you head back to your website in your browser, you'll see that it now really is a skeleton site. We need to add some content!

Planning the site

We've got a skeleton site, with no content. The first thing I suggest you do is plan out what you want to include on your site. What content are you going to publish there?

You don't have to decide on everything just yet, but having a good plan before you start will make things a lot easier.

Wordpress is so flexible that you can use it to create just about any type of website. In this book, I am going to create a site that I think will cover most of what you might want to do. Here is a basic model of the site:

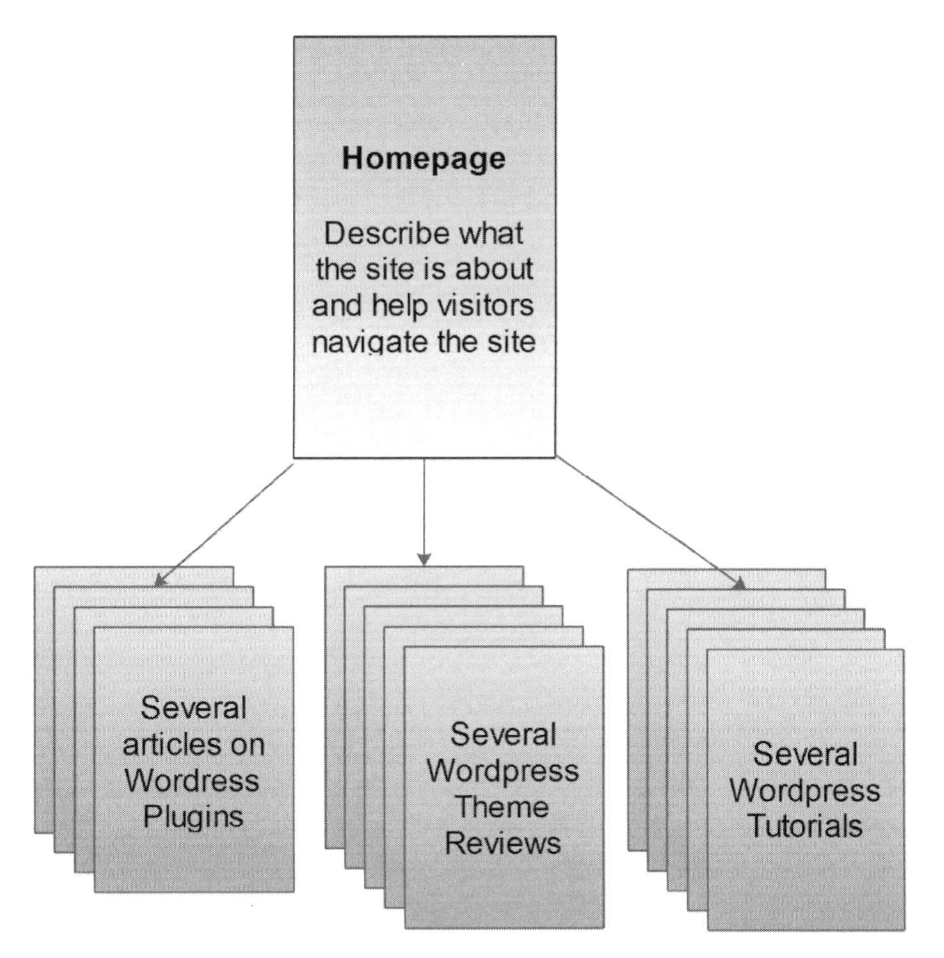

So, my homepage will introduce the site to my visitors and tell them what the site is about. The homepage will also help my visitors find what they are looking for. The site will have three main sections (for now, at least, but this will increase over time). There will be a section with several articles on Wordpress plugins, another section with articles on Wordpress themes, and then some Wordpress tutorials.

In addition to this website "content", here are a few other things you need:

1. About Us page (for the visitors, and Google likes to see one).

2. Contact Us form (for the visitors and Google likes to see one)
3. Privacy Policy (for a little legal coverage)
4. Terms of Use (for a little legal coverage).

From the above, we can see that there are two distinct types of content.

There are those articles that we are writing to engage our visitors on the topic of our site, in this case Wordpress. These articles can typically and conveniently be grouped into "categories" and we will call this type of article **"web site content"**.

The other type of content is the stuff that is not directly related to the topic of the site, but is required to make the site complete and more professional (as well as provide ourselves with a little legal protection). This type of content is what I call the "legal pages". These "legal" pages are typically very similar for all sites you build, irrespective of topic.

When we come to build our site, we will create the "website content" using POSTS, and the "legal pages" as PAGES. We'll look at how and why we use posts and pages in a little while. Before we do that, there are a few Wordpress settings we need to change.

Getting the House in Order

Wordpress comes installed with a number of default settings that really aren't in our best interests. In this section, we will make some changes and set up a few things. We are getting our house in order, ready for the first content.

I won't go into details on why we are changing these things. I'll give you a brief overview, but all you need to do is go where I tell you, click what I say and save your changes. After this next section, your site will be ready to start adding content.

Wordpress Settings

Let's make the changes.

Checkpoint #1 - Author Profile

From the Users menu in the left sidebar, select **Your Profile**.

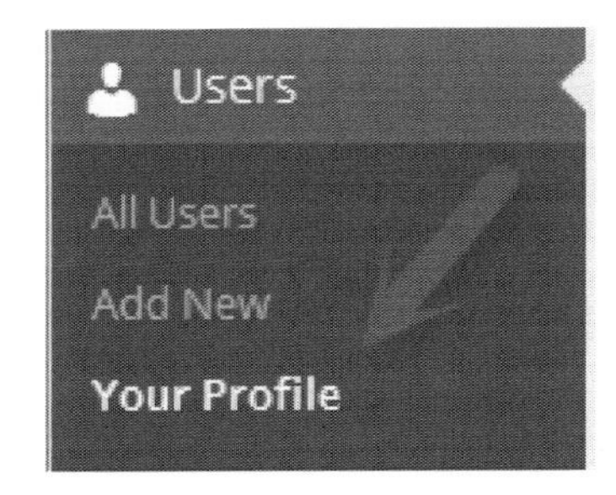

On this screen at the top:

First Name	Andrew
Last Name	Williams
Nickname *(required)*	Andy
Display name publicly as	Andy ▾

Contact Info

E-mail *(required)*	
Website	

You cannot edit the username.

Enter your first and last name. In the Nickname, enter your name. This will be prefilled with your username, but I would change it to your first name.

In the **Display name publicly as**, select the way you want your name appearing on the website. The options available will include first and last name, nickname, username etc.

Make sure you have a valid email address in the contact info box.

Finally on this screen, add a little information about yourself in the **Biographical Info** box. This information will be used on your author page, which lists all of the posts you have written.

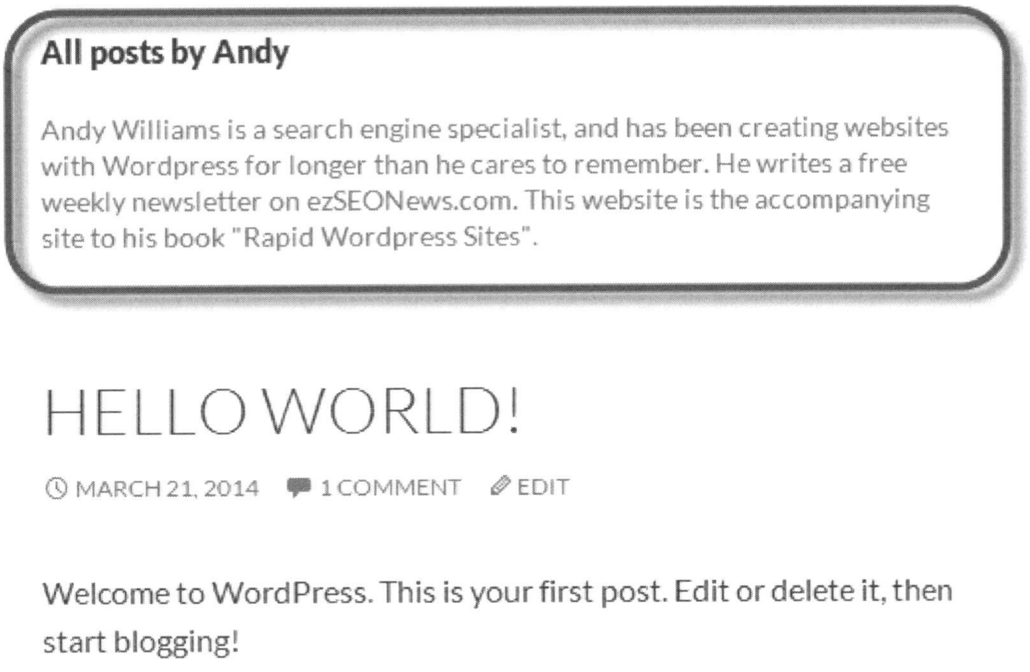

All posts by Andy

Andy Williams is a search engine specialist, and has been creating websites with Wordpress for longer than he cares to remember. He writes a free weekly newsletter on ezSEONews.com. This website is the accompanying site to his book "Rapid Wordpress Sites".

HELLO WORLD!

MARCH 21, 2014 1 COMMENT EDIT

Welcome to WordPress. This is your first post. Edit or delete it, then start blogging!

Incidentally, if you want to find your own author page, visit the "post page" for any of your posts (visit the homepage and click a post title), and look for your author name under the title:

Welcome to WordPress. This is your first post. Edit or delete it, then start blogging!

ONE THOUGHT ON "HELLO WORLD!"

Mr WordPress

MARCH 21, 2014 AT 12:36 PM EDIT

Hi, this is a comment.
To delete a comment, just log in and view the post's comments. There you will have the option to edit or delete them.

REPLY

Just click that and you'll be taken to the author page.

Checkpoint #2 – Update Services

Go to the **Writing** menu in the **Settings** menu in the left sidebar. You will see a large box labeled **Update Services.** At the moment, there is just one entry.

Essentially, whenever you post new content (or update an existing article) on your site, each of the sites listed in the update service will be notified. This can mean your content gets indexed and included in the search engines within minutes. However, we can do better than just one update service.

Do a Google search for **Wordpress update services 2014**, and find a list someone else has put together. Copy and paste it into your own "ping list", and save. Each URL in the list needs to be separated by a line break, so one per line only please.

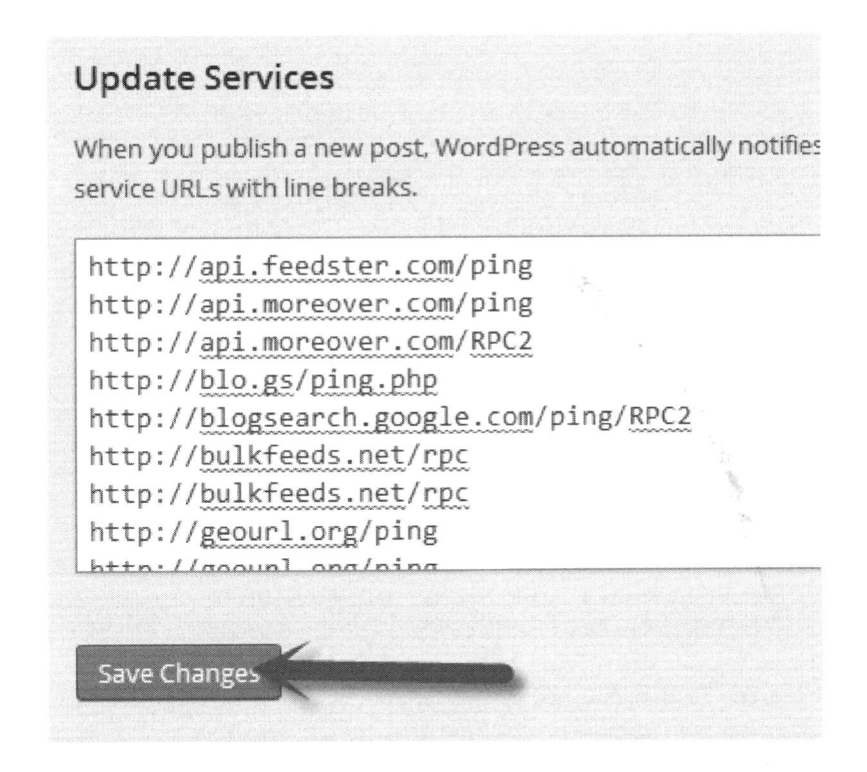

Checkpoint #3 - Reading Settings

Go to **Reading** in the **Settings** menu in the left sidebar:

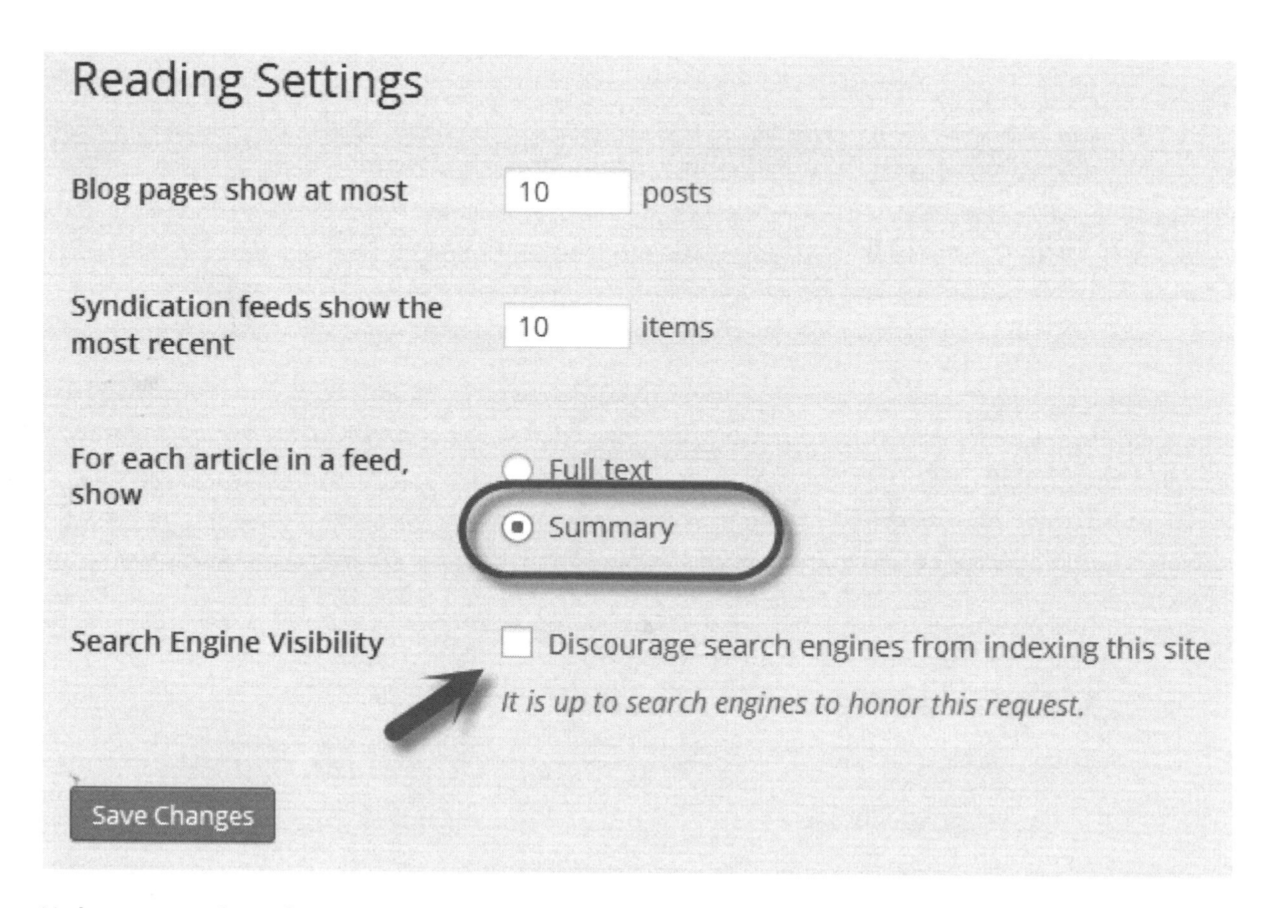

Make sure that **Summary** is selected, and that the search engine visibility box is UNCHECKED. If you check this option, the search engines WILL NOT index your pages or include them in the search engines.

Checkpoint #4 - Discussion Settings

Go to **Discussion** in the **Settings** menu in the left sidebar.

Most of these options can be left as they are. The ones to change are listed below:

Change 1:

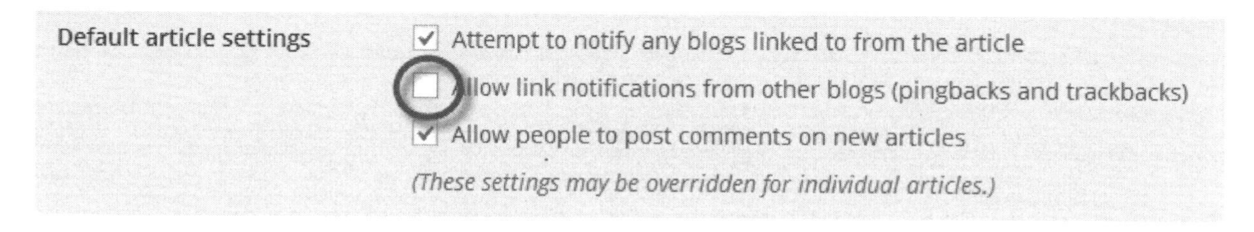

Uncheck the option above, to help prevent spammy "comments" on your site.

Change 2:

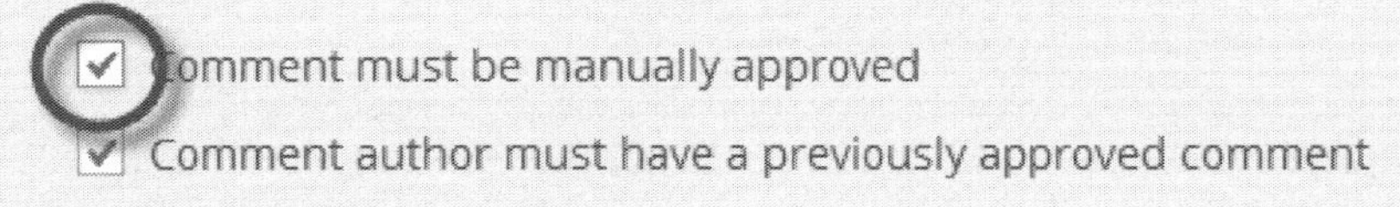

Check the option to manually approve all comments.

Change 3:

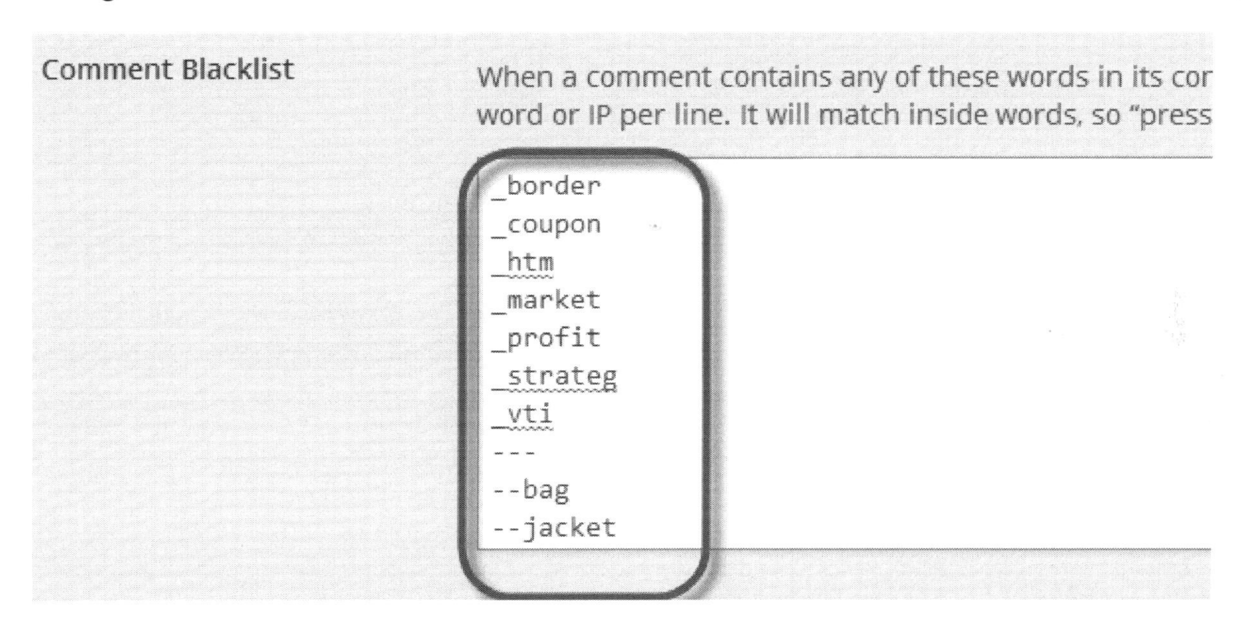

The comment blacklist will help sort out a lot of spam comments before you even see them. You simply enter all of the words you want to be considered spam, and if those words appear in a comment, the comment is marked as spam and sent to the spam folder. Now, you don't have to think of the words yourself, as others have created lists for us. Do a Google search for **Wordpress comment blacklist**, and find a list you can copy and paste into your own comment blacklist.

Change 4:

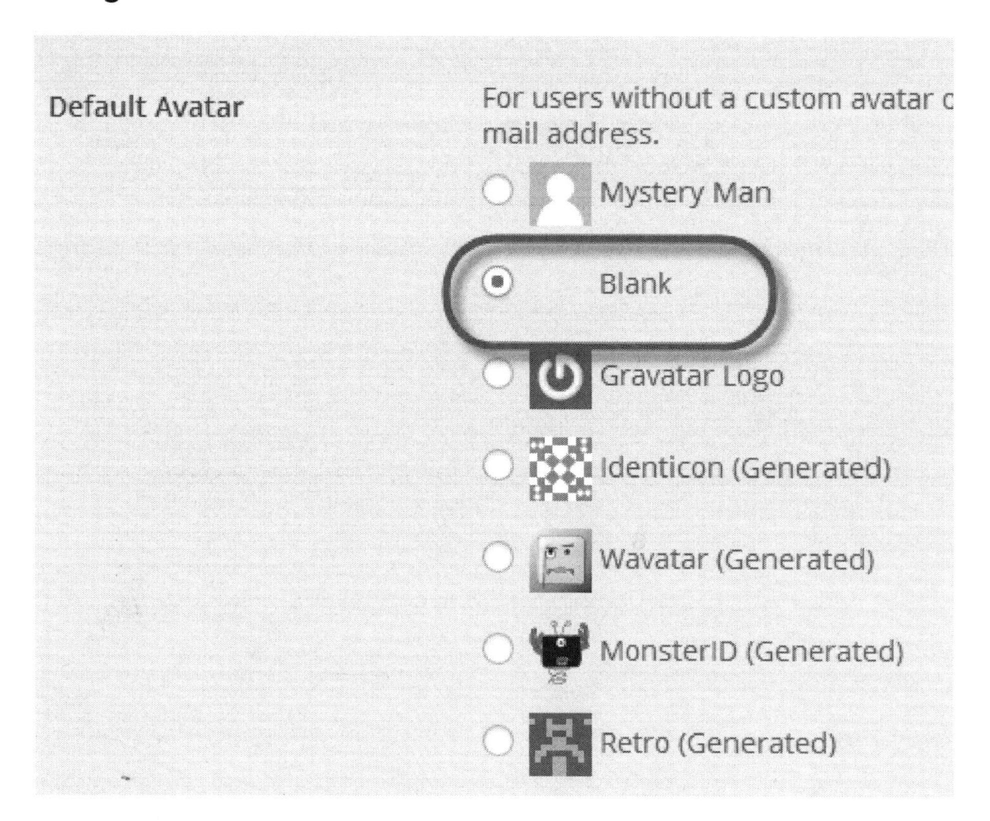

Under the default Avatar section, select **Blank**.

Reason: If someone leaving a comment does not have a Gravatar set up, then their image will be omitted if you set this to "Blank". You can set it up to use any of those other images as the default image, but by using an image, you are slowing down the load times of your web pages. Imagine having 100 comments on a post, with 90 people not using a Gravatar. That would be 90 "default" images that need to load. Best save images for those times when people have bothered with the Gravatar, so select Blank, and an image will only appear when there is a valid Gravatar attached to the commenter's email address.

Checkpoint #5 - Permalinks

Under the **Settings** menu, go to **Permalinks.**

This is an important one. By default, Wordpress will create the URL (web address) of the articles you post on your site using the following format:

http://rapidwpsites.com/?p=123

.. where p = the number of the post in the database.

From a search engine point of view, it is far better to be more descriptive with your URLs. What I recommend you do is add the category and post name to the URL. Don't worry what that means right now, just make the following change:

Select **Custom Structure**, and enter:

/%category%/%postname%/

Save your changes.

To give you an idea of what this has done, look at this before and after scenario.

The "Hello World" post URL was:

http://rapidwpsites.com/?p=1

After the change it is:

http://rapidwpsites.com/uncategorized/hello-world/

The word "uncategorized" in the URL is the category of the "Hello World" post, which is called "uncategorized". Of course, when we come to add content to our site, we will give our categories meaningful names.

Checkpoint #6 - Limit Login Attempts

This is only an option if you chose to include this plugin when installing Wordpress earlier.

Go to **Limit Login Attempts** inside the **Settings** menu.

You can actually leave these options as they are, but I like to tighten them up a little. Here are my settings:

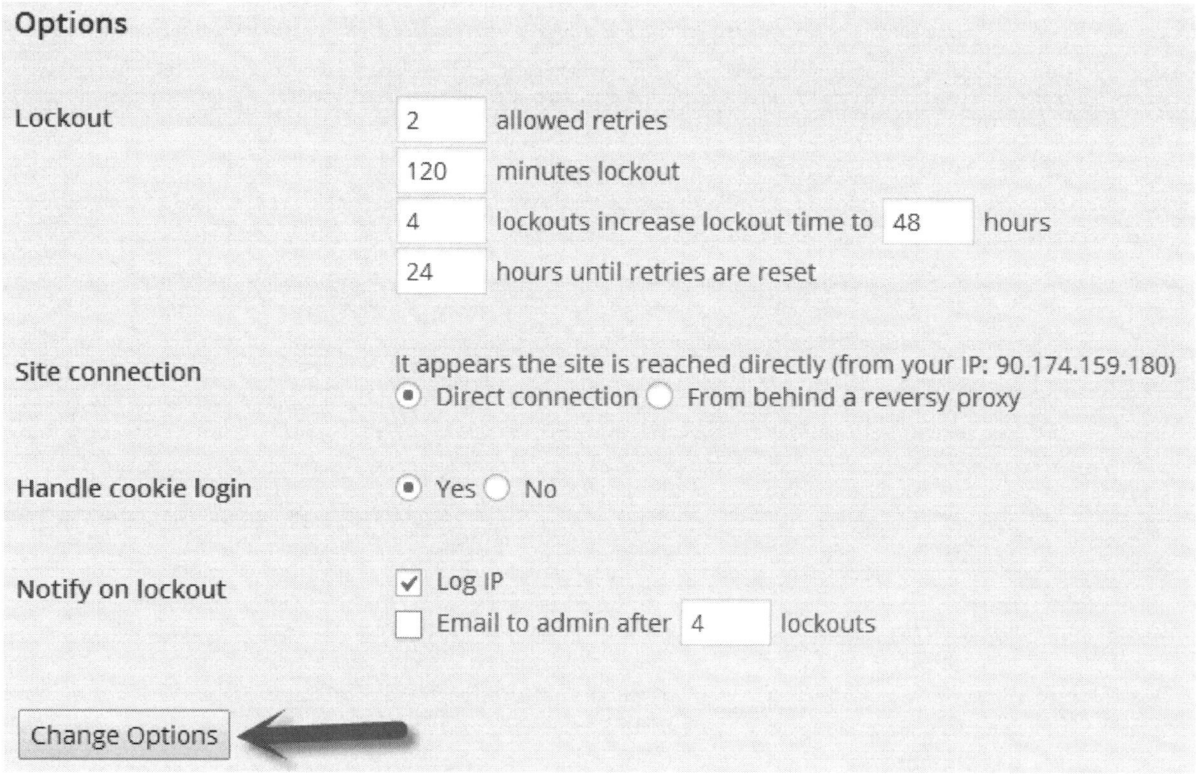

Options

Lockout
2 allowed retries
120 minutes lockout
4 lockouts increase lockout time to 48 hours
24 hours until retries are reset

Site connection
It appears the site is reached directly (from your IP: 90.174.159.180)
Direct connection From behind a reversy proxy

Handle cookie login
Yes No

Notify on lockout
Log IP
Email to admin after 4 lockouts

Change Options

NOTE: If you are in the habit of mistyping, or do not use a password manager like Roboform or Lastpass, then be careful with the settings on this screen. With my settings above, you have 2 attempts to login, and if you get them both wrong, you will be locked out of your own Dashboard for 2 hours. If you then have 2 more incorrect login attempts in a row, you're out for 48 hours. I highly recommend you use a password manager so that this does not happen. If it does happen to you, you are better off disabling this plugin and not using it, but that does make your site less secure.

Checkpoint #7 – Plugins

Click on the Plugins menu in the left sidebar. There will be a few plugins that were installed with Wordpress.

The first is Akismet. Akismet is a plugin that helps prevent comment spam, and it is extremely effective at what it does. However, if your site is commercial in nature (you make any money from the site), then you need the paid version of this plugin. Akismet can only be used for free if your site is a personal, non-profit website. If that's you, then head on over to Akismet, sign up to get your API key, and plug it into the Akismet settings. See the Akismet site for details on how to do this.

If you are not going to be using a plugin, you should delete it, since leaving unused plugins on your server can increase the security risk of your site. Old plugins can have vulnerabilities that hackers use, and if you have old and unused plugins with these vulnerabilities on your server, you are a target.

To delete a plugin, click the delete link under the plugin.

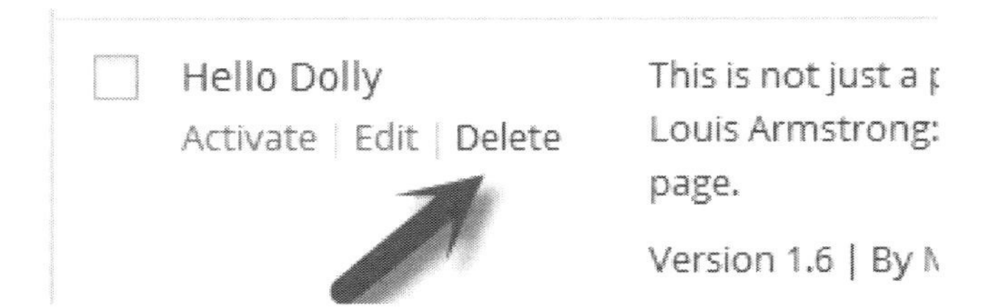

Hello Dolly can be deleted, as can Akismet if you are not using it. When you click the delete link, you'll get this choice:

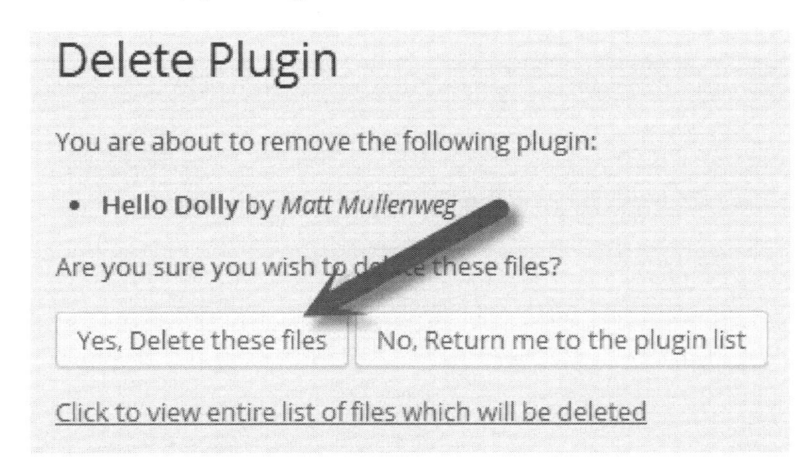

Select **Yes, Delete these files.**

Checkpoint #8 - Gravatars

Gravatars are images that we can associate with our email address. If you look at the top right of your Dashboard, you will see your name, and then a placeholder image where your photo could be. Here is mine:

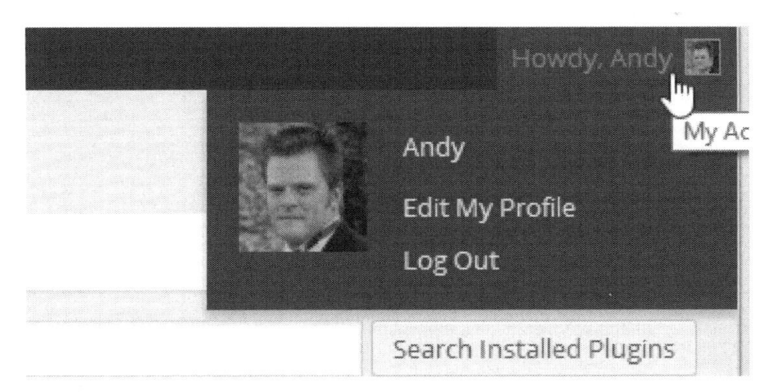

My photo is appearing there because I am using Gravatars. Essentially, I have this photo attached as a Gravatar to my Admin email address. If I use that email to post a comment on any other blog, my photo appears with my comment. Here is an example:

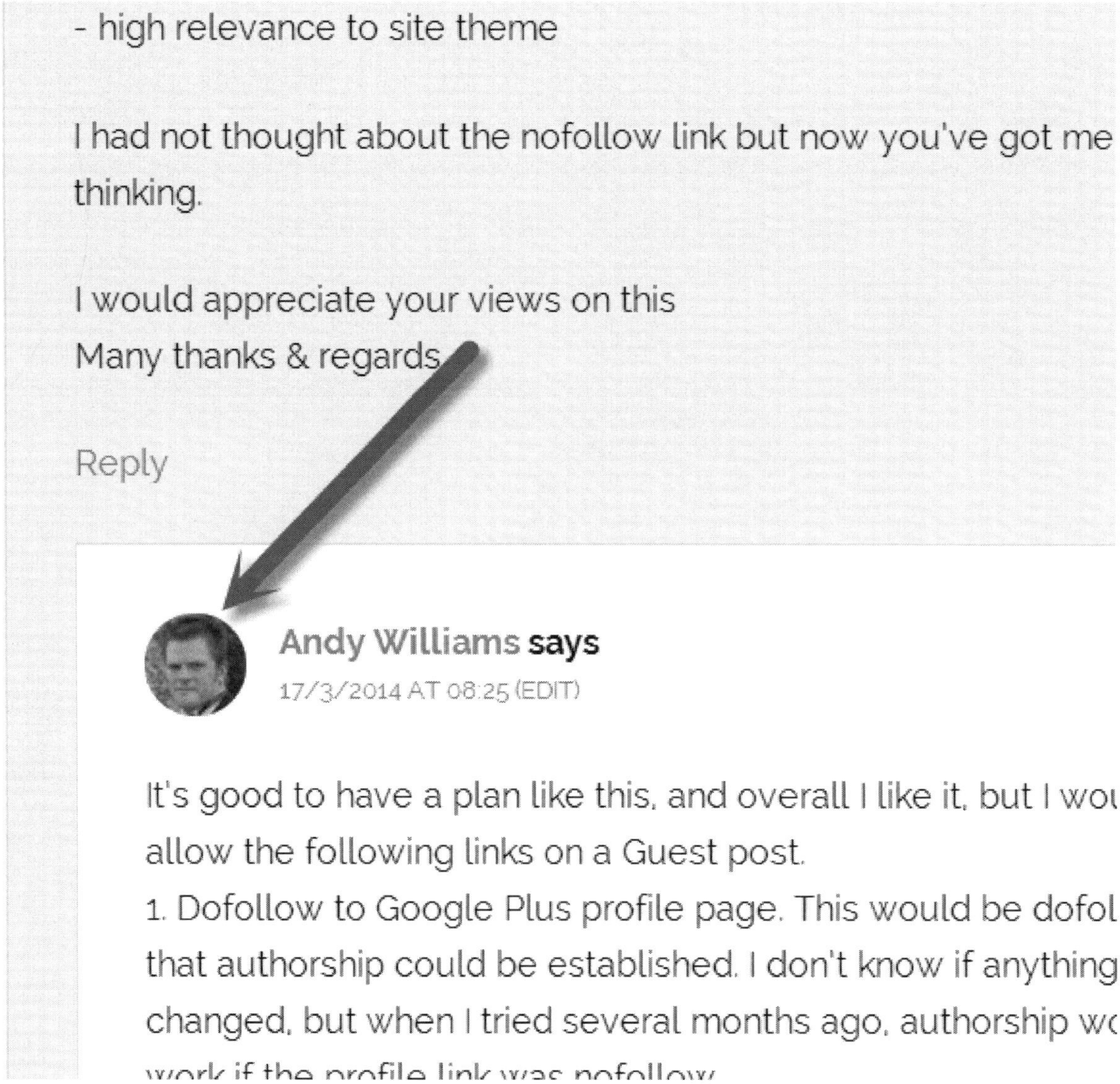

- high relevance to site theme

I had not thought about the nofollow link but now you've got me thinking.

I would appreciate your views on this
Many thanks & regards

Reply

Andy Williams says
17/3/2014 AT 08:25 (EDIT)

It's good to have a plan like this, and overall I like it, but I wou
allow the following links on a Guest post.
1. Dofollow to Google Plus profile page. This would be dofol
that authorship could be established. I don't know if anything
changed, but when I tried several months ago, authorship w
work if the profile link was nofollow

In the screenshot, I am replying to a comment. My Gravatar shows because I used my admin email when I commented.

Gravatars are a great way to brand yourself and I highly recommend you use a Gravatar for your own Admin email address. Visitors to your site love to know who they are dealing with, so get over your shyness and put your face on your site.

To sign up for a Gravatar, head on over to http://en.gravatar.com/

Look for the link to **Create your own Gravatar**, and follow the instructions. Now, whenever you post a comment on any website that is related to your own, use the email address that has your Gravatar attached, and your face will show up next to your comments on these other sites (unless of course they have Gravatars disabled, but very few do).

Checkpoint #9 – Adding a Sitemap

A sitemap is essentially a list of pages on your site, and it is used mainly by the search engines to find all of your content. It is therefore a good idea to have one. The best way to add a sitemap, is to use a plugin.

Click on **Add New** in the **Plugins** sidebar menu.

Search for **Google XML Sitemaps** and find this plugin by Arne Brachhold:

Name	Version	Rating	Description
Google XML Sitemaps Details | Install Now	3.4	★★★★☆	This plugin will generate a special XML sitemap which will help search engines like Google, Bing, Yahoo and Ask.com to better index your blog. With such a sitemap, it's much easier for the crawlers to see the complete structure of your site and retrieve it more efficiently. The plugin supports all kinds of WordPress generated pages as well as custom URLs. Additionally it notifies all major search ... By Arne Brachhold.

Click the **Install Now** link under the plugin title.

Now click the **Activate Plugin** link:

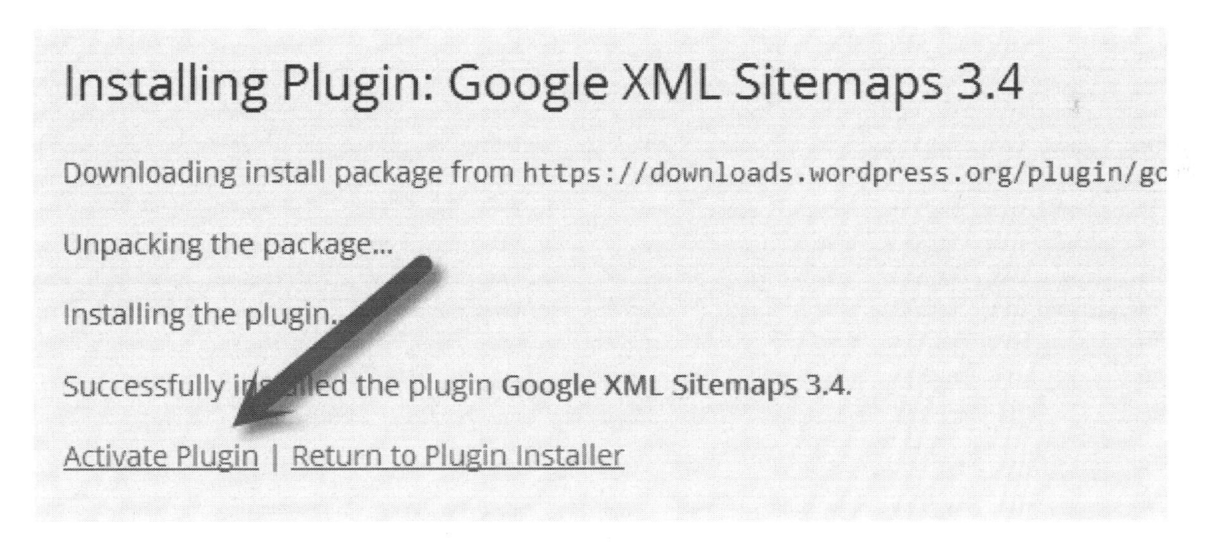

Installing Plugin: Google XML Sitemaps 3.4
Downloading install package from https://downloads.wordpress.org/plugin/gc
Unpacking the package...
Installing the plugin...
Successfully installed the plugin Google XML Sitemaps 3.4.
Activate Plugin | Return to Plugin Installer

You will now have a new menu item in the **Settings** sidebar menu:

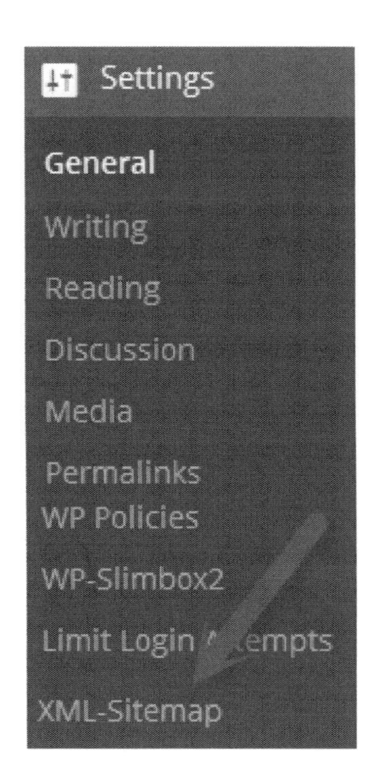

Click on XML-Sitemap to enter the settings.

Scroll down to the **Sitemap Content** section, and copy my settings here:

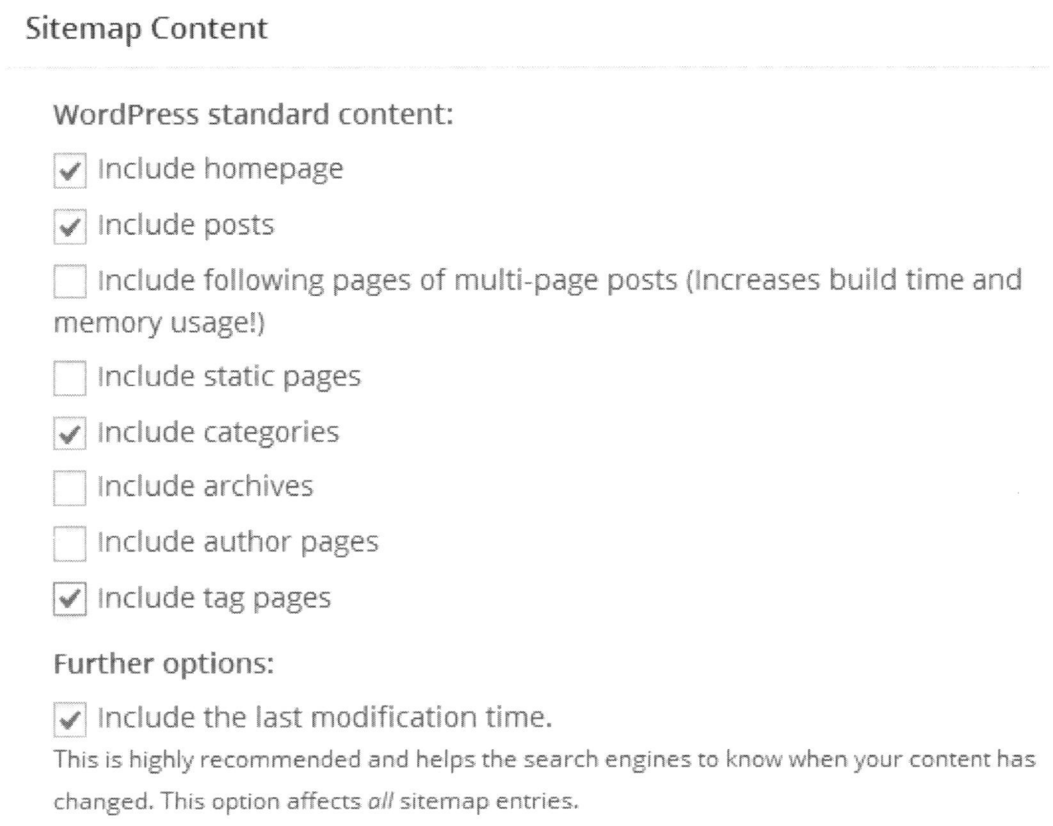

Sitemap Content

WordPress standard content:

- [x] Include homepage
- [x] Include posts
- [ ] Include following pages of multi-page posts (Increases build time and memory usage!)
- [ ] Include static pages
- [x] Include categories
- [ ] Include archives
- [ ] Include author pages
- [x] Include tag pages

Further options:

- [x] Include the last modification time.

This is highly recommended and helps the search engines to know when your content has changed. This option affects *all* sitemap entries.

Scroll to the very bottom and click the Update Options button.

Once the options are saved, you'll be back at the top of the options page, which will tell you that your sitemap has not yet been built:

The sitemap wasn't generated yet.

The sitemap wasn't built yet. Click here to build it the first time.

If you encounter any problems with t build process you can use the debug function to get more information.

There is a new beta version of this plugin vailable which supports the new multi-site feature of WordPress as well as m ny other new functions! More information and download

Click the link to build it for the first time.

You can then click the link to view your sitemap:

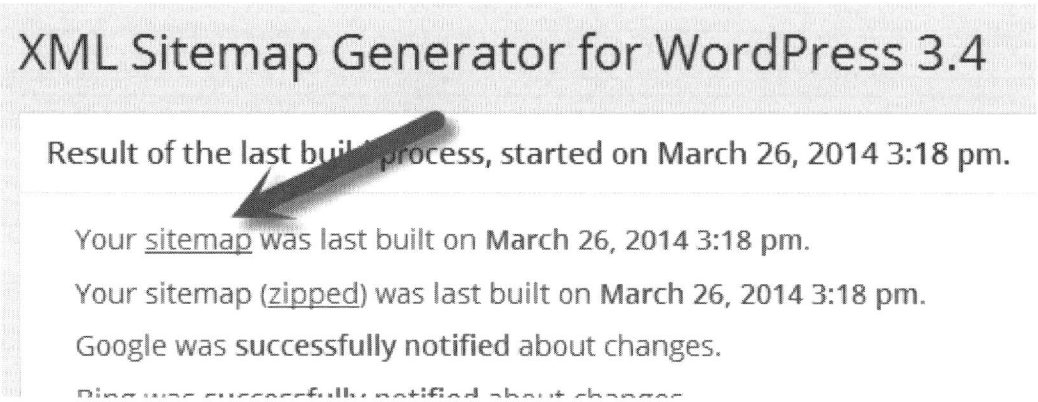

XML Sitemap Generator for WordPress 3.4

Result of the last build process, started on **March 26, 2014 3:18 pm.**

Your sitemap was last built on **March 26, 2014 3:18 pm.**

Your sitemap (zipped) was last built on **March 26, 2014 3:18 pm.**

Google was **successfully notified** about changes.

You won't see much there yet, because you haven't added any content. Here is a screenshot of mine, shortly after adding my first article:

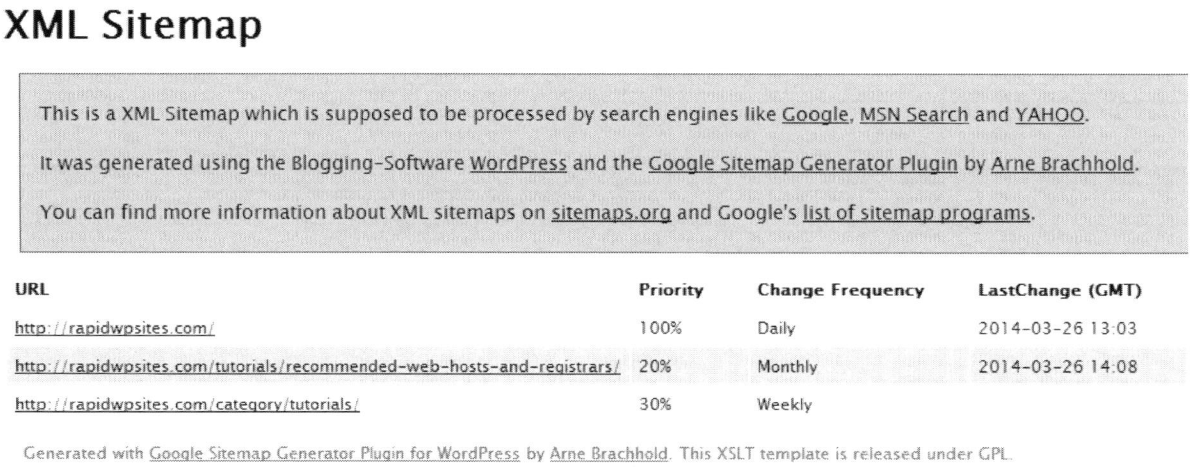

XML Sitemap

This is a XML Sitemap which is supposed to be processed by search engines like Google, MSN Search and YAHOO.

It was generated using the Blogging-Software WordPress and the Google Sitemap Generator Plugin by Arne Brachhold.

You can find more information about XML sitemaps on sitemaps.org and Google's list of sitemap programs.

URL	Priority	Change Frequency	LastChange (GMT)
http://rapidwpsites.com/	100%	Daily	2014-03-26 13:03
http://rapidwpsites.com/tutorials/recommended-web-hosts-and-registrars/	20%	Monthly	2014-03-26 14:08
http://rapidwpsites.com/category/tutorials/	30%	Weekly	

Generated with Google Sitemap Generator Plugin for WordPress by Arne Brachhold. This XSLT template is released under GPL.

Now, whenever you add a new post to your site, it will automatically be added to this sitemap, and Google will be notified of the new addition. You should find that once your site becomes established, new content will be indexed and found in Google within minutes of you clicking the "publish" button.

Pages v Posts

Wordpress gives you two options for adding new content to your site. These are confusingly called "Pages" and "Posts". Both use the exact same "What You See Is What You Get" (WYSIWYG) editor, making it easy to add them, but you need to decide which one to use. That is what this chapter is for. I'll explain the differences between pages and posts, and tell you which one to use and when.

From now on, whenever I talk about posts, I am referring to Wordpress POSTS, and whenever I talk about pages, I am talking about Wordpress PAGES.

Wordpress was originally designed with bloggers in mind, and Wordpress "posts" were the tool given to the blogger so they could add updates to the blog. These Wordpress posts were designed to be date-dependent, so that posts could be listed in chronological order. Think of it much like a diary. Things happen, and you enter them in the order they happen. If you then ordered the posts in date order, with the oldest posts at the top, you'd have a chronological list of posts over time.

So what about Wordpress "pages"?

Well, pages are not date-dependent. They are stand alone pages, and each page is usually unrelated to any other piece of content on the site.

Post Categories

Another major difference between posts and pages is that posts can be grouped and categorized, whereas pages cannot (this isn't strictly true, but it helps if you think it is).

On my RapidWPSites.com website, I want to have a number of articles reviewing Wordpress plugins. All of these articles are related to each other, because they are all about "plugins". I will have another set of articles reviewing Wordpress themes, and again, these will all be related to one another because of their common topic - Wordpress themes.

The beauty of grouping and categorizing content on your site is that Wordpress makes it easy for us to manipulate these groups of posts.

If a visitor lands on my review of the Thesis Wordpress theme, doesn't it make sense to show that visitor a list of other theme reviews to give them more information before they choose one to buy? Wordpress makes this easy. We can simple add a "Related Posts" section to each post, listing other posts in the same category. This type of thing is not possible with Wordpress pages (at least no easy way to do it, because pages were designed to be separate, standalone pieces of content that were not related to any other).

So, all posts are given a category, whereas pages are not. Earlier in this book, I showed you the URL of the "Hello World!" post after we made the change to the permalink structure. This was the URL:

http://rapidwpsites.com/uncategorized/hello-world/

The word "uncategorized" in the URL is the category of the post.

Uncategorized is a default category that Wordpress added when it was installed. We can, and will, change that later. However, think about my RapidWPSites website. The URLs of my theme reviews might look like this:

http://rapidwpsites.com/themes/thesis

http://rapidwpsites.com/themes/avada

http://rapidwpsites.com/themes/genesis

Some of my plugin reviews might look like this:

http://rapidwpsites.com/plugins/yarpp

http://rapidwpsites.com/plugins/wordpress-seo

http://rapidwpsites.com/plugins/wp-db-manager

.. and so on. You can instantly see that the first three posts are related (they are all themes) and the second three posts are related (they are all plugins).

This is a major SEO (Search Engine Optimization) benefit of posts as well. The search engines see these posts in the same category, and this helps them categorize and rank your content. The search engines know that the first three posts are related, and that the second three posts are related. The search engines can then categorize sections of your site. Wordpress actually helps out even more.

For every category you create (I have two in the examples above - themes and plugins), Wordpress creates a "Category page" that lists all of the posts in that category. Therefore there will be a "plugins category page" with a URL that looks like this:

http://rapidwpsites.com/category/plugins/

That page will list all posts in the plugins category. Again, the search engines know that the category page lists related posts, so it automatically knows that all of the posts listed on that category page are about plugins.

So, we can assign categories to posts. In fact, a post can be given more than one category. However, I don't recommend it. Categories are the top level of organization of posts, and I want you to stick to only using ONE category per post.

In my example above, it does not make sense to put my review of the YARPP plugin in both the plugins and themes category, does it? It's a plugin, so goes in the plugins category.

However, what if I had a category called "reviews". My theme review posts could then go in both the themes category and the reviews category.

Similarly my plugin reviews could go in the plugins category AND the reviews category.

If you have this dilemma, then you probably have the wrong categories for your site, so simplify the structure even more. In this case, just leave the review category out.

Post Tags

So, categories are the main way we categorize and group posts. Wordpress also give us a secondary method for categorizing content, called Tags. These are just words or phrases we assign to a post, like keywords related to the post.

Each post can have multiple tags assigned to it.

When you think about posts, think ONE category, MULTIPLE tags.

Let me give you an example of when you might use a tag.

Suppose you have a site on vacuum cleaners. You have decided on categories like Dyson, Hoover, Eureka, Kirby, Dirt Devil and so on. In other words, you are using the manufacturer names as categories. All Dyson vacuum reviews go in the Dyson category, all Kirby reviews go in the Kirby category.

This makes sense, because as webmaster, you decided that most visitors know the brand of vacuum they want, so grouping by brand helps them more easily find the model that suites them best.

However, sometimes a visitor does not know the brand of vacuum he wants. All they know is that they want a hand-held vacuum, or a canister vacuum, or maybe a vacuum designed to deal with pet hair.

This is where I would use tags.

I'd have the following tags:

Upright, canister, pets, hand-held, HEPA filter, etc.

Therefore my Dyson DC31 Animal review would be put in the Dyson category, but I could tag is with pets and hand-held.

The beauty of tags is that we can manipulate them in the same way we do with categories. If someone on your site is interested in a "hand-held vacuums", but not sure which manufacturer, you can show them a list of all vacuums "tagged" with "hand-held".

In fact, Wordpress even creates a "tag page" for each tag you use. That tag page lists all posts that have used that particular tag.

So Wordpress would create a page for you that lists all "hand-held" vacuum reviews.

Sound familiar? Yes, it's very much like the category pages we mentioned earlier.

So, posts can have categories and tags assigned to them.

I do have a few rules on using categories and tags that will keep you out of trouble. Here they are:

1. Only one category per post.
2. You can have multiple tags, but try to limit each post to 5 or fewer tags. The more tags you use on a post, the more spammy your site begins to look to Google.
3. Never use a tag if only one post will be tagged with it (you could be even stricter with this. I personally never use a tag if it will only ever be used on one or two posts). Tags, like categories, are there to help organize and GROUP your posts. If there is only one post using a tag, it's not a group. Remember that Wordpress creates a "tag page" for each tag you use. If you only have one post using a tag, then that tag page will basically just contain one post. That would be considered duplicate content by Google, since you already have that one post on its own "post page", as well as on a category page.
4. Never create a tag with the same name as a category.

never create a Tag with same name as a category.

Tags are ultimately there to help you make your site better for your visitors. Don't abuse them.

Post Excerpts

Another great feature of posts is **excerpts.** When you enter a post, you have the option of entering an excerpt as well.

By default, Wordpress hides the excerpt entry box on the edit post page, so we need to unhide it. To hide and unhide various aspects of the Dashboard, Wordpress has "Screen Options", which you can see in the top right of your dashboard.

Click where it says "Screen Options" to open the menu:

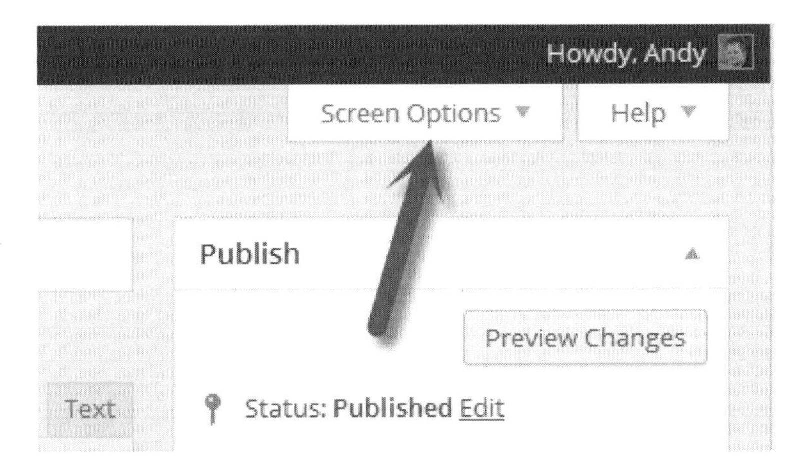

Clicking that button will expand it:

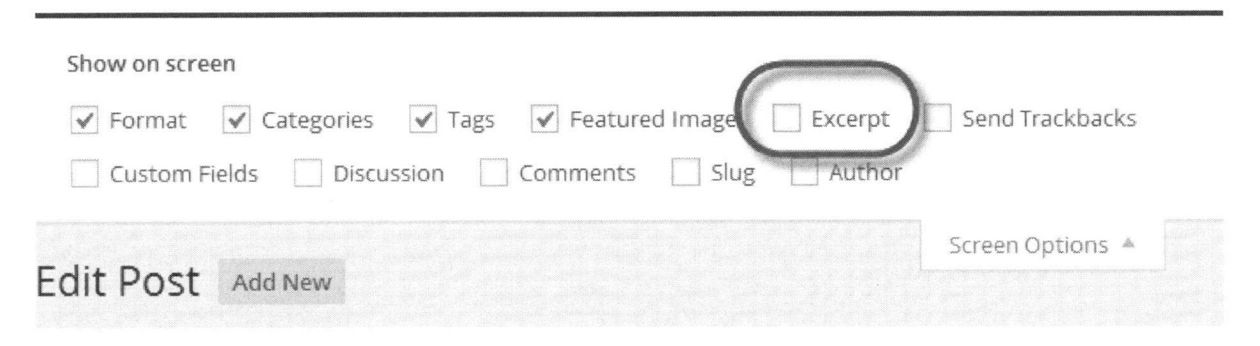

As you can see, the excerpt is turned off. If we check that box, the Edit post screen adds this new entry box:

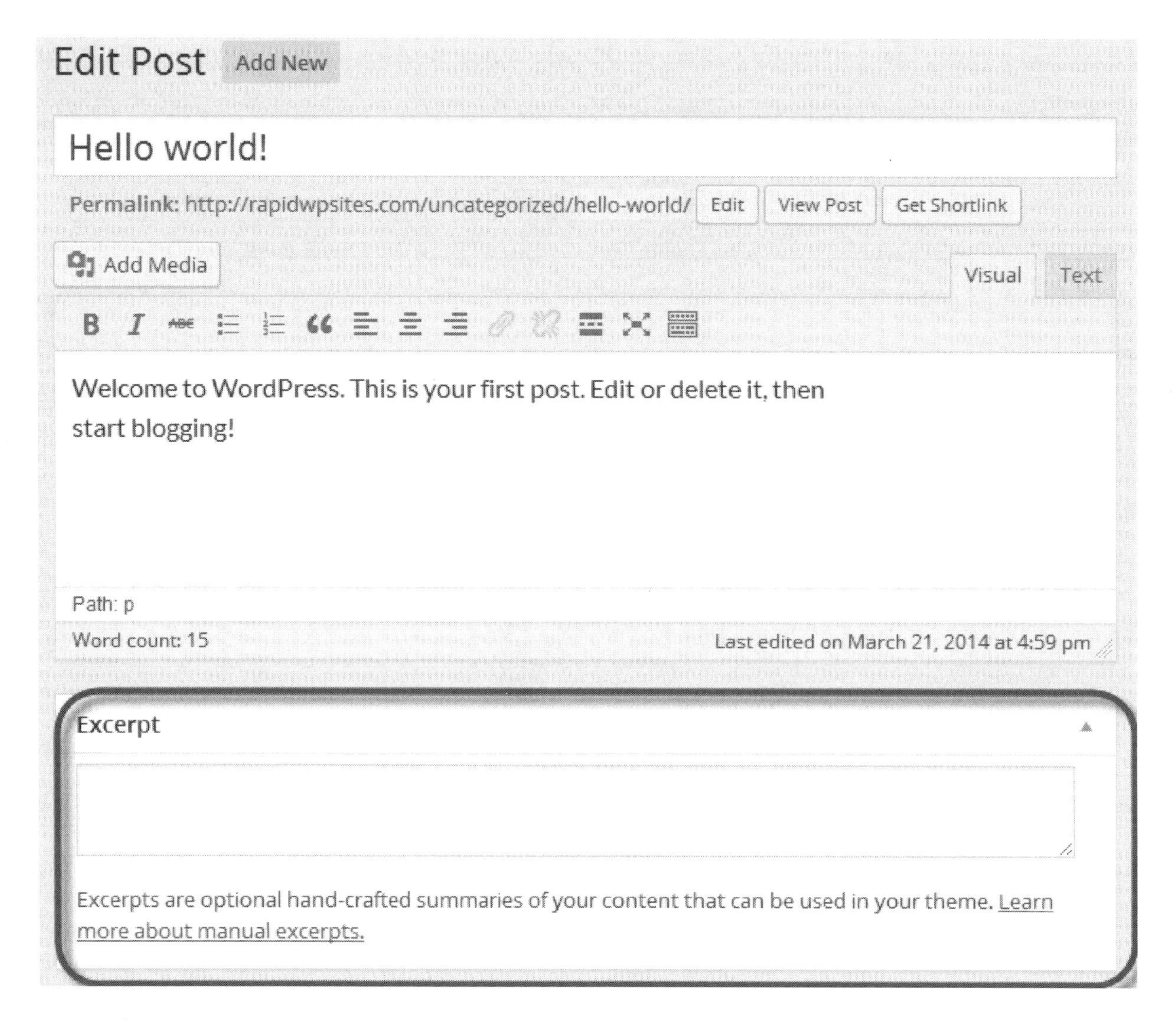

Now when I enter a post, I can also enter a separate excerpt.

Note that the "Screen Options" are dynamic, and will show you just the options that are relevant to the Dashboard screen you are viewing. In the screenshots above, I am in the Edit post screen, so the options I am given relate to the Edit posts screen.

OK, so let's go back to our discussion of excerpts, and look at what they are, and why we would use them.

An excerpt is a short summary or description of a post. Some Wordpress themes and some plugins can use the excerpt and display it as the description of a post to your visitors.

Let's see an example of an excerpt being used properly on a site. This screenshot shows the sidebar of a website that is using a plugin to display recent posts in a category:

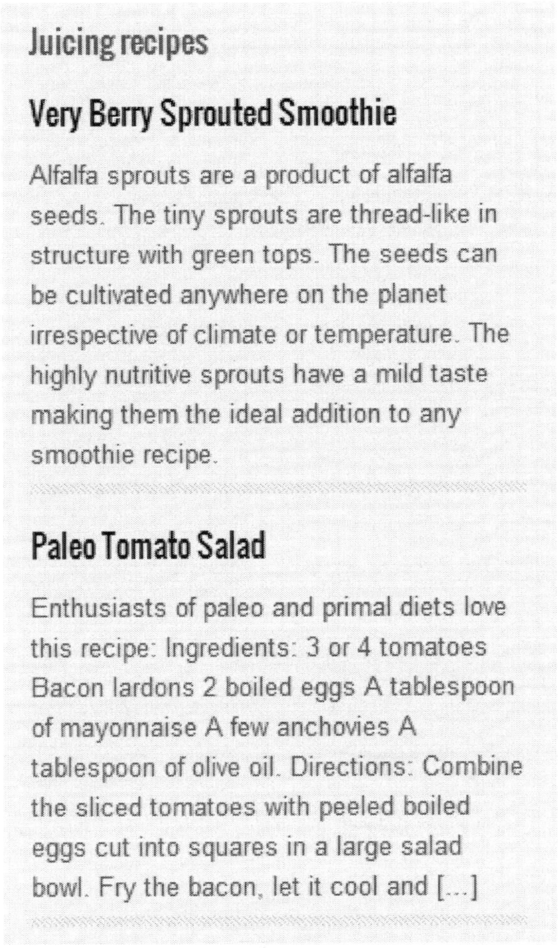

Juicing recipes

Very Berry Sprouted Smoothie

Alfalfa sprouts are a product of alfalfa seeds. The tiny sprouts are thread-like in structure with green tops. The seeds can be cultivated anywhere on the planet irrespective of climate or temperature. The highly nutritive sprouts have a mild taste making them the ideal addition to any smoothie recipe.

Paleo Tomato Salad

Enthusiasts of paleo and primal diets love this recipe: Ingredients: 3 or 4 tomatoes Bacon lardons 2 boiled eggs A tablespoon of mayonnaise A few anchovies A tablespoon of olive oil. Directions: Combine the sliced tomatoes with peeled boiled eggs cut into squares in a large salad bowl. Fry the bacon, let it cool and [...]

Notice the top one. The description of the post is nicely defined and "complete". The one lower down however, is not. Notice that the description for the second one ends with [...].

This particular plugin looks for an excerpt to use as the post description. If it finds an excerpt, it will use it. If it does not find one, it will use the first bit of text in the article and create a description from that. When it does that, you end up with a description that is not complete, copied from the start of the article, and ends with [...].

You can see how using excerpts makes your site look more professional, and better for your visitors.

It's also better for the search engines because they see different content in the description, instead of just part of the first paragraph of the post.

Posts and RSS Feeds

Another important difference between posts and pages is that posts appear in RSS feeds, pages do not.

Wordpress sites automatically create RSS feeds. These are special files that contain lists of your most recent posts on your site.

Wordpress creates an RSS feed for your site as a whole, but it also creates separate feeds for each category, each tag, all posts by a particular author, etc.

RSS feeds are important tools to notify people, and other websites, that you have published new content. Personally, I monitor the RSS feeds (using a free service over at Feedly.com) of my favorite websites, and when they post new content, the feed is updated (automatically by Wordpress) and I get notified of that new content.

OK; so when do you use Posts, and when Pages?

The rule is fairly simple.

Use Pages for your "legal pages" (remember those), and posts for "website content" (the articles you write to engage your visitors).

Note that Wordpress is extremely flexible and you could create an entire site using just pages. Or, you could create a site that uses pages for "main articles", then posts as a type of blog attached to your site (and I will cover this option later). However, I think that when you are just starting out with Wordpress, you need to use the tools Wordpress gives you in the way they were designed to be used, and that is what I am teaching you in this book.

Now you know the main differences between posts and pages, it's time to create some. However, before we do that, let's take a look at the editor we use to enter content.

Using the WYSIWYG Editor

Whether you are entering a post or a page, it all starts with the same WYSIWYG editor. You can see it if you go to **Add New** in the **Posts** menu in the left sidebar. Go on; add a new post so that you can use it as a test document to explore the editor.

The first thing to do is click that button on the right of the toolbar.

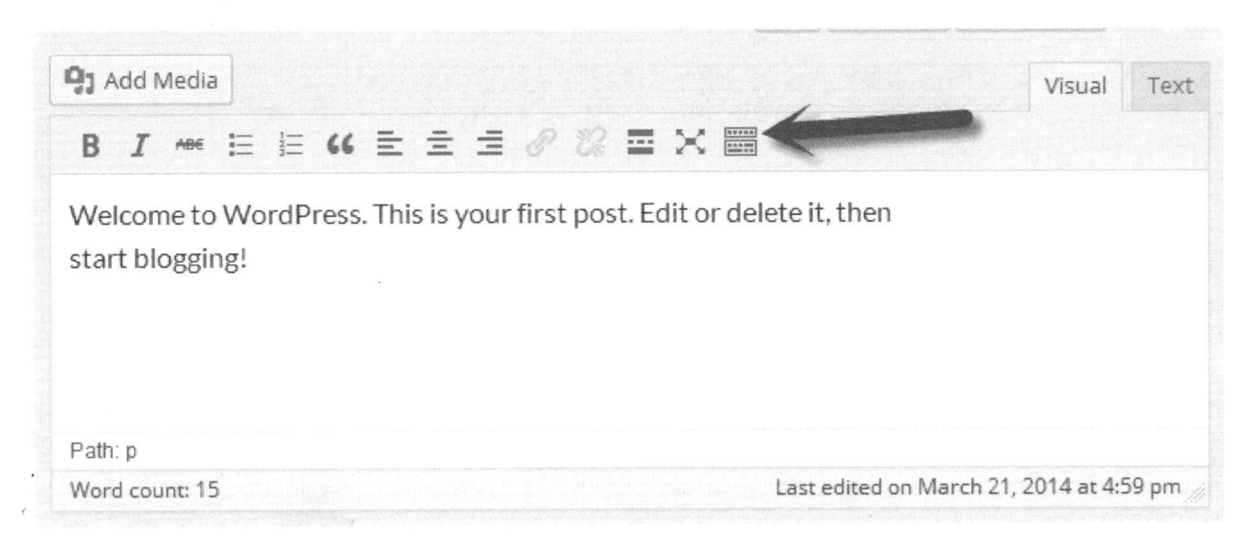

That's better.

You now have another row of buttons to help you enter and format your article.

If you are familiar with a Word processor, you will intuitively know how to use this editor.

The large white area under the buttons is where you type text. Go on, try typing in the box. As you type, you will see that the editor automatically wraps text onto the next line when you get to the end of the line. This is the first tip for beginners.

When you are typing text into this editor, never press the return key on your keyboard to try a word wrap. Let the editor wrap the text for you. Only press the return key ONCE at the end of a paragraph.

As you are typing, you may find the box you are typing in is a little small. You can make it bigger by clicking and dragging the bottom right corner of the editor window. Move your mouse there and you'll see the cursor change.

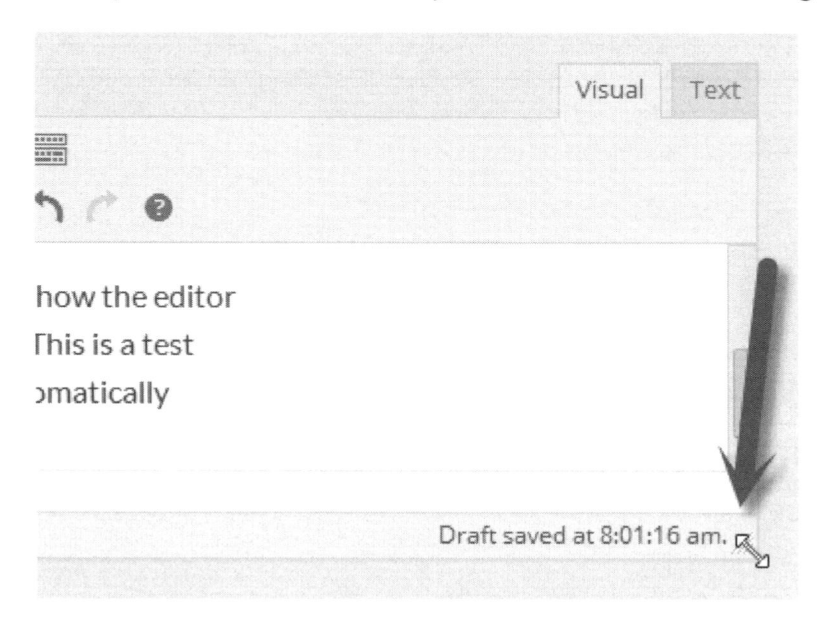

Left click and hold the click. Now drag the window down to the desired height, and then release the button.

OK, you can see how easy it is to type plain text into the window.

Headlines in your document

The main headline on any post or page will be created by Wordpress for you, from the text you type into the "Enter title here" box:

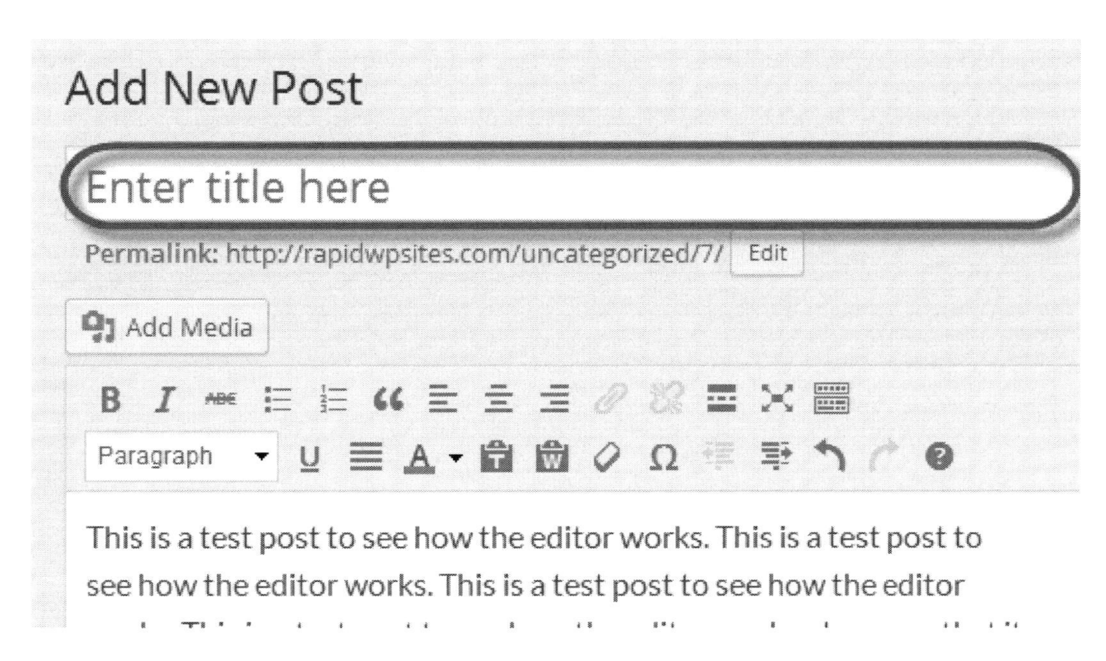
Add New Post
Enter title here
Permalink: http://rapidwpsites.com/uncategorized/7/
Edit
Add Media
Paragraph
This is a test post to see how the editor works. This is a test post to
see how the editor works. This is a test post to see how the editor

Go on, type in a title for your test document.

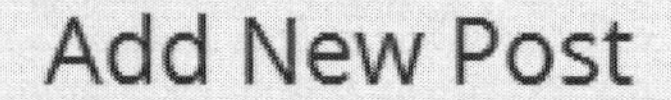

This is my test document

Permalink: http://rapidwpsites.com/uncategorized/7/ Edit

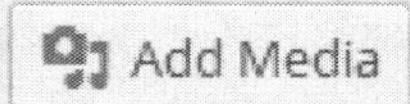

Paragraph

This is a test post to see how the editor works. This is a test post to see how the editor works. This is a test post to see how the editor works. This is a test post to see how the editor works. I can see that it automatically wraps onto the next line when it gets to the end.

This is the second paragraph. This is a test post to see how the editor works. This is a test post to see how the editor works. This is a test post to see how the editor works. I can see that it automatically wraps onto the next line when it gets to the end.

Over on the right of the editor screen, in the **Publish** options, you will see a **Preview** button, so you can check to see what your post will look like when it is live on your site.

Click the button and your test post will open in a new browser tab:

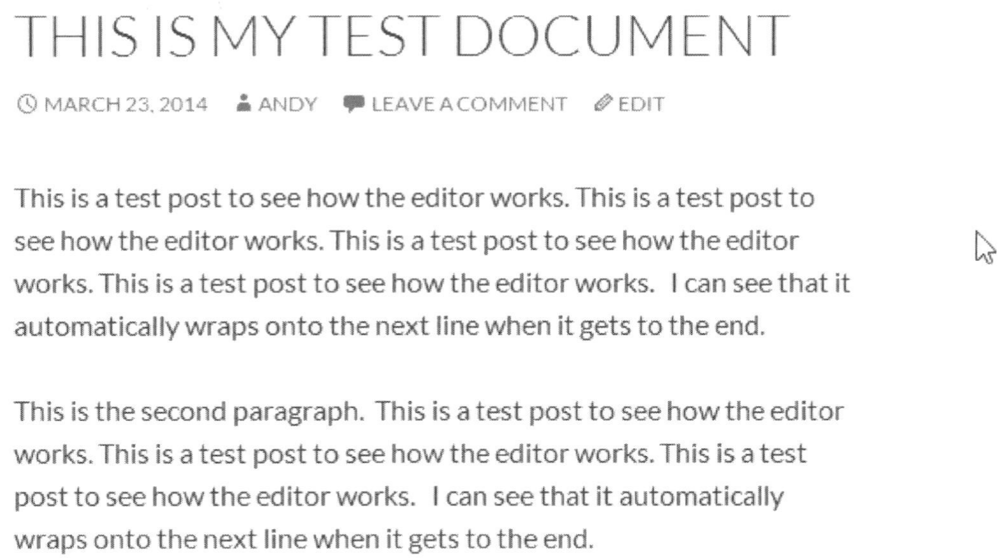

THIS IS MY TEST DOCUMENT

MARCH 23, 2014 ANDY LEAVE A COMMENT EDIT

This is a test post to see how the editor works. This is a test post to see how the editor works. This is a test post to see how the editor works. This is a test post to see how the editor works. I can see that it automatically wraps onto the next line when it gets to the end.

This is the second paragraph. This is a test post to see how the editor works. This is a test post to see how the editor works. This is a test post to see how the editor works. I can see that it automatically wraps onto the next line when it gets to the end.

As you can see, the post title is there above the content of my post.

It is always a good idea to add sub-headers, bullets and other formatting to make your posts look better to the visitor. Let's add a sub headline before the second paragraph.

Back in the editor, position your mouse where you want the sub-headline to appear, and left click your mouse to set the editing position.

NOTE: You won't be able to set the cursor in the white space between the paragraphs, so just click at the very start of the second paragraph.

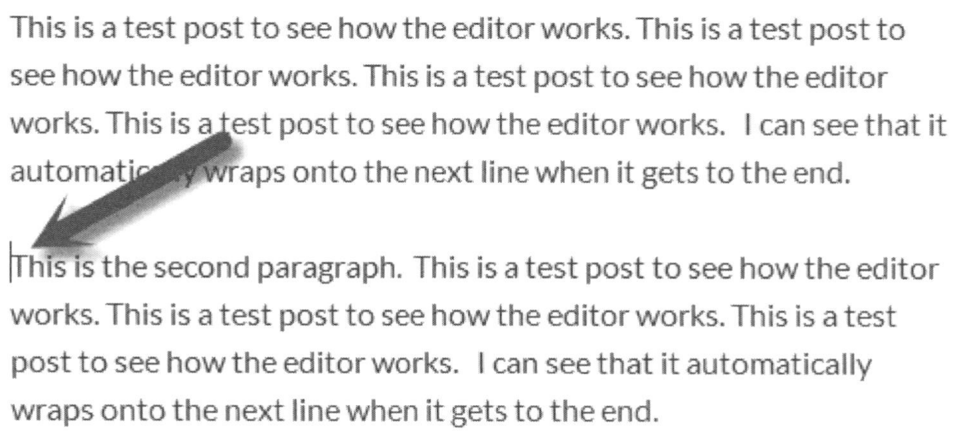

This is a test post to see how the editor works. This is a test post to see how the editor works. This is a test post to see how the editor works. This is a test post to see how the editor works. I can see that it automatically wraps onto the next line when it gets to the end.

This is the second paragraph. This is a test post to see how the editor works. This is a test post to see how the editor works. This is a test post to see how the editor works. I can see that it automatically wraps onto the next line when it gets to the end.

You will see a blanking cursor which marks the point you selected. This “edit cursor” (as we will call it from now on) is a short, thin, vertical line, and it marks the position that text will appear if you type.

Since we want to type a sub-headline at this point, just start typing the headline,

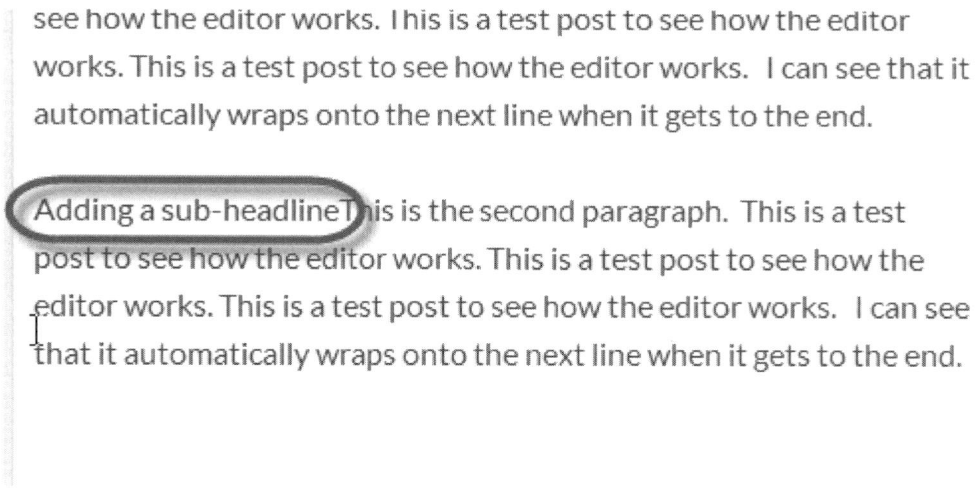

see how the editor works. This is a test post to see how the editor works. This is a test post to see how the editor works. I can see that it automatically wraps onto the next line when it gets to the end.

Adding a sub-headlineThis is the second paragraph. This is a test post to see how the editor works. This is a test post to see how the editor works. This is a test post to see how the editor works. I can see that it automatically wraps onto the next line when it gets to the end.

.. and when you finish the headline, press the return key to move the second paragraph down one.

This is a test post to see how the editor works. This is a test post to see how the editor works. This is a test post to see how the editor works. This is a test post to see how the editor works. I can see that it automatically wraps onto the next line when it gets to the end.

Adding a sub-headline 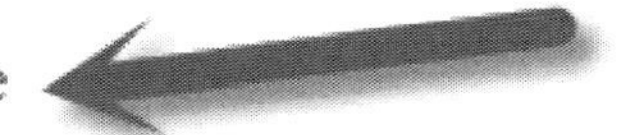

This is the second paragraph. This is a test post to see how the editor works. This is a test post to see how the editor works. This is a test post to see how the editor works. I can see that it automatically wraps onto the next line when it gets to the end.

OK, we now have the headline, but if you preview the post again, you will see it is normal text, and does not look like a headline. We need to format it.

Using your mouse, select the headline. You can do this by clicking at the start of the headline, holding the click, and dragging your mouse to the end of the headline. When selected, the headline is highlighted.

This is a test post to see how the editor works. This is a test post to see how the editor works. This is a test post to see how the editor works. This is a test post to see how the editor works. I can see that it automatically wraps onto the next line when it gets to the end.

Adding a sub-headline

This is the second paragraph. This is a test post to see how the editor works. This is a test post to see how the editor works. This is a test post to see how the editor works. I can see that it automatically wraps onto the next line when it gets to the end.

OK, with the headline selected, we need to choose the headline style to use. In the editor toolbar, you can see a drop down box that currently says “Paragraph”. This is on the second row of buttons, and you may not see this row if you didn’t click the top right toolbar button earlier (in which case, do that now).

Click where you see the word "Paragraph" and the drop down box opens up, giving you options.

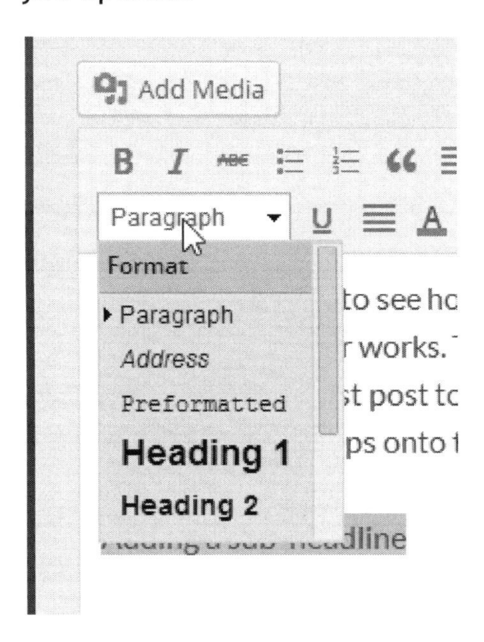

You can see Heading 1 and Heading 2 at the bottom. If you scroll down that box, you will see other headline options as well.

When Wordpress creates the post, the headline at the top of the page (which we saw earlier) is set as Heading 1, which is the largest headline.

You should only ever have ONE Heading 1 per post/page.

Sub-headings should therefore be Heading 2, and if you have sub-headings inside a Heading 2 section, these should be Heading 3, and so on.

OK, select Heading 2 from the list, and your headline will change formatting in the editor.

This is a test post to see how the editor works. This is a test post to see how the editor works. This is a test post to see how the editor works. This is a test post to see how the editor works. I can see that it automatically wraps onto the next line when it gets to the end.

Adding a sub-headline

This is the second paragraph. This is a test post to see how the editor works. This is a test post to see how the editor works. This is a test post to see how the editor works. I can see that it automatically wraps onto the next line when it gets to the end.

If you accidentally select the wrong formatting, just highlight the headline again, and reselect.

To change the formatting of any text in the editor, you follow the same routine. Select the text you want to format, and then select the formatting option in the toolbar.

Try it with bold and italic text. Select a bit of text in your test post, then click the Bold and/or Italic button in the toolbar.

Other useful formatting options on the top row of the toolbar include the list buttons. There are bullet lists and numbered lists:

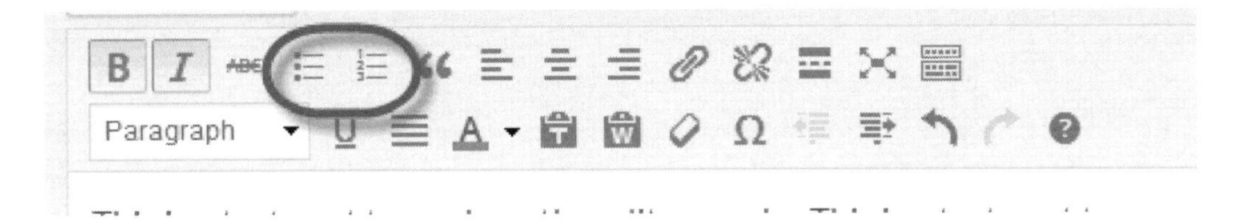

To create a bullet list, type the first item you want in your list on its own line in the editor, just like you did when entering the sub-heading.

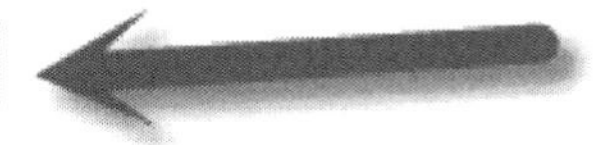

see how the editor works. This is a test post to see how tl
works. This is a test post to see how the editor works. I c
automatically wraps onto the next line when it gets to th
this is item one in my list
Adding a sub-headline
This is the second paragraph. This is a test post to see ho
works. This is a test post to see how the editor works. This i
to see how the editor works. I can see that it automatica
onto the next line when it gets to the end.
Path: p

You do not have to select that line of text to create a bullet point. Simply click so that the edit cursor is somewhere on the line. Now click the bullet button. The line will become a bullet point. Clicking the bullet button again will toggle the bullets off/on. This can be useful if you end up with a bullet point at the end of your list:

works. This is a test post to see hov
automatically wraps onto the next
this is item one in my list
this is the second item
this is the third

Just move your edit cursor to that line, and press the bullet button to toggle bullets off for that line.

To add another bullet point to the list, move the edit cursor to the end of the first bullet point, and press the return key on your keyboard. A second bullet point appears, ready for typing in the next item in the list.

When you get to the end of your bullet list, you can simply move the edit cursor away from the list, and carry on working on other areas of your document.

On the top toolbar, you also have options for aligning your paragraphs. Typically you won't want to change this, but the options are there to center and right align if you need them.

One of the more important formatting options in the top toolbar is the ability to add hyperlinks in your content. A hyperlink is simple a link to another web page.

To add a hyperlink, highlight the text you want to use as the link text, and then click the **Insert/Edit link** button.

A popup will appear where you can enter the details of the link:

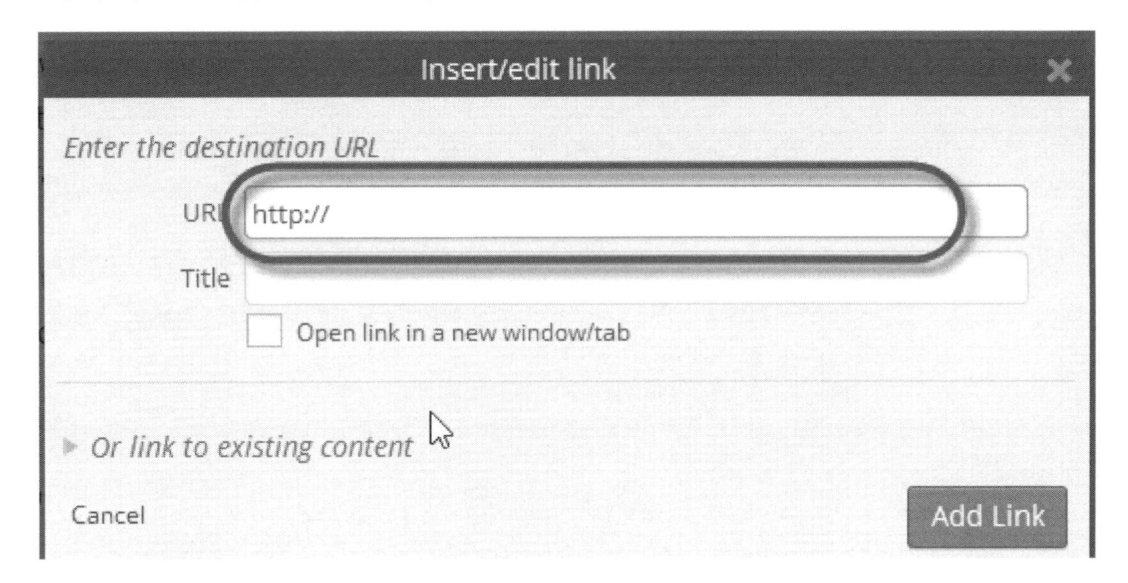

Enter the URL of the page you want to link to in the top box. If you want this link to open in a new browser tab when someone clicks on it, check the **Open link in a new window/tab** checkbox.

I do not recommend adding a "Title" for the link. It is not something that will help your visitors, and could get you into trouble with the search engines if you abuse the feature.

If you want to link to another page on your site, you can either enter the URL in the URL box, OR, select the other post from the options at the bottom of this popup. See the little triangle next to "Or link to existing content"? That triangle means some options have been collapsed and you can expand them by clicking the triangle, or the text next to it.

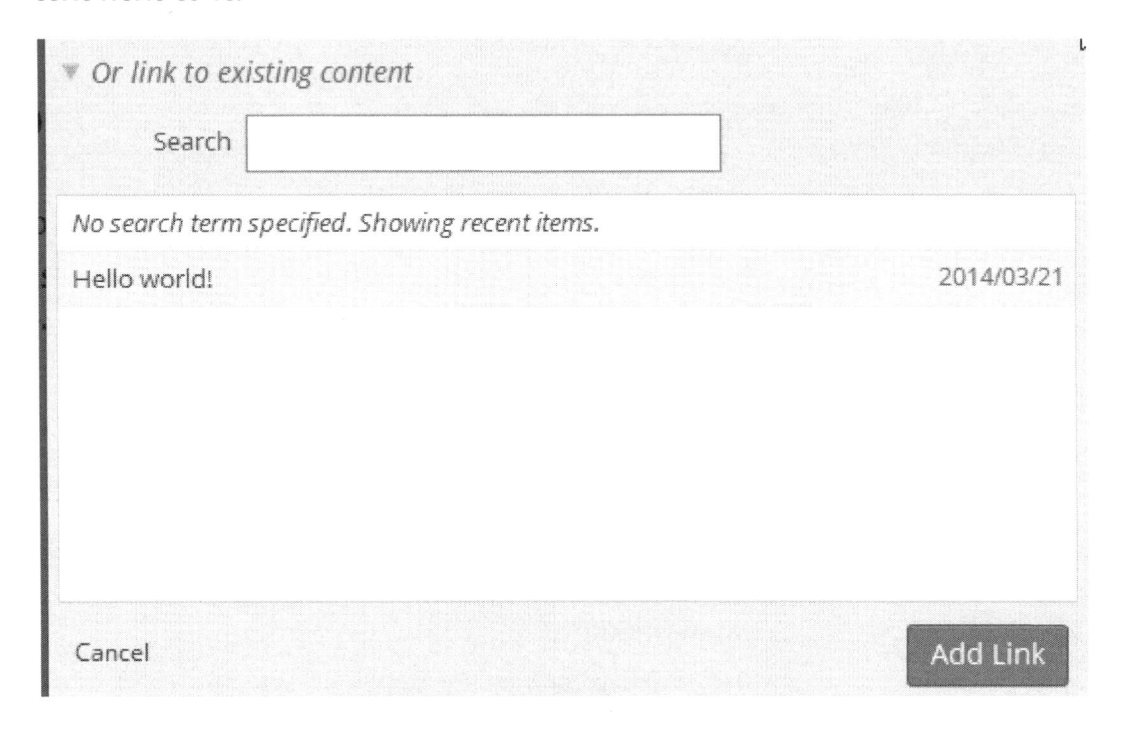

If you have a lot of content on your site, you can search for the post you want to link to using the search box at the top. A list of posts will appear below (you can see my "Hello World" post is still there). Clicking it adds the URL of the post into the URL box, but will also put the title of the post into the "Title" box. Since I don't recommend using the Title attribute, if I want to link to another page on my own site, I'll open the page in my browser, copy the URL from the address bar, and paste it into the URL box in the Insert/edit link screen.

When you insert a link, you will see the text you had previously selected has now changed, to indicate it is now a hyperlink:

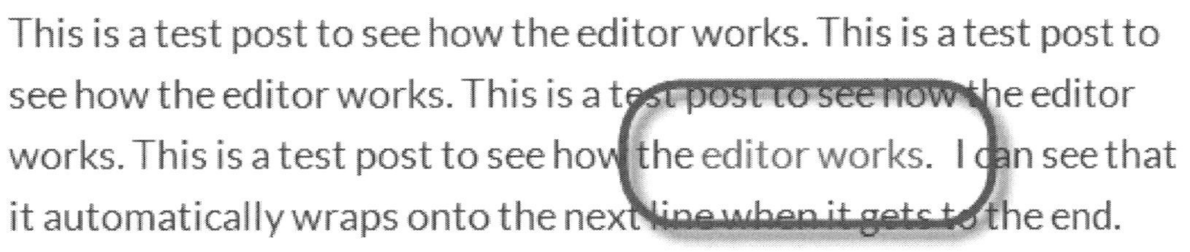

This is a test post to see how the editor works. This is a test post to see how the editor works. This is a test post to see how the editor works. This is a test post to see how the editor works. I can see that it automatically wraps onto the next line when it gets to the end.

The way the links look in published posts on your site will be determined by the theme you are using. Some themes just make links a different color, while others will add an underline to the text. The default Wordpress theme we are currently using on this site does both:

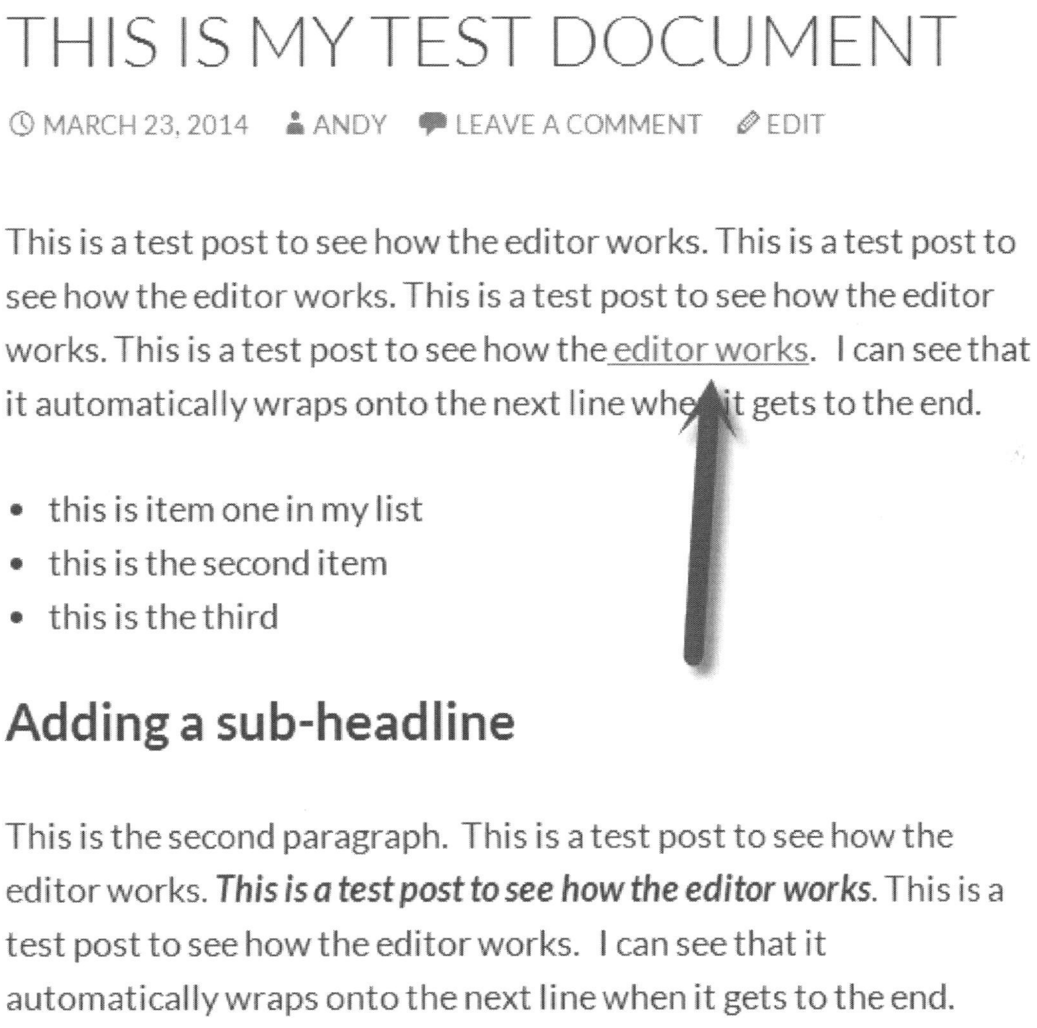

THIS IS MY TEST DOCUMENT

MARCH 23, 2014 ANDY LEAVE A COMMENT EDIT

This is a test post to see how the editor works. This is a test post to see how the editor works. This is a test post to see how the editor works. This is a test post to see how the editor works. I can see that it automatically wraps onto the next line when it gets to the end.

- this is item one in my list
- this is the second item
- this is the third

Adding a sub-headline

This is the second paragraph. This is a test post to see how the editor works. ***This is a test post to see how the editor works***. This is a test post to see how the editor works. I can see that it automatically wraps onto the next line when it gets to the end.

To remove a link in your post, click somewhere in the link to place the edit cursor inside the link text. Now click the **Unlink** button in the toolbar (it's right next to the insert/edit link button).

The final option I want to cover on the top row of toolbar options is the **Insert More Tag** button. This is used to insert a break in your post, to stop any further text from appearing. This break will be obeyed by Wordpress on all web pages where the post appears, EXCEPT the actual post page. Therefore the more tag is obeyed on the homepage, category pages, tag pages, author pages etc. When Wordpress find a more tag, it truncates your post at that point, offering the visitor a "more" link to read the rest of the post.

OK, let's try this.

Insert a "More tag" after your first paragraph.

If you preview the post, you won't notice any difference, since the preview is showing you the "post page", and this is the only page where the more tag is ignored. To see the more tag in action, click the **Publish** button:

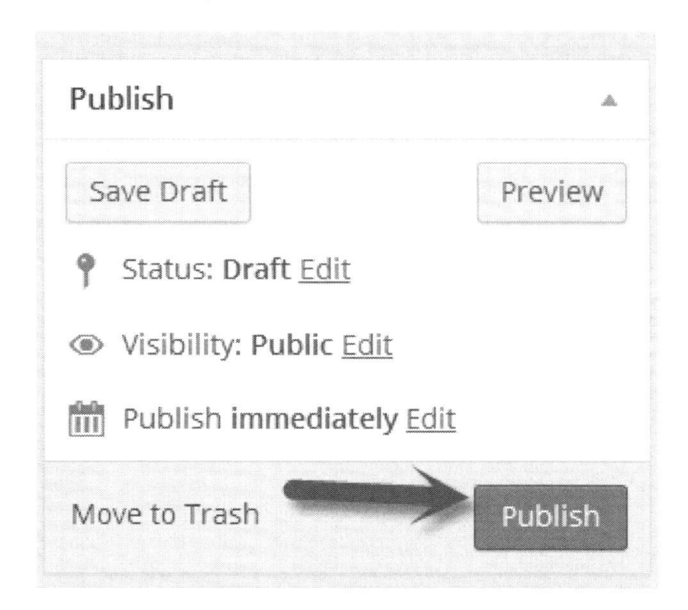

This makes the post live on your site. If you now visit the homepage of your site, you'll see your test post is now truncated where you added the more tag:

THIS IS MY TEST DOCUMENT

MARCH 23, 2014 LEAVE A COMMENT EDIT

This is a test post to see how the editor works. This is a test post to see how the editor works. This is a test post to see how the editor works. This is a test post to see how the editor works. I can see that it automatically wraps onto the next line when it gets to the end.
Continue reading →

Notice that Wordpress is offering you a link to "Continue reading".

Clicking that opens up the full post page, with the screen scrolled down to the position of the more tag, so your visitor can carry on reading the post. Go on, click the "Continue reading" link to understand how this all works.

On the bottom row of the toolbar, there are a couple of options I want to tell you about. The first one is the clipboard with the "W" inside. This button allows you to paste in text from a Word document, which Wordpress will then handle gracefully to insert that Word document into a post. If you simply try to paste content from a Word document into the main editor window, you'll end up in a mess. If you use Word to write your documents ahead of time, you MUST use the **Paste from Word** button.

When you click it, you are given a box to paste your Word document into. Just follow the instructions, and your Word document should be correctly formatted and inserted.

The only other toolbar buttons I want to mention are the redo/undo buttons:

You are probably already familiar with undo and redo features of your Word processor. If you do something wrong, you can click the undo button to undo it. If you undo something and need to redo it, click the redo button.

The Visual / Text editors

You may have noticed two tabs at the top right of the editor – "Visual" and "Text".

The visual editor is selected at the moment, and with the visual editor we can design our content visually using the WYSIWYG editor and formatting buttons.

Click onto the Text tab, and you'll see the contents of your post as HTML code.

You are unlikely to need to modify the HTML code directly, so I won't discuss the Text editing screen and its options. Just know it's there. We will revisit this tab later when we look at inserting a Youtube video into a post.

Inserting Media into your post

Media can be images, video or sound files. You insert them the same way in each case, by using the Media Library.

To insert an image, move your edit cursor to the position of your document where you want to insert the image.

Now click the **Add Media** button.

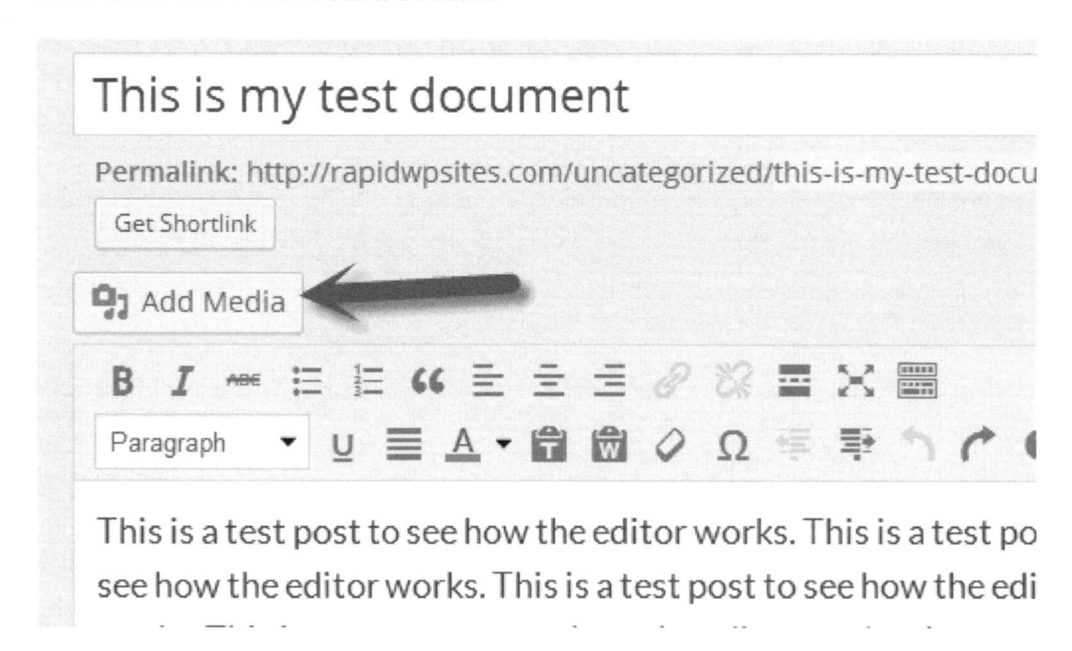
This is my test document
Permalink: http://rapidwpsites.com/uncategorized/this-is-my-test-docu
Get Shortlink
Add Media
Paragraph
This is a test post to see how the editor works. This is a test po
see how the editor works. This is a test post to see how the edi

The **Insert Media** screen opens.

You can drag and drop any media files from your computer to this screen.

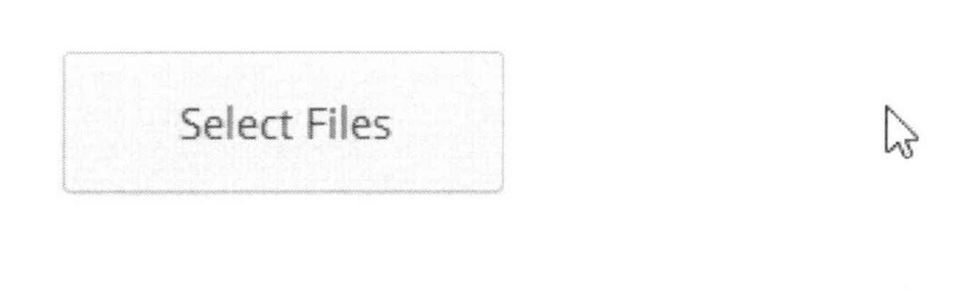

If you prefer, you can also select the files from your computer by clicking the **Select Files** button. Both of these options will add the files to your media library.

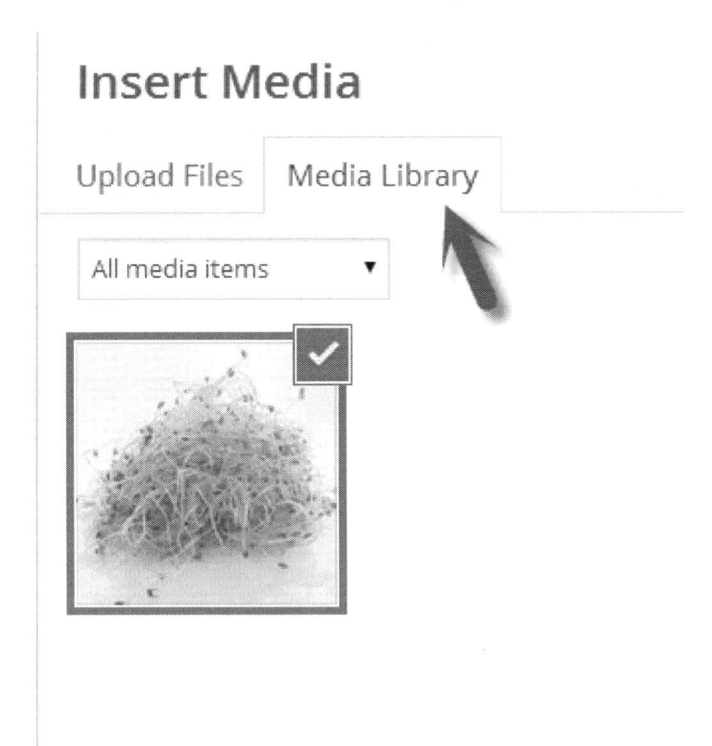

On the Media Library screen, you can select any of the images you have added to your library, and insert them into your post.

Above the **Insert into Post** button, you have a few options.

I recommend you set the alignment to either right or left, as this will make the text of your post flow around the image.

Adding a sub-headline
This is the second paragraph. This is a test post to see how the editor works. ***This is a test post to see how the editor works.*** This is a test post to see how the editor works. I can see that it automatically wraps onto the next line when it gets to the end.

When you want to add an image to your post, you can either upload a new image, as we have just done, or go to the Media Library (by clicking the Media library tab at the top of the Insert Media screen) and select an image that you uploaded previously.

Wordpress 3.9 gave us a second option for inserting images into post. We are now able to drag and drop an image from our computer, directly into the post.

Find the file you want to add to your post, and click and hold the mouse to drag the image into your post. As your mouse goes over the post, you'll see the screen change:

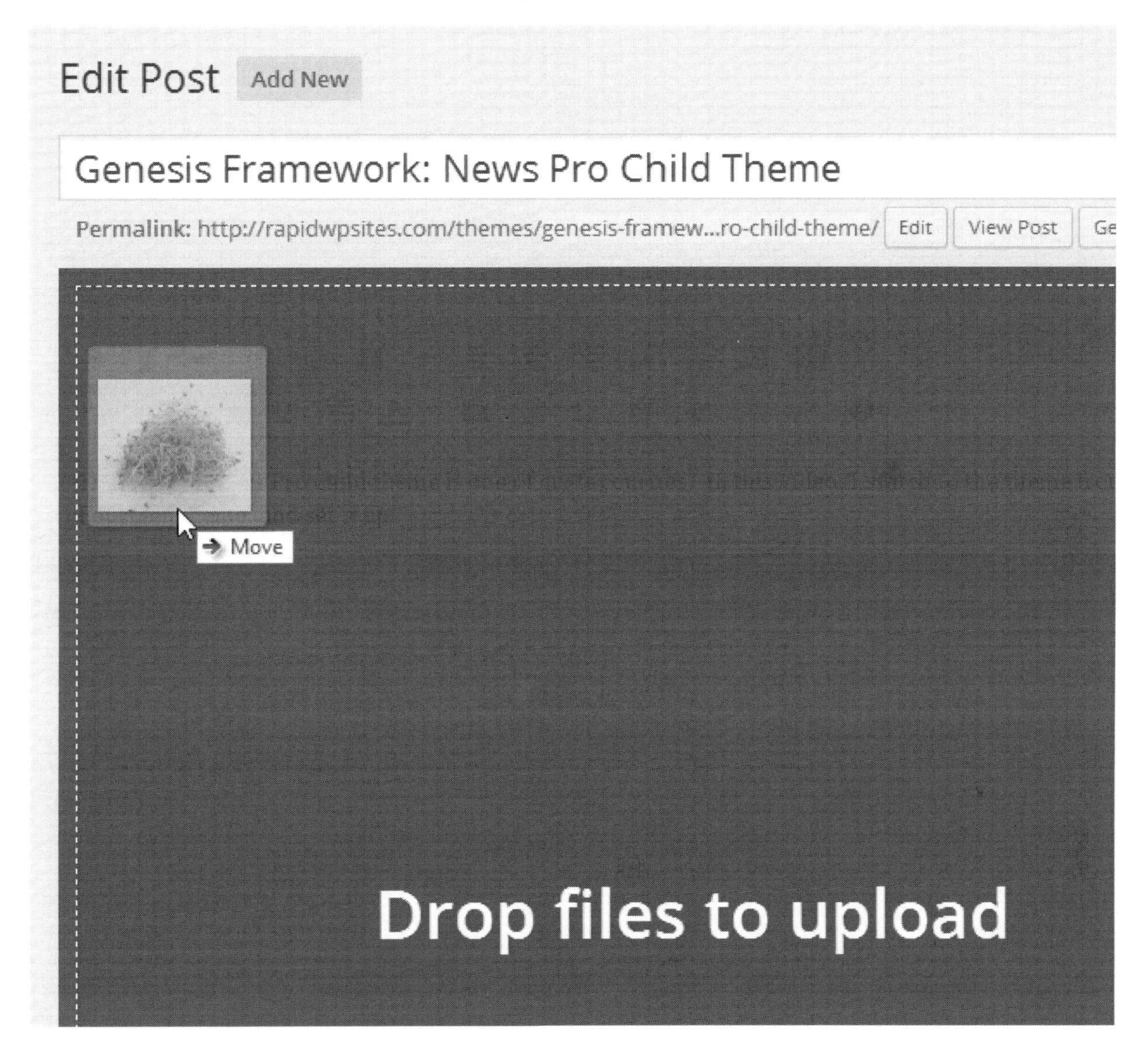

You can now drop the image into the post. When you do, Wordpress will upload the image to your media library.

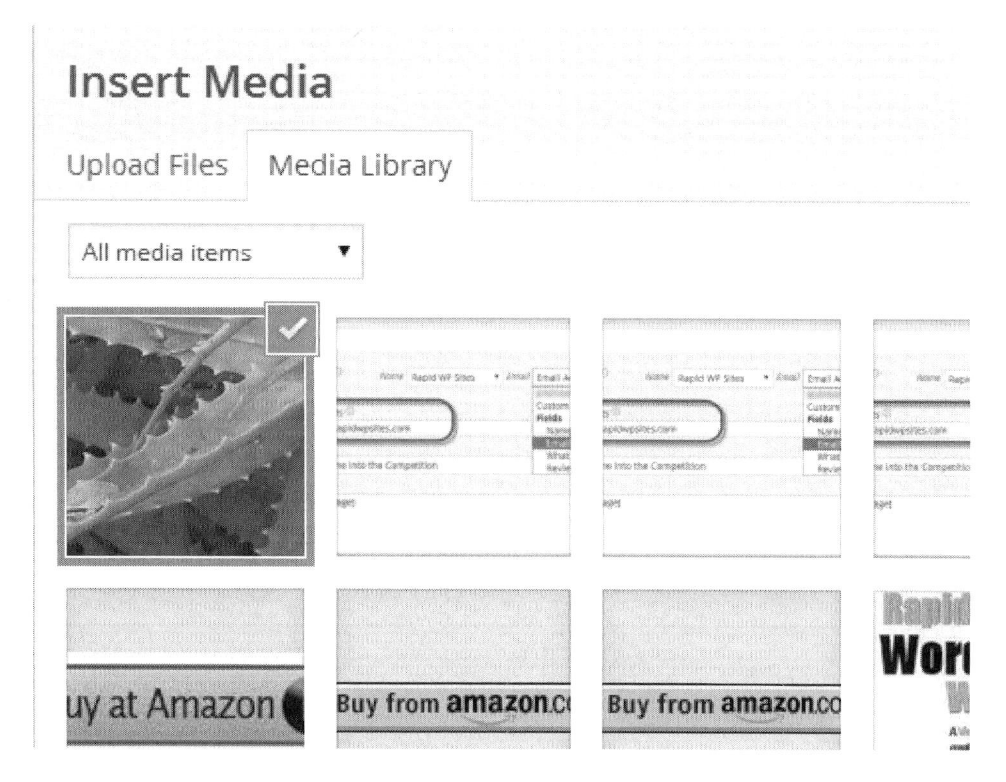

You can see the image I just dropped top left.

Now just click the **Insert into post** button to insert the image into your post.

With Wordpress 3.9 you can also drag and move your image around the post to put it in the correct location.

Image Lightbox

When you insert an image into your post, the default settings in Wordpress are to make the image a link to itself. You can see this if you preview your page, and click on the image. The image loads in a browser screen, all by itself:

For most types of image, you don't want the image to be a hyperlink. We can turn this off when we insert the image, or after an image has already inserted.

Remember when we inserted the image; there were some options above the **Insert into Post** button?

One of those options was a drop down box, labeled **Link To**:

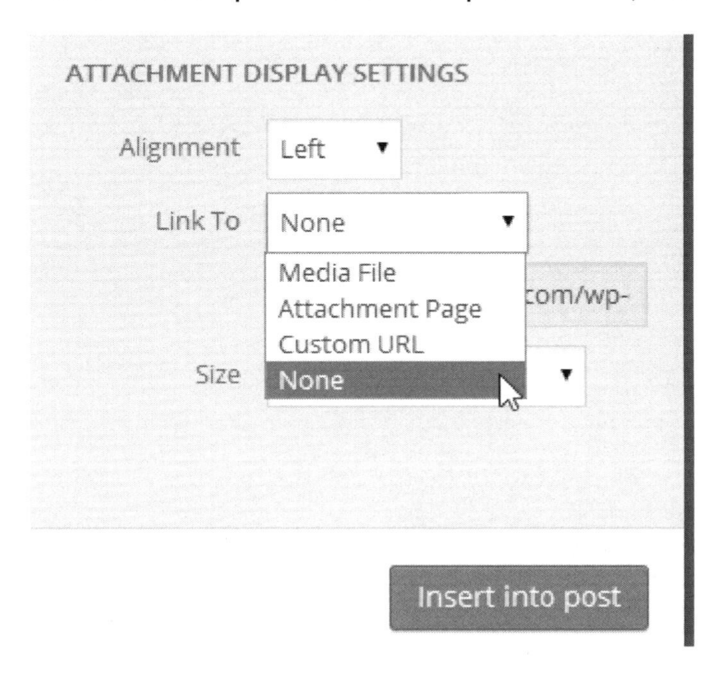

The default was set as "Media file", meaning the image linked to itself. To stop the image linking to itself, select **None** from this drop down box.

If you have already inserted an image and want to turn off the self-linking, click on the image in your WYSIWYG editor. A couple of icons appear top left in the image:

The icon on the right allows you to delete the image. The icon on the left allows you to edit the image details:

Image Details

Caption

Alternative Text aloevera-and-frog

DISPLAY SETTINGS

Align Left Center Right None

Size Full Size - 285 × 220

Link To Media File

http://rapidwpsites.com/wp-content/uploads/2014/04/aloev

ADVANCED OPTIONS ▲

Image Title Attribute

Image CSS Class

Open link in a new window/tab

Link Rel

Link CSS Class

Edit Original Replace

At the bottom of the **Display** Setting, you can see a section called **Link To**. Just select **None** from the list, to remove the self-link. After any changes, click the Update button at the bottom of the image details screen.

Since changing the image actually changes the post, you'll need to click the update button on the edit post screen.

OK; so we can turn off the self link, but some people actually want to display their images when a visitor clicks on them. There is a nice way of doing this with a plugin.

First thing we need to do is make sure the image links to itself. We just removed that in the preceding section, so add it back again.

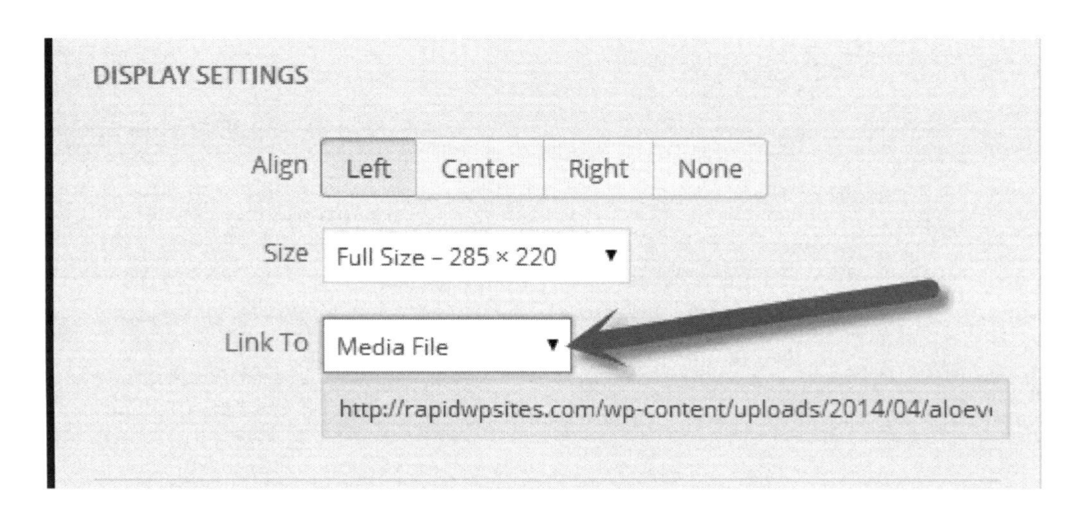

You can do this in the image details screen, by selecting the **Media File** option from the drop down list. This will insert the URL of the image in the **Link To** field.

Down below the Display Settings, you'll see the **Advanced Options**. These may be collapsed, so click the little arrow next to them to unfold them. You can now see an option to **open link in a new window/tab**.

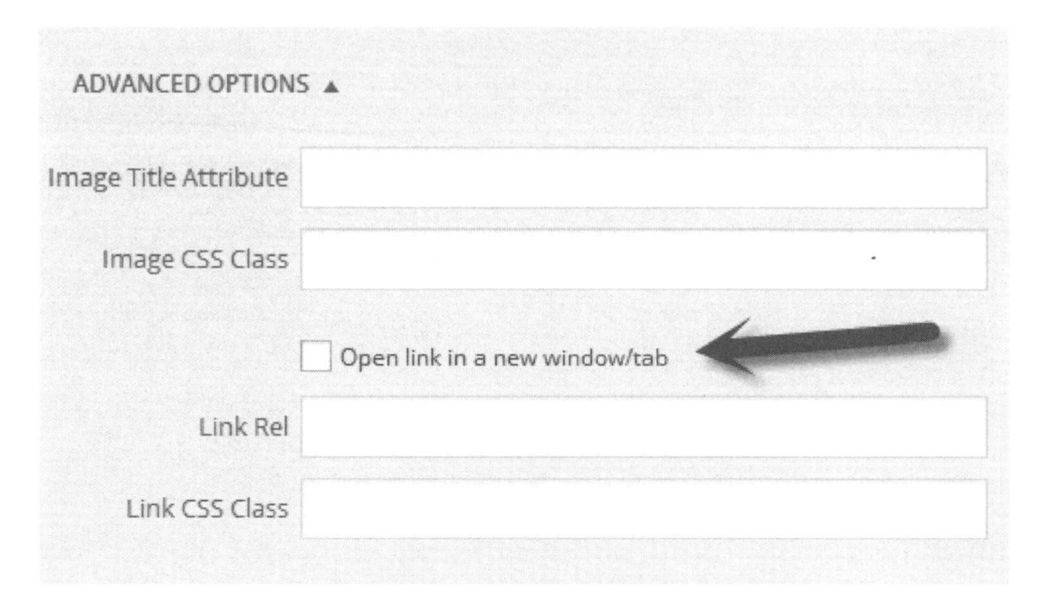

Click the checkbox to **Open link in a new window**, then click **Update** to save the change.

Click the **Update** button for your post as well, to save the changes to the post.

If you now preview the page, and click the image, it opens in a new browser window.

This doesn't look very pretty, so let's install an image lightbox plugin to handle the image display more gracefully.

Click on the **Add New** item in the Plugins sidebar menu.

You'll be taken to the **Install Plugins** screen. In the search box at the top, type in WP-slimbox2, and click the search button:

Name	Version	Rating	Description
WP-Slimbox2 Plugin Details | Install Now	1.1.3.1	★★★★☆	A WordPress implementation of the stellar Slimbox2 script by Christophe Beyls (an enhanced clone of the Lightbox script) which utilizes the jQuery library to create an impressive image overlay with slide-out effects. Almost, if not all, options are configurable from the administration panel. For more on the settings and what they do check out the Slimbox2 page. Support forums are generously host... By Greg Yingling (malcalevak).

Make sure you locate the correct plugin (shown above) and click the **Install Now** button. You'll get a popup asking if you are sure. Just click OK.

Once the plugin is installed, you'll have the option to **Activate Plugin**.

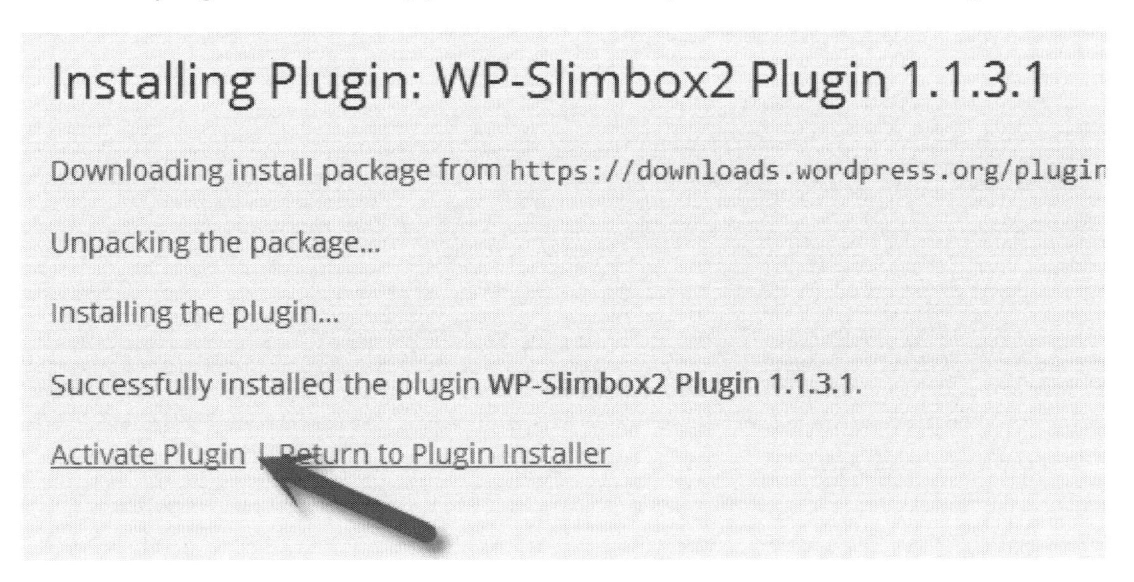

Installing Plugin: WP-Slimbox2 Plugin 1.1.3.1
Downloading install package from https://downloads.wordpress.org/plugin
Unpacking the package...
Installing the plugin...
Successfully installed the plugin WP-Slimbox2 Plugin 1.1.3.1.
Activate Plugin | Return to Plugin Installer

Click that link.

Once installed and activated, the plugin should start working immediately.

If you visit a post on your site and click on an image, the image will open in a "lightbox".

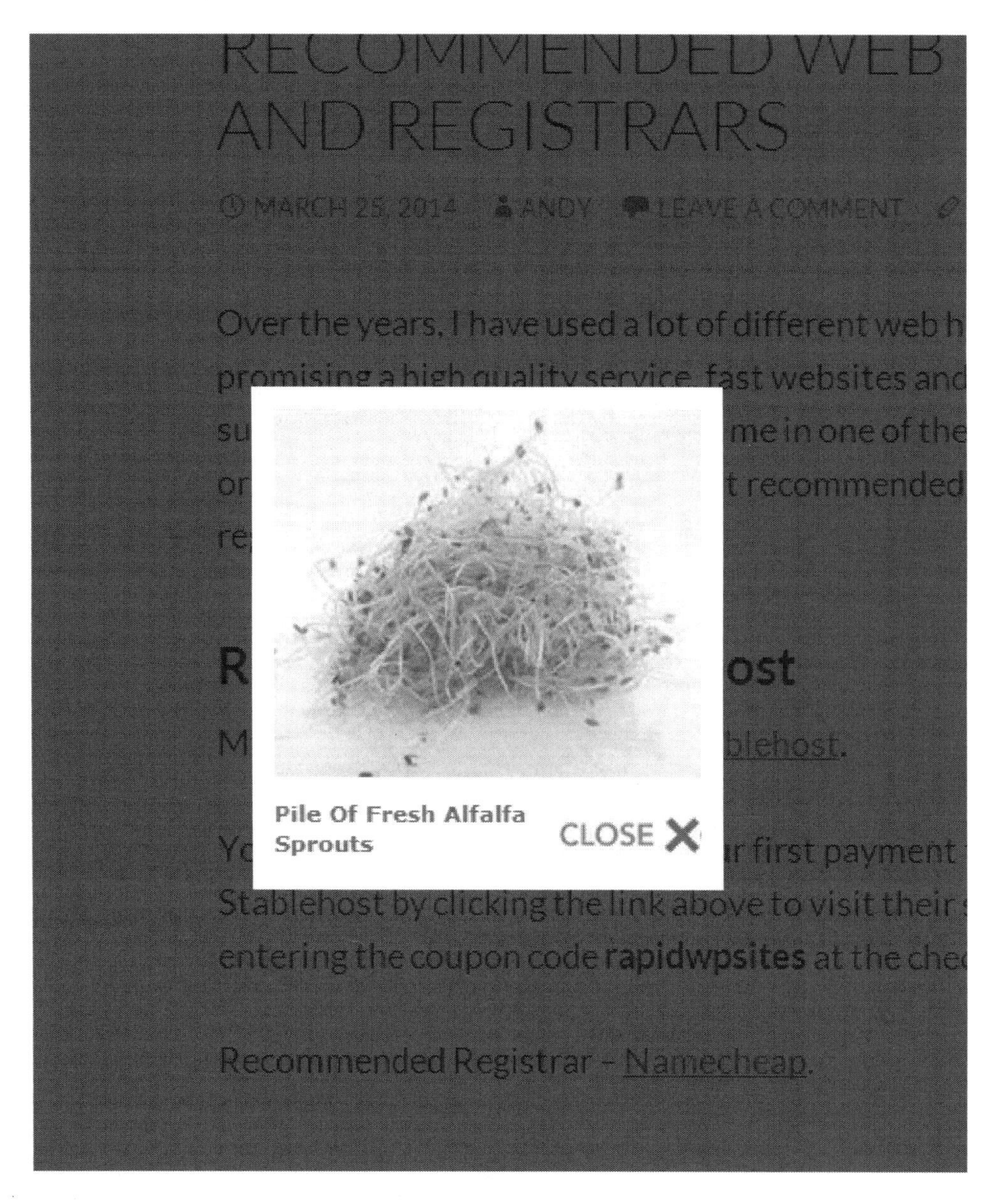

AND REGISTRARS
MARCH 25, 2014 ANDY LEAVE A COMMENT
Over the years, I have used a lot of different web
fast websites and
me in one of the
recommended
ost
Pile Of Fresh Alfalfa Sprouts
CLOSE
first payment
Stablehost by clicking the link above to visit their
entering the coupon code rapidwpsites at the
Recommended Registrar – Namecheap.

After installing this plugin, you'll have a new item in the Settings menu in the left sidebar:

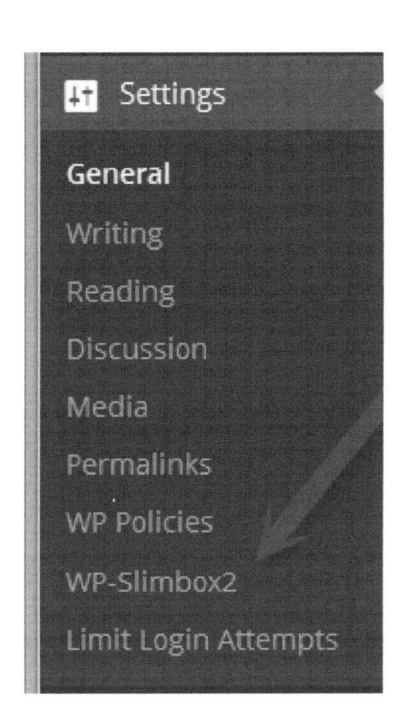

This will take you to some settings for the plugin, so you can customize the look of the lightbox.

The only important option should already be checked by default:

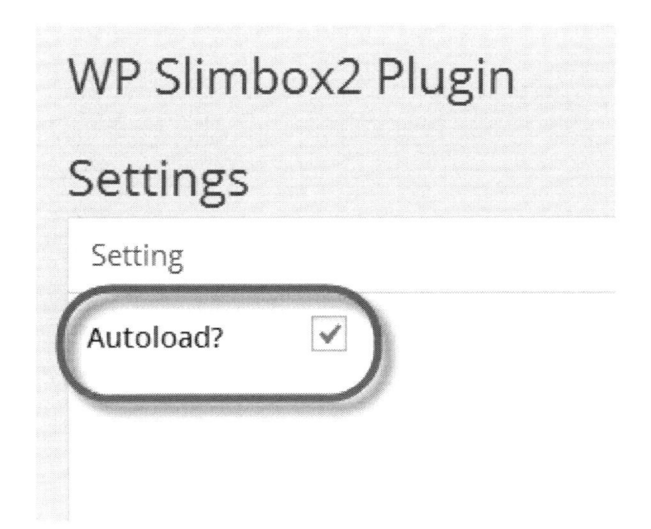

You might also like to check this one, so the lightbox works on mobile devices:

You can look over the other options for yourself, and consult the documentation of the plugin if you need more help with this.

Adding a Youtube Video

If you want to add a video from a video sharing site, like Youtube, that's easy.

Find the video on Youtube.

Under the video, look for the **Share** link. Click it, and then you'll see another menu open with an **Embed** link. Click it.

Under the "embed" link you'll see the code you need to copy and insert into your post.

Copy the code, then head back to your editor. Now switch to the "Text" tab:

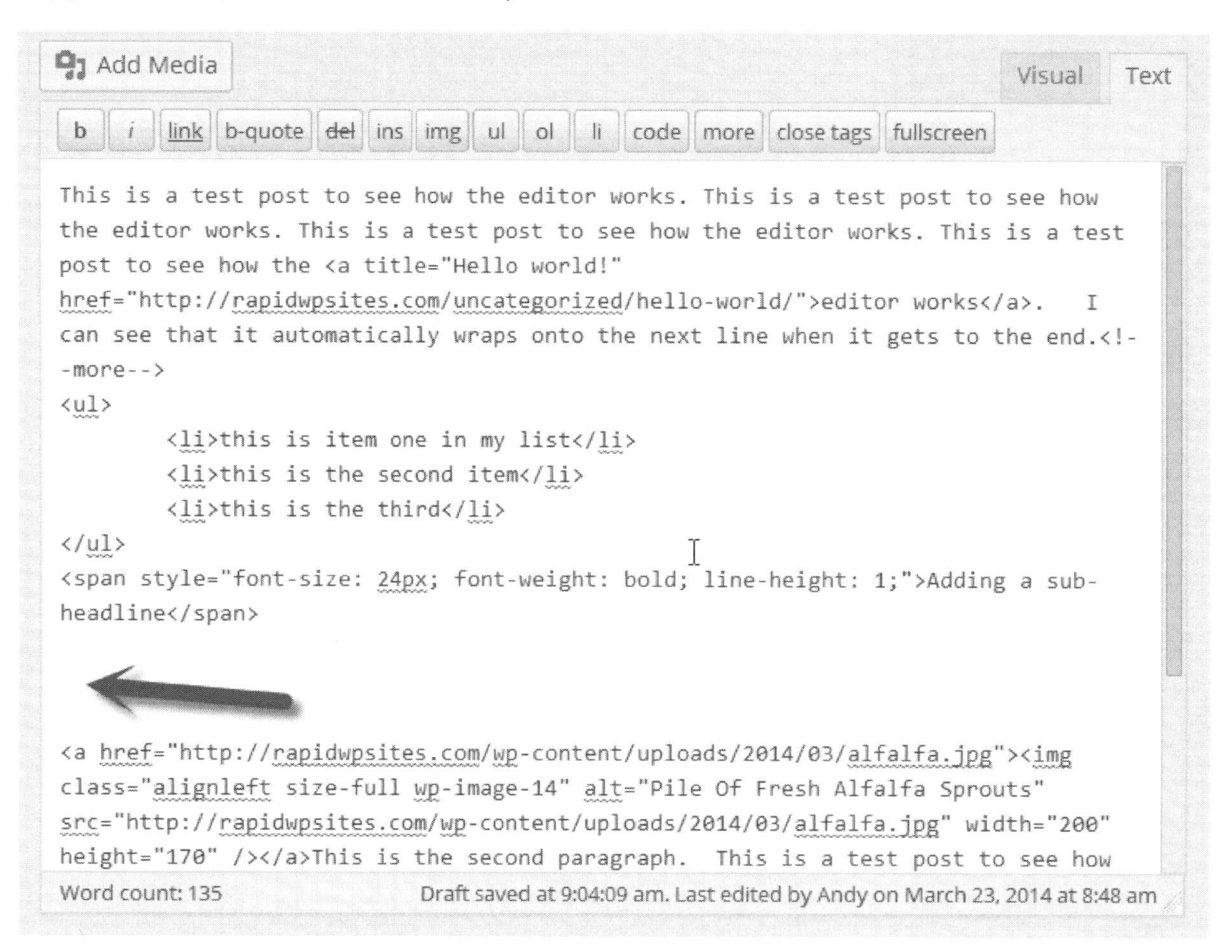
Add Media
Visual
Text
b
i
link
b-quote
del
ins
img
ul
ol
li
code
more
close tags
fullscreen
This is a test post to see how the editor works. This is a test post to see how
the editor works. This is a test post to see how the editor works. This is a test
post to see how the <a title="Hello world!"
href="http://rapidwpsites.com/uncategorized/hello-world/">editor works</a>. I
can see that it automatically wraps onto the next line when it gets to the end.<!-
-more-->
<ul>
<li>this is item one in my list</li>
<li>this is the second item</li>
<li>this is the third</li>
</ul>
<span style="font-size: 24px; font-weight: bold; line-height: 1;">Adding a sub-
headline</span>
<a href="http://rapidwpsites.com/wp-content/uploads/2014/03/alfalfa.jpg"><img
class="alignleft size-full wp-image-14" alt="Pile Of Fresh Alfalfa Sprouts"
src="http://rapidwpsites.com/wp-content/uploads/2014/03/alfalfa.jpg" width="200"
height="170" /></a>This is the second paragraph. This is a test post to see how
Word count: 135
Draft saved at 9:04:09 am. Last edited by Andy on March 23, 2014 at 8:48 am

You'll see the HTML code for your page, so try not to change anything. Look for the position in your post that you want the video to appear.

Move the edit cursor to that position, and paste the video code into your post. Now if you switch back to the HTML editor tab, you can see where the video will appear. If you preview your post, you can see the video embedded, and even click on it to play:

- this is item one in my list
- this is the second item
- this is the third

Adding a sub-headline

This is the second paragraph. This is a test post to see how the editor works. ***This is a test post to see how the editor***

OK, you have all the tools you need to create content for your site. Let's create some web pages.

Creating Pages - About, contact & terms

The first web pages we are going to create on the site are the ones I call "legal" pages. Remember? We talked about them earlier. These are the web pages that are not specifically written to engage our visitors, but are required to make the site complete, and more professional.

Let's start with the Contact Us page. This will allow your visitors to contact you by filling out a form on your site. For this, we are going to use a plugin.

Click **Add New** in the Plugins sidebar menu.

In the search box, type **contact form 7**

You should see this plugin:

Name	Version	Rating	Description
Contact Form 7 Details | Install Now	3.7.2		Contact Form 7 can manage multiple contact forms, plus you can customize the form and the mail contents flexibly with simple markup. The form supports Ajax-powered submitting, CAPTCHA, Akismet spam filtering and so on. Docs & Support You can find docs, FAQ and more detailed information about Contact Form 7 on contactform7.com. If you were unable to find the answer to your question on the FAQ... By Takayuki Miyoshi.

Click the **Install Now** link under the title.

You'll be asked to confirm that you want to install it, so just click OK.

Finally, activate the plugin.

You will now have a new menu in the sidebar, labeled **Contact**.

Under the Contact menu, click **Contact Forms.**

The plugin installed a demo form for you, and that serves our purpose.

Highlight the shortcode for the form and copy it.

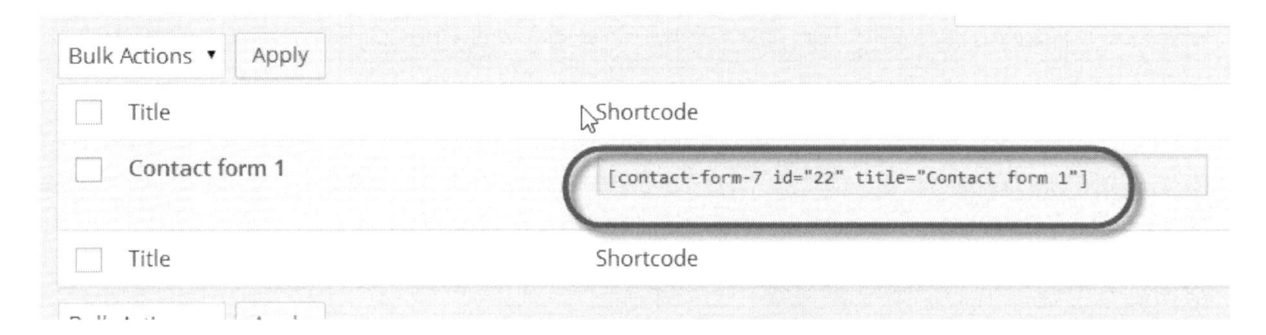

We now need to go and create a Page. Under the **Pages** menu, click **Add New**.

For the title, type **Contact** or **Contact Us**.

In the WYSIWYG editor, paste the contact form shortcode you copied earlier.

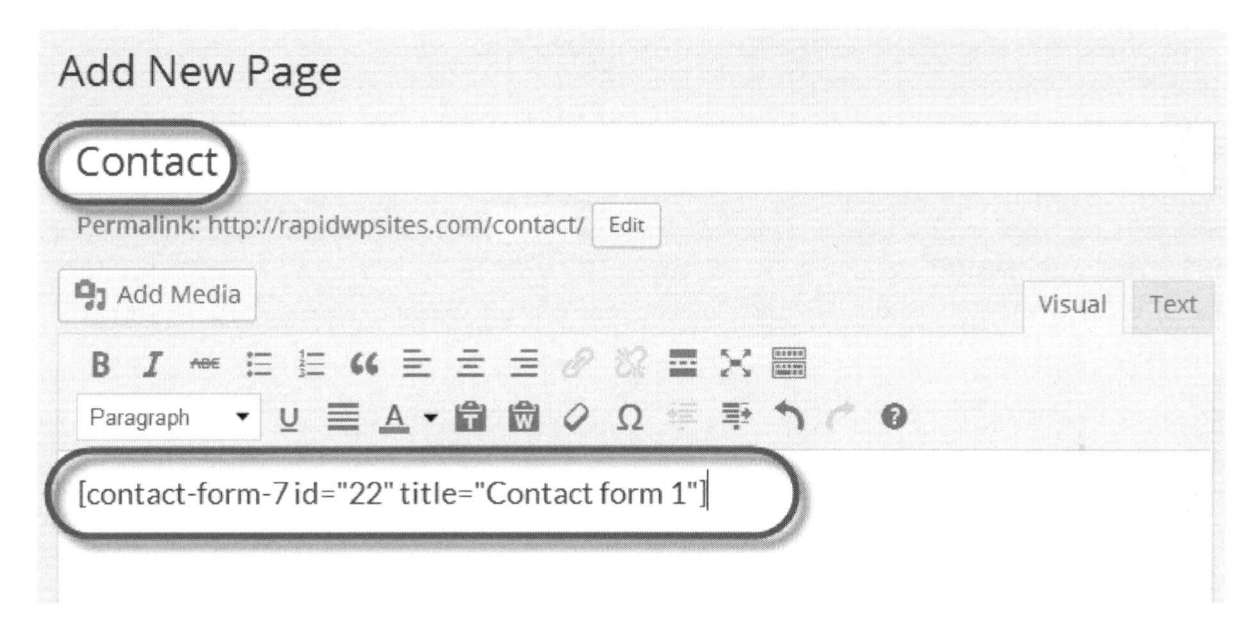

Click the **Publish** button to publish the page.

If you now visit your homepage, you will see the link to the contact page in the top right menu.

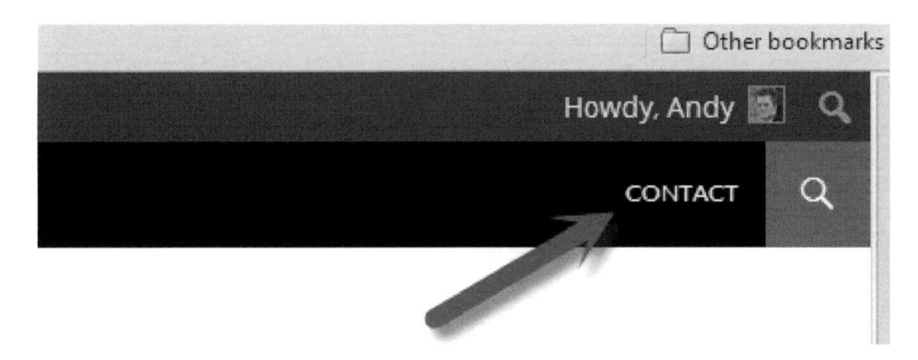

Click to visit the contact page.

You will see your contact form on the page. If you fill it in and send a test message, you should receive it at the email address you entered as your admin email when you set Wordpress up.

NOTE: When you are working in the Dashboard and want to go visit your site, click the **Visit Site** link in the menu located top left (the menu will be your site name).

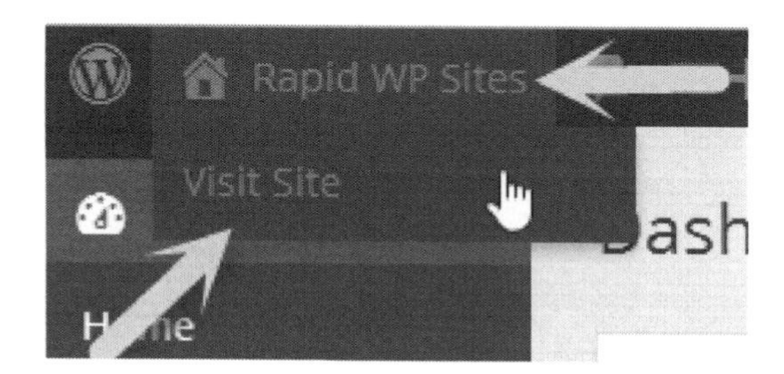

This will open the site in the same browser window, but you can right click it and open in a new window if you prefer.

There is one more thing to do.

Notice that at the bottom of the Contact page, there is a comment form? We don't want to allow comments on the contact page, since comments should be restricted to posts only. If we left it in place, and accepted comments, then the comments would appear at the bottom of the contact page, and that isn't really something we want.

You need to turn comments off on this page (and every other page), and only allow comments on posts.

To turn comments off for n the contact form, open the page edit screen for the contact page.

In the edit page screen, click on the Screen Options top right:

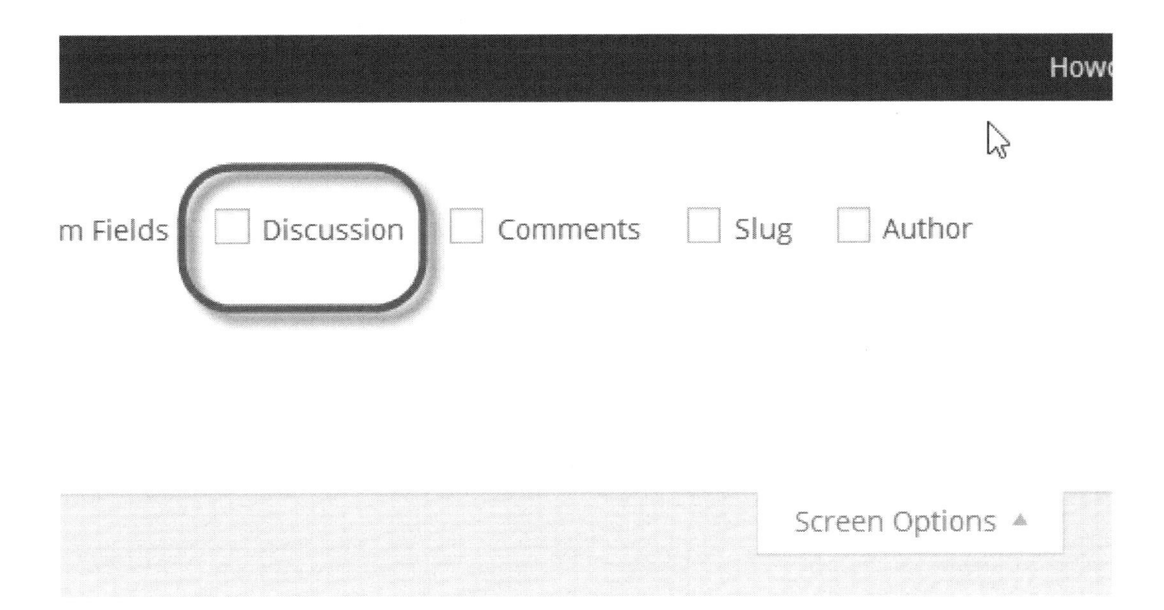

.. and then check the **Discussion** checkbox.

This will make the discussion options visible on the Edit Page screen:

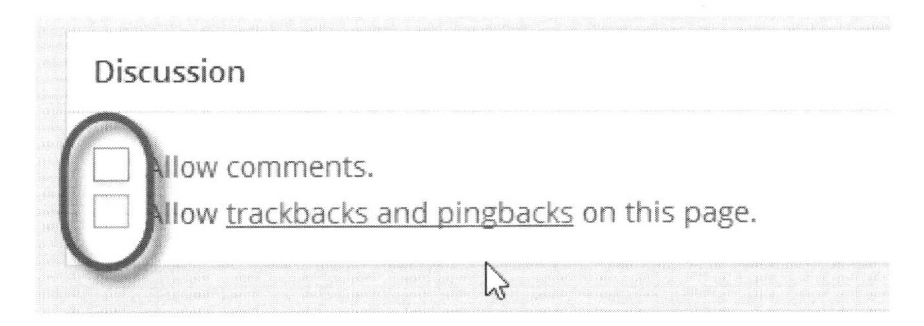

Uncheck both of these boxes to prevent comments and trackbacks/pingbacks.

You can now re-publish your page. If you have already published the page, the "Publish" button is now labeled **Update**.

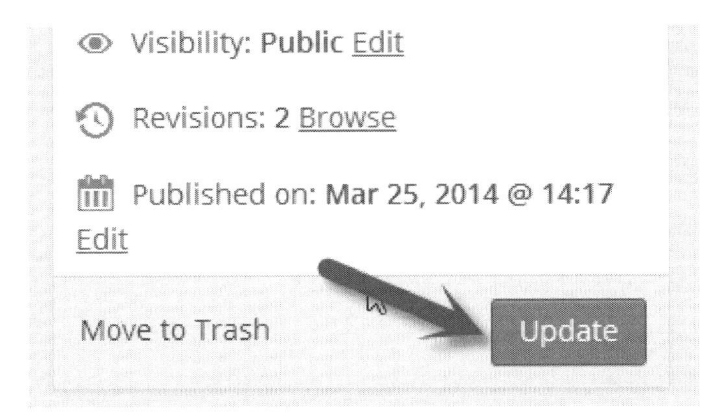

Once updated, go back to your contact page and you should find the comment form has gone.

That's the first page complete.

OK, now for the "About Us" page. This is where you have a chance to write a little bit about yourself and your site, so your visitors know about the person/company behind the site. The "About Us" page is often the most visited page on many websites, so bear that in mind.

Click **Add New** from the **Pages** sidebar menu.

This will start a new page.

For the title, use something simple, like "About", "About Me" or "About Us".

Now in the WYSIWYG editor, write the contents of your "About" page.

What should you include? Well obviously that is your choice, but here are some things I try to include in mine:

1. I like to begin by stating the goal of my web site, but usually approach this from the point of view of the visitors. What are their problems or interests and how can my site help them.
2. Add your name and photo.
3. Add a bit of information about yourself.
4. Break up the page with bullet points and sub-headings to make it easier to read or scan.
5. Include your contact details, or at the very least a contact form (or a link to your contact form).

Once you have entered the text for your about page, click the **Publish** button to make it live on your site.

Here is my About Us page:

http://rapidwpsites.com/about/

You will notice I included a photo, plus a link to my contact form at the end.

Visit your own about page.

You will find the comment form at the bottom of the page. Go in and turn it off in the same way we did for the Contact form. You should not need to edit the **Screen Options** again, since these are remembered between sessions.

The final pages we want to create are as follows:

1. Disclaimer
2. Privacy Policy
3. Terms of Use

While you can create these pages manually, and add your own legal documents, I prefer to get them up quickly using another plugin.

Click **Add New** from the plugins menu.

Now search for **WP Policies**

Install and activate this one:

Name	Version	Rating	Description
WP Policies Details | Install Now	1.0	★★★★☆	WP Policies allows you to quickly add pre-written privacy policy and disclaimer statements to your Wordpress blog. The plugin currently comes with 10 policies that you can edit depending on your blog. By Offline Marketing Tools.

You will now have a new menu item under **Settings** called WP Policies.

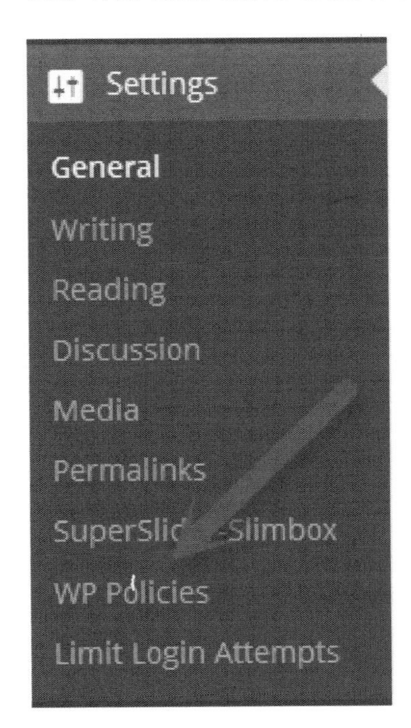

Click it.

Scroll down to the **Contact Details** section.

Enter your site name and email address. You should also enter your Company name if applicable, Address and phone number. However, be aware that these details will appear on the legal documents.

Once you have entered these, click the **Update options** button.

Now scroll to the very bottom and click **Import files**. This will create pages for a lot of different "policies".

You can see these when the page refreshes:

Current Policy Pages	Manage	Edit	Delete
anti-spam_policy	Manage	Edit	Delete
disclaimer	Manage	Edit	Delete
dmca_notice	Manage	Edit	Delete
e-mail_policy	Manage	Edit	Delete
earnings_disclaimer	Manage	Edit	Delete
external_links_policy	Manage	Edit	Delete
medical_disclaimer	Manage	Edit	Delete
privacy_policy	Manage	Edit	Delete
terms_of_use	Manage	Edit	Delete
testimonial_disclaimer	Manage	Edit	Delete

You can delete any of the ones you don't want. At the bare minimum, I'd say you need the disclaimer, privacy policy and terms of use.

You don't need to delete any of these, even if you don't want to use them. You never know what you might want later.

If you click **Pages** in the left sidebar, you can see that you now have a number of different pages. The two you created manually (Contact and About), plus the ones the WP Policies plugin created. If you open up one of the pages created by this plugin, you will not see the "legal" text of the page. In fact, the Visual editor of the WYSIWYG editor is blank. If you click on over to the Text editor tab, you will see this:

The page will load the content from a file called "privacy_policy.dat" when someone loads the page in their browser. This file was installed on your server with the plugin, and you can edit it if you want to.

Preview one of these pages in your browser.

You will notice that these pages also have the comment form. You will need to manually turn the comment form off on each of these pages, in the same way we saw earlier.

Top Navigation Menu

When we created the contact and about us page, these pages were added to the top menu of our site. However, the policies created with the plugin were not.

To offer our visitors links to all of the important "legal" pages, we need to replace that default menu that Wordpress created for us, with a custom menu that we will create now.

Under the **Appearance** menu in the left sidebar, select **Menus**.

At the top, click the link to create a new menu:

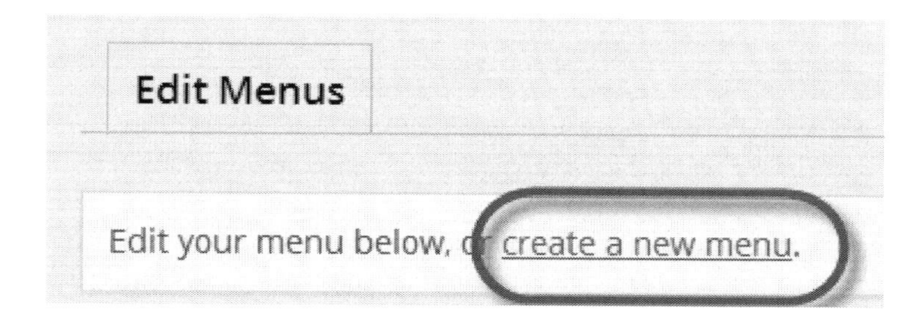

You will now be able to enter a name for your menu:

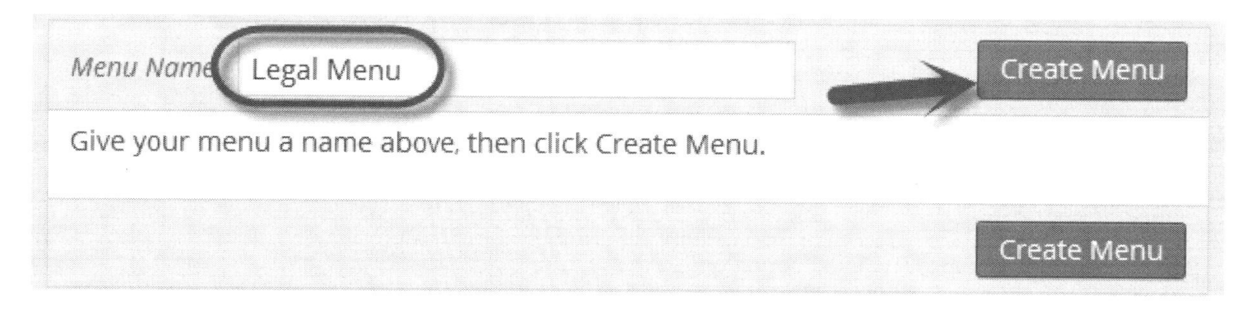

I call this menu my "legal" menu, so that is what I enter here.

Next click the **Create Menu** button.

This creates an empty menu that we can add items to.

On the left, you'll see a list of your pages:

Click on the **View All** tab.

You can now place a check mark next to the pages you want in your menu. I've clicked:

- Home
- About
- Contact
- Disclaimer
- Privacy Policy
- Terms of Use

Note that we are selecting the "About" and "Contact" pages as well, because the menu we are creating will replace that default one that Wordpress has created on the site.

Once you have them checked, click the **Add to Menu** button.

You will now see your list of pages in a column on the right. You can click and drag these pages so that they are in the order you want them to appear on your site.

You can also nest menu items, like this:

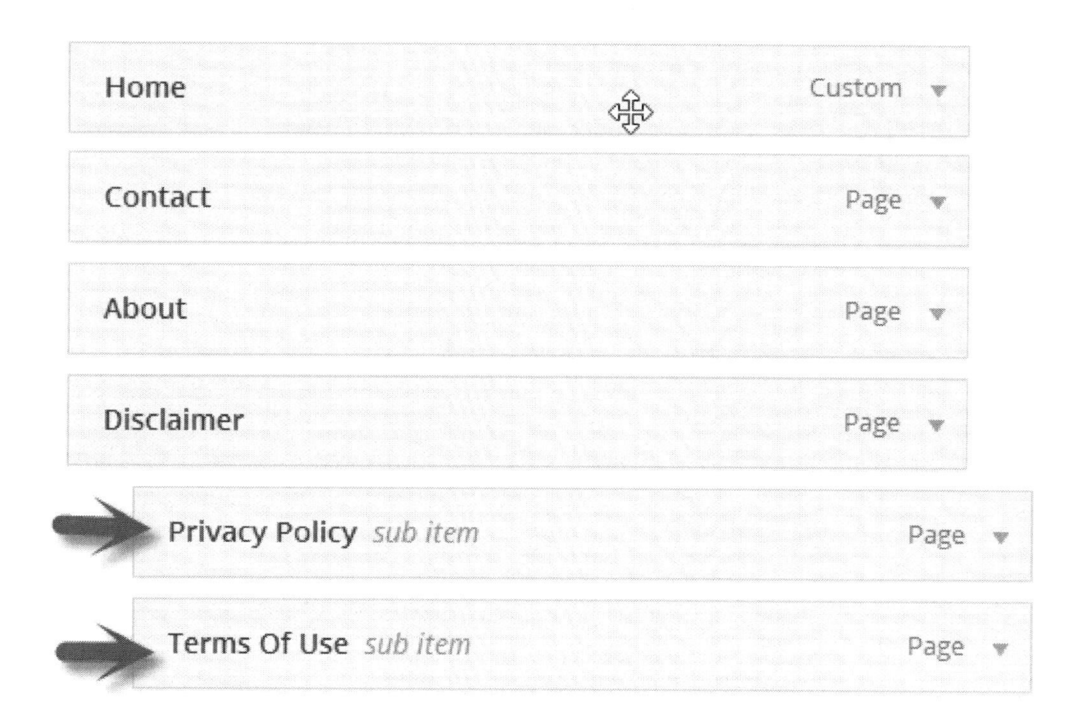

See how the Privacy Policy and the Terms of Use are indented under the "parent" Disclaimer page?

When you indent pages in a menu, only the parent pages show in the menu on your site, but when a visitor moves their mouse over the parent page, a drop down menu appears showing the indented pages.

Here it this menu on my site.

.. and if I mouse-over the Disclaimer menu item:

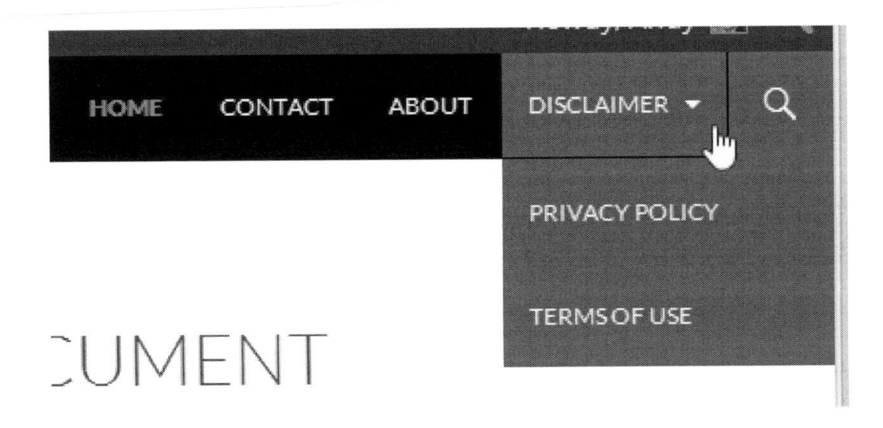

This type of nesting of menu items is useful to stop your menu becoming too big. You indent items like this, simple dragging the menu item to the right a little, underneath the "parent" page.

To display your menu at the top of your website, you need to tell Wordpress to use your newly created menu instead of the default menu.

At the top of the **Menus** screen, click on the **Manage Locations** tab.

When designers are creating Wordpress themes, they design them with menu locations in mind. Most themes will allow a menu at the top of the page, usually under the main site logo, but some themes will have two locations designed for menus.

In the Twenty Fourteen theme that Wordpress uses by default, there are two possible locations where you can put your menu.

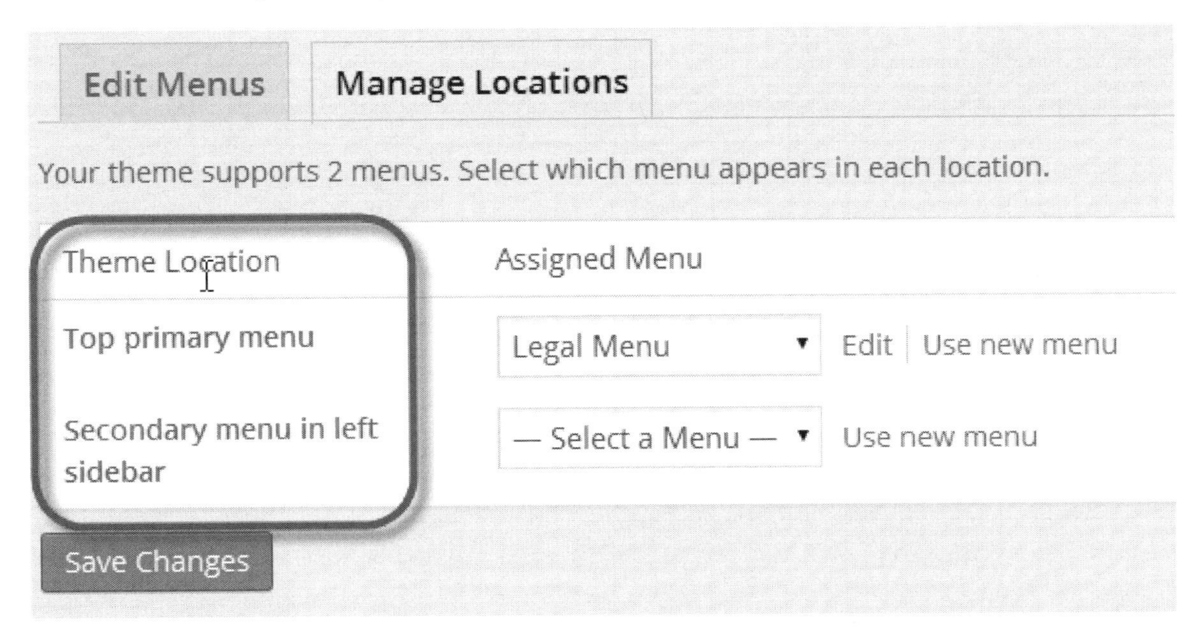

The first location is at the top of the page, where we previously saw the "Contact" and "About" pages listed. This theme also allows us to add the menu to the left sidebar.

Put your "legal" menu in the **Top Primary menu** location and click **Save changes.**

If you now visit your website, your menu will be visible top right. Try clicking items in your menu. You should be taken to the corresponding pages on your site.

If you want, you can try adding the menu to the other location, just to see where it ends up. Here is my legal menu in my left sidebar location.

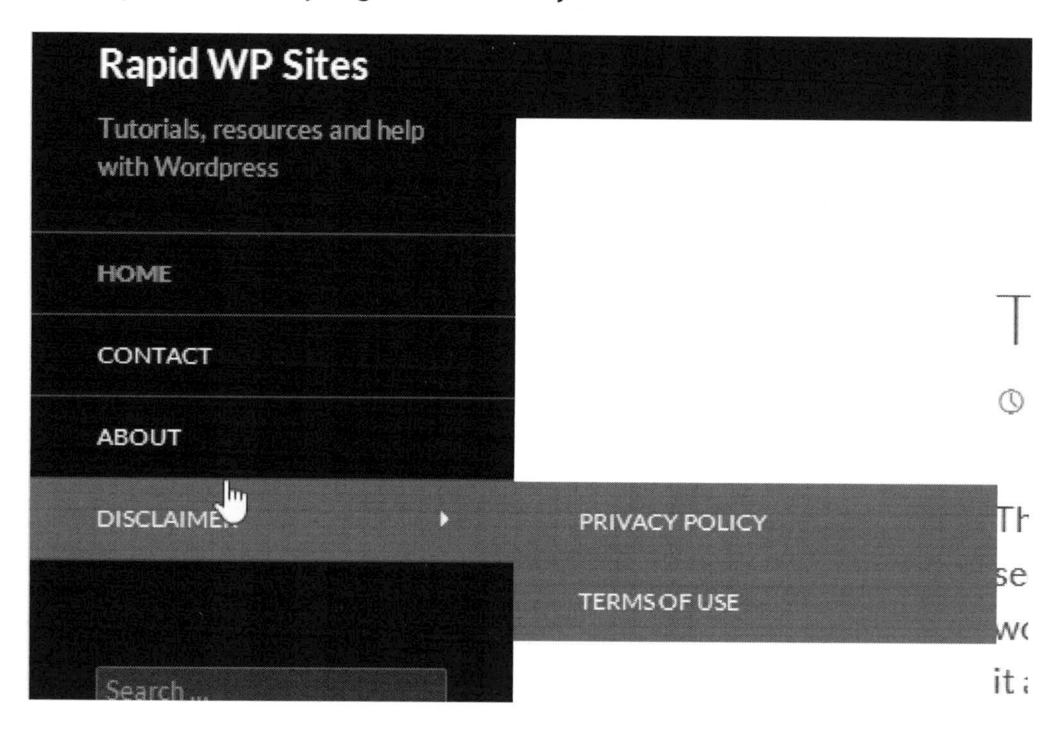

The parent menu now expands horizontally to display the privacy and terms pages.

I typically use a menu in the sidebar to point to my most important POSTS, or categories of posts, but not usually my legal menu.

When you have finished playing with your menus and locations, make sure your legal menu is only displayed ONCE on your site. I'd recommend the top menu option. If and when you decide to change to a different Wordpress theme later, you may have to re-arrange your menu(s).

Note that although this theme has a "designed location" in the left sidebar, you can actually add any menu to the sidebar of your site using widgets. We'll look at widgets later.

Creating the Categories

OK, so the site is starting to take shape. Next we need to add the real website content. That is, the content that we WANT our visitors reading. This is where we start adding posts.

Setting up the Categories

I always like to start by creating the first few categories for the posts I know I want write. You can create categories on the fly, as you need them, but since I have already planned my site, I know three categories I will be using. Remember this:

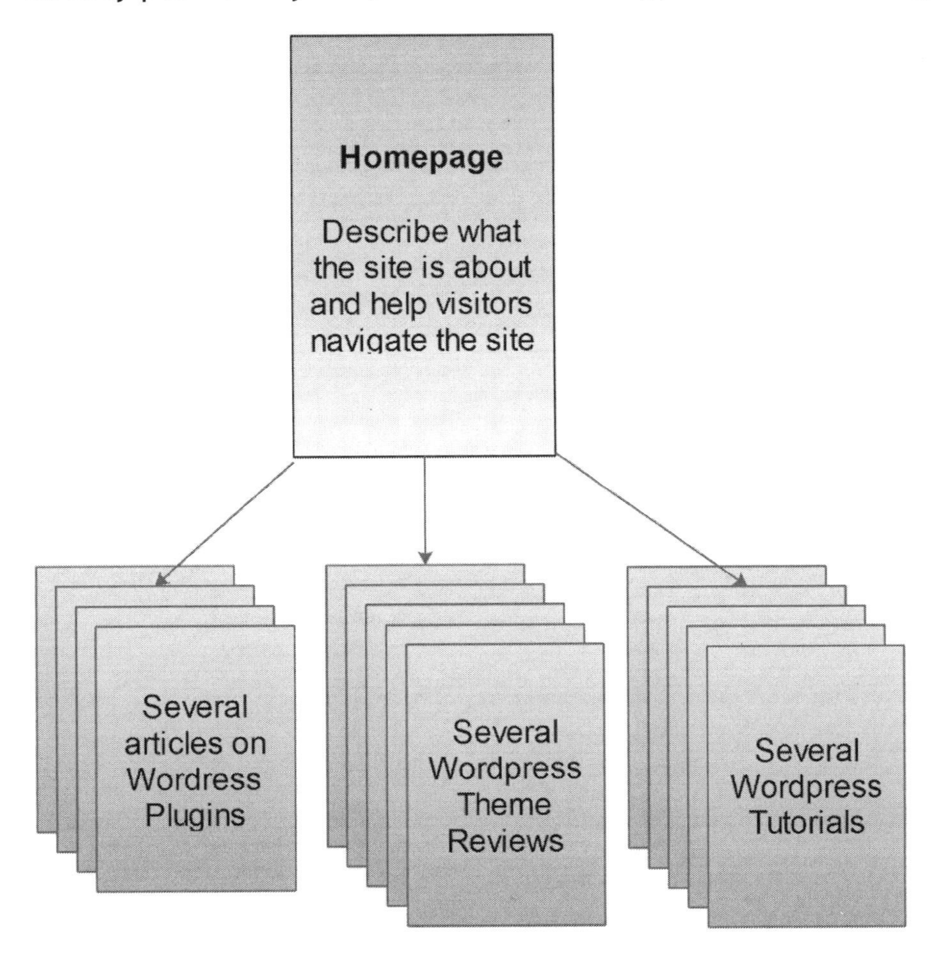

So, I have categories for:

1. Plugins
2. Themes
3. Tutorials

Let's set up those categories now. They won't appear on the site until a post is added to the category, so you don't end up with empty categories.

Click **Categories** under the **Posts** menu in the left sidebar.

On the right of the categories screen, you can see a list of all existing categories. The only one you have now is **Uncategorized**. This is the one that Wordpress set up to be used as a default category. If you enter a post, and forget to select a category, Wordpress chooses this one by default.

I actually want my "tutorials" category to be the default category, and the easiest way to do this is to edit the "Uncategorized" category.

If you move your mouse over "Uncategorized", a menu appears:

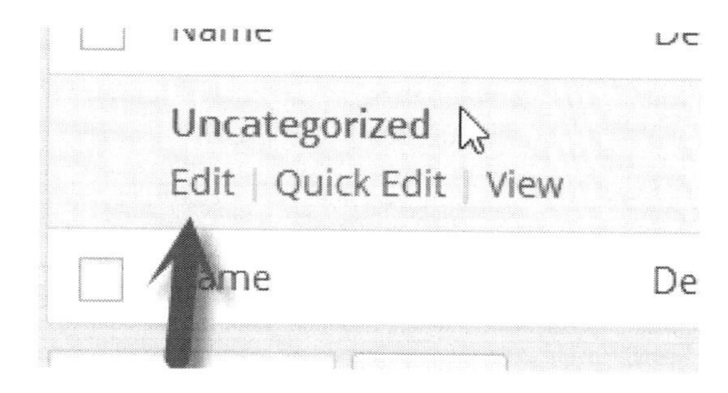

Click **Edit**.

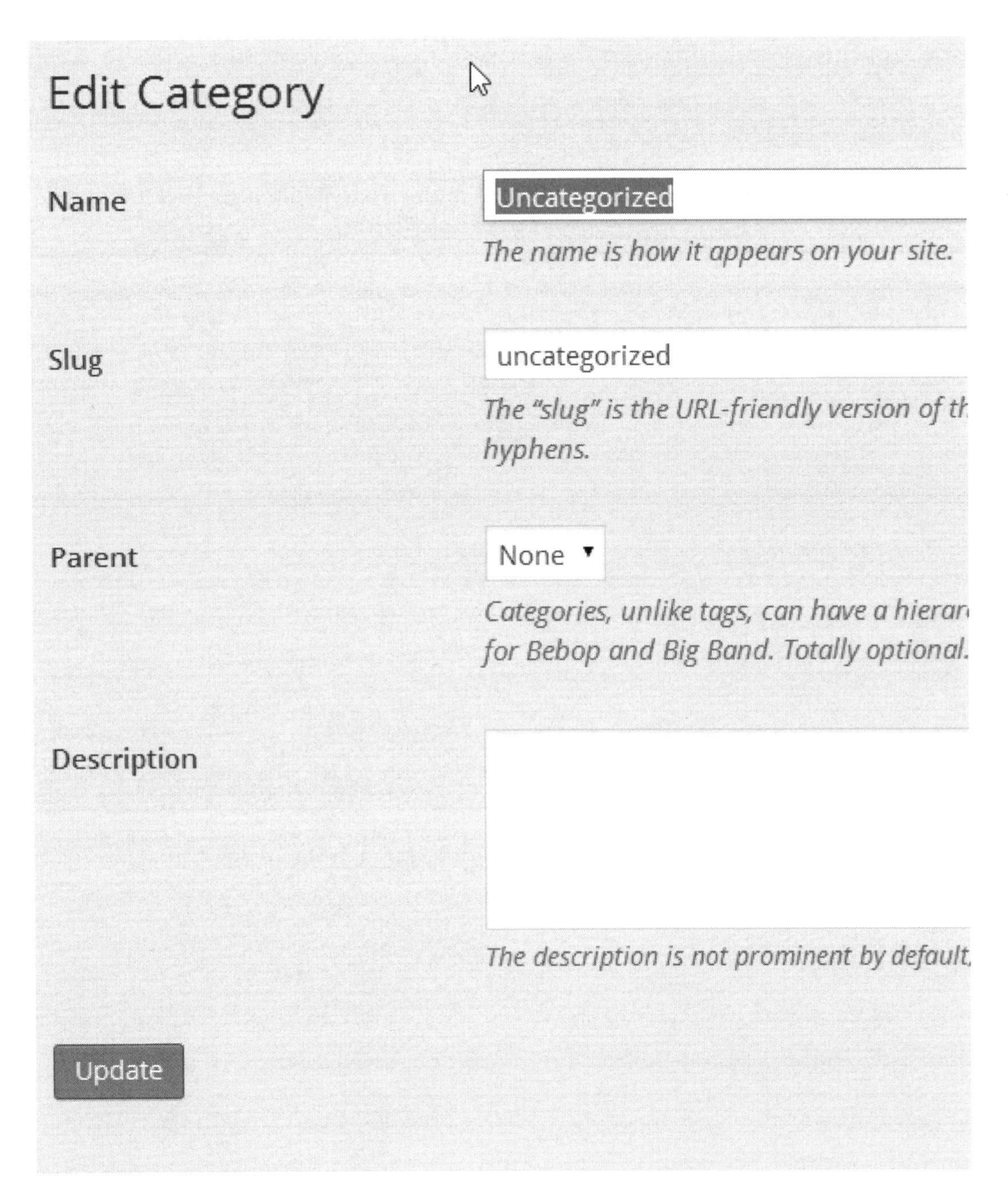
Edit Category
Name
Uncategorized
The name is how it appears on your site.
Slug
uncategorized
The "slug" is the URL-friendly version of th
hyphens.
Parent
None
Categories, unlike tags, can have a hierar
for Bebop and Big Band. Totally optional.
Description
The description is not prominent by default,
Update

You can now edit this category.

Enter the name of your chosen default category. In my case, it's "tutorials".

Delete the contents of the **Slug** box, and leave it empty. The slug is the text that will be used in the URL of posts in this category. If the slug is blank when you save your category, Wordpress will use the category name to create a slug, with spaces being replaced by dashed.

Leave the **Parent** box as **None**. Choosing a parent allows you to nest categories in much the same way we did with menu items when constructing the legal menu. I don't want nested categories, so no "Parent".

In the description box, enter a few sentences to describe the purpose of the category.

When you have finished, click the **Update** button.

Your new default category will now be listed in place of the old "uncategorized" category:

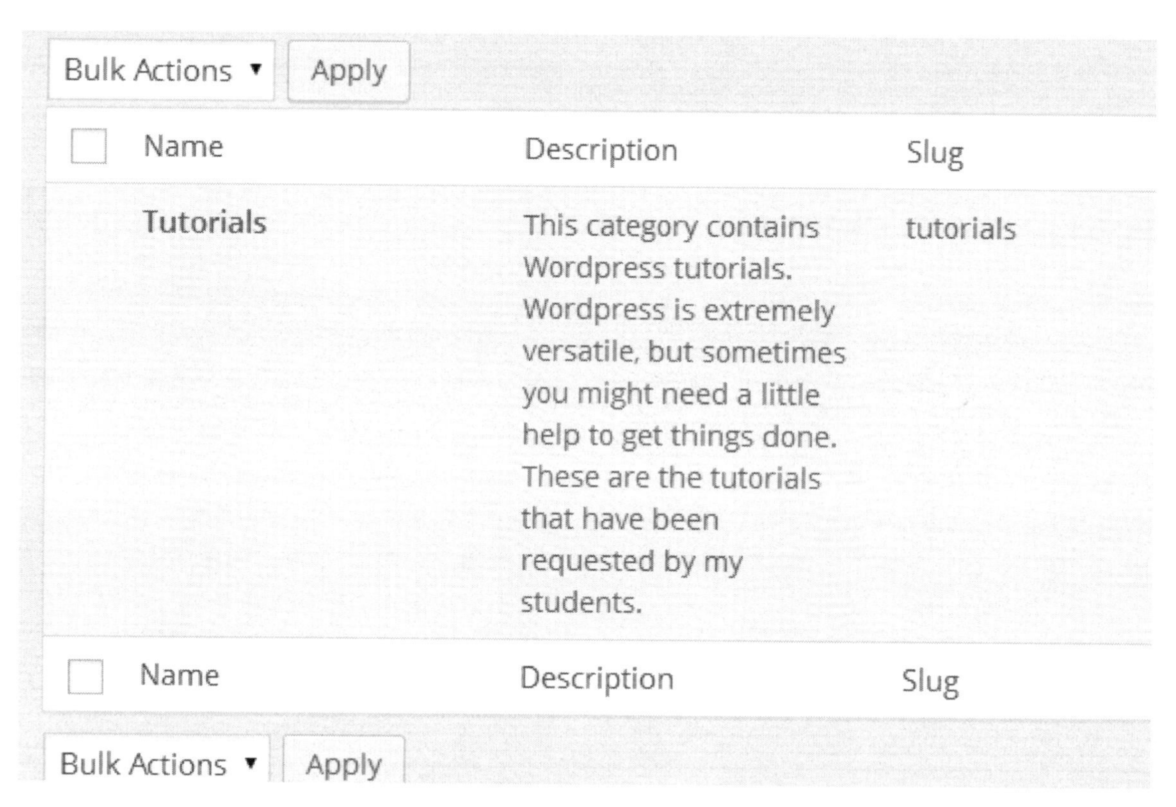

Note that third column "Slug". Wordpress has given my "tutorials" category the slug "tutorials". That is, exactly the same as the category name. This will now create URLs that look like this:

http://rapidwpsites.com/tutorials/using-an-image-for-the-logo

OK, I've just got the "plugins" and the "themes" categories to set up, and I'll be ready to enter posts.

To enter new categories, just add the information on the category page and click the **Add New Category** button:

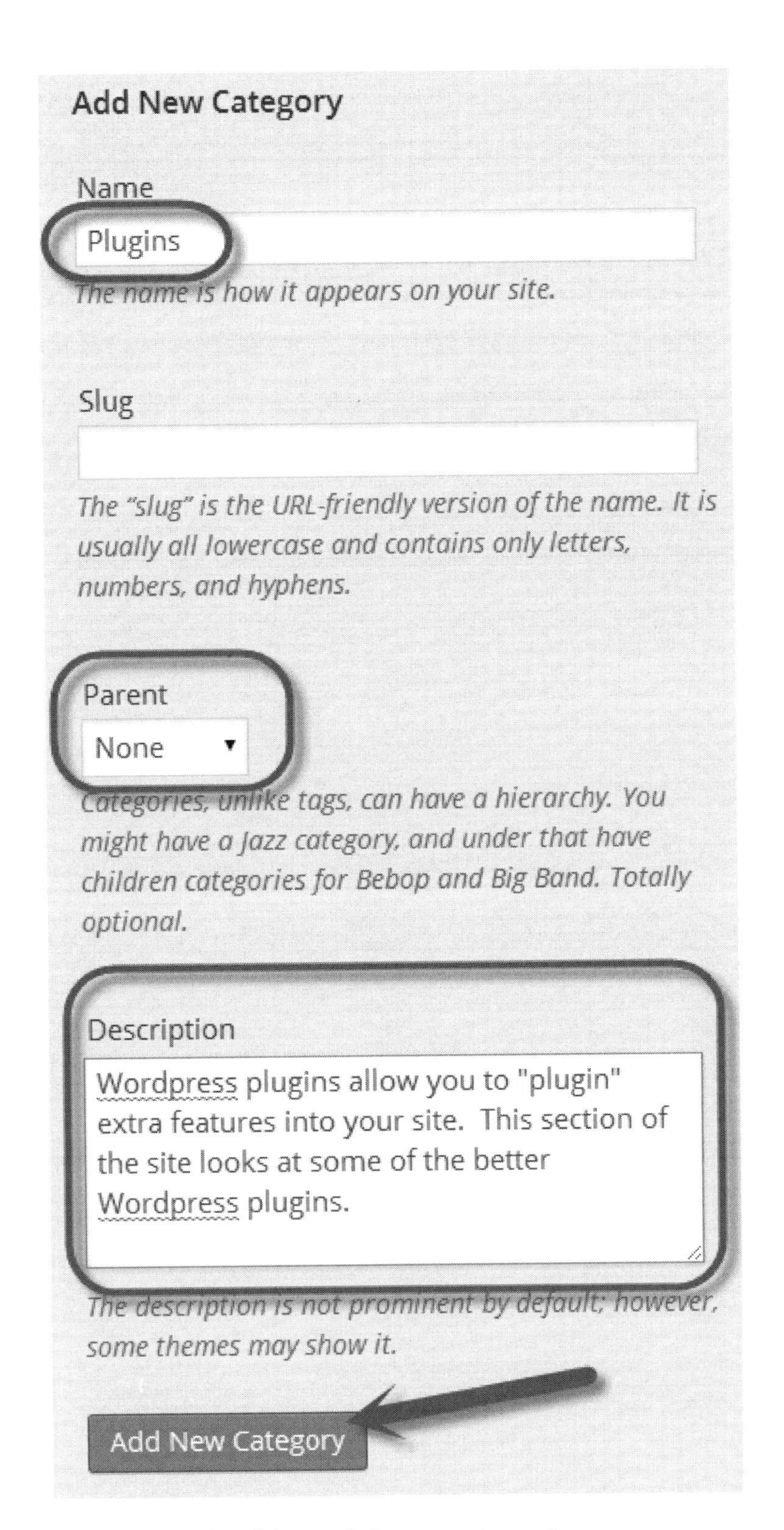

Here is my final list of three categories.

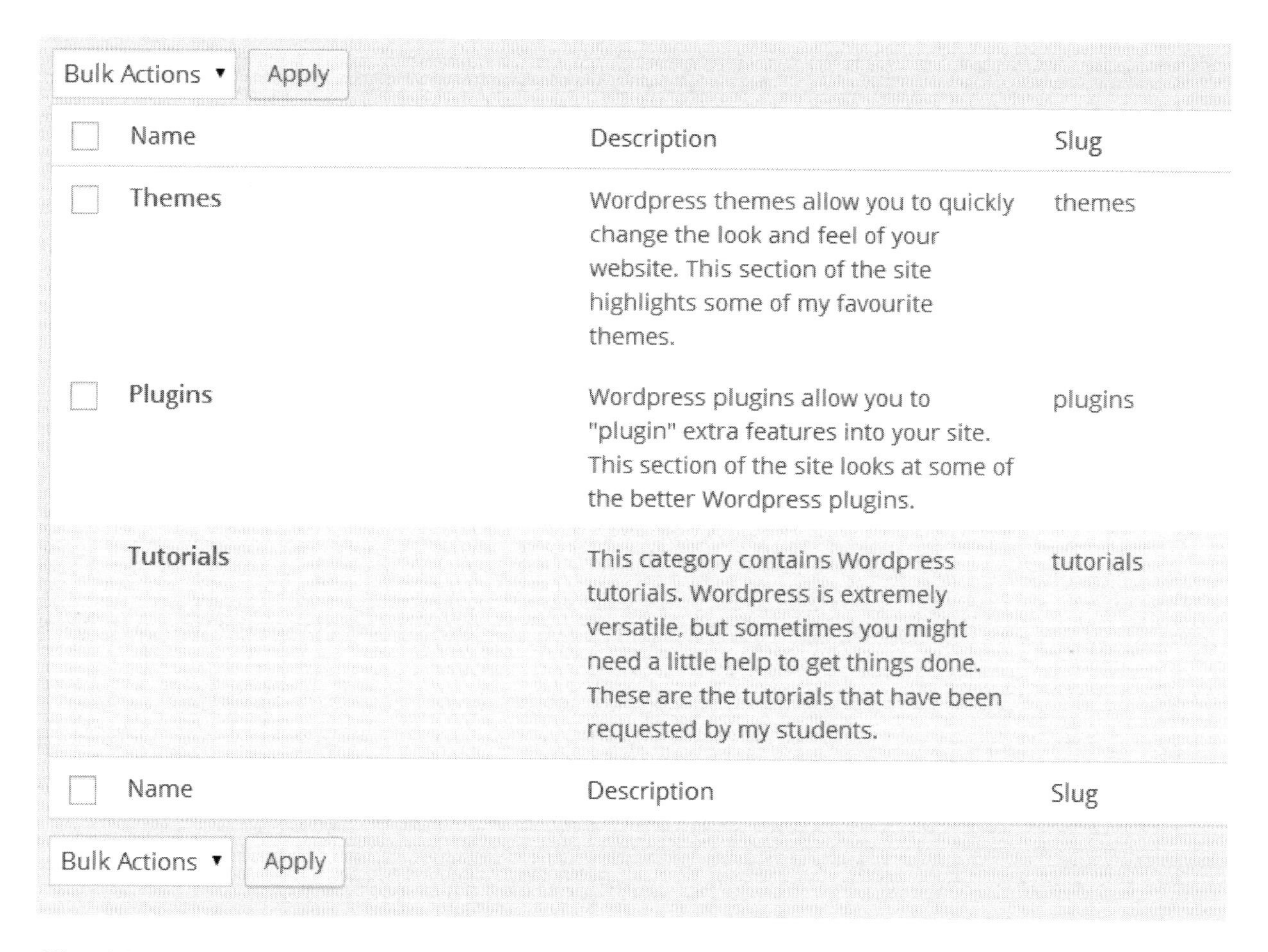

Bulk Actions ▼ Apply

Name	Description	Slug
Themes	Wordpress themes allow you to quickly change the look and feel of your website. This section of the site highlights some of my favourite themes.	themes
Plugins	Wordpress plugins allow you to "plugin" extra features into your site. This section of the site looks at some of the better Wordpress plugins.	plugins
Tutorials	This category contains Wordpress tutorials. Wordpress is extremely versatile, but sometimes you might need a little help to get things done. These are the tutorials that have been requested by my students.	tutorials
Name	Description	Slug

Bulk Actions ▼ Apply

I'll add more as and when I need them.

OK, let's enter the first post.

Creating Posts

Create a new, bank post. To do this, select **Add New** from the **Posts** menu in the left sidebar.

You now have a blank post, ready for entry.

Enter the title

Add a title. Make sure the title tells a visitor what the post is about, without being overly long. For my first post, I'll call it:

"Recommended Web Hosts and Registrars"

This will be my post on which web hosting companies I recommend, as well as which registrar. This is an important page for readers of this book, because my recommendations may change. However, you will always have the most up to date recommendations on this page, even if your copy of the book is out of date.

Typing in the post content

You can type your content directly in the WYSIWYG editor and that is what I will be doing. However, some people actually prefer to write their content in Microsoft Word first, and then copy it across to Worpdress.

Before Wordpress version 3.9, you needed to use a special "Paste from Word" button to insert any content that you copied from Microsoft Word. However, for Wordpress 3.9 or higher, you can simply write and format your post in Word and copy and paste it into the WYSIWYG editor.

When formatting in Word, use the normal text format for the body and Heading 2 & Heading 3 for headers (remember Wordpress will create a Heading 1 out of your title). Bullet points are also excellent to include, as they break up big blocks of text and make it easier for your visitors.

OK; for me, it's back to the WYSIWYG editor to enter my first post.

Select a category

OK, so my post is complete. The next thing I need to do is choose a category for this post. I have three to choose from (though I could create another one if needed).

I want to use "tutorials" for the category of this post, because I will probably end up adding short video tutorials to this post at a later date.

You select the category by checking the appropriate box in the **Categories** section of the **Edit Post** screen:

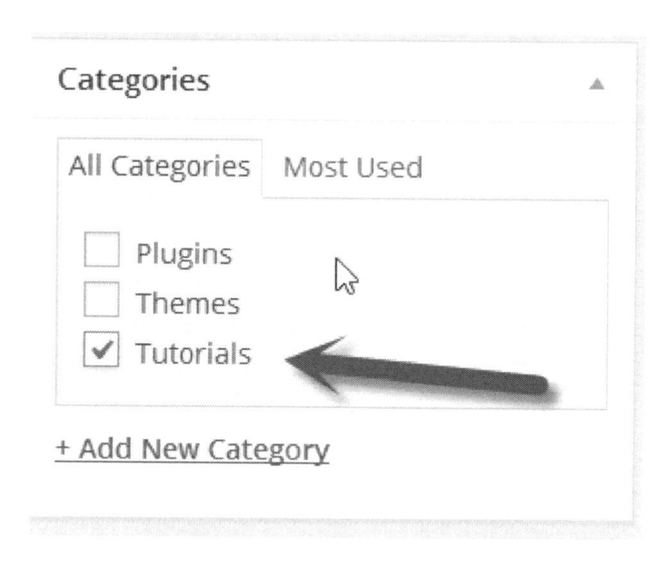

Note that there is a link underneath the existing categories, which allows you to quickly add other categories when you need them. However, adding a category via this link will not give you the option of adding a category description, so I personally add categories the way I showed you earlier.

Do you need tags?

Since this is my first post, I won't be adding any tags. As I add more posts to the site, I will consider whether they are needed. It is easy enough to go back in and add them to posts, so you don't have to do everything at the time of publishing.

Add an Excerpt

We talked about excerpts earlier in the book. I recommend you add an excerpt for all posts on your site. We toggled the visibility of the excerpt box earlier in the book, so you should have it on your "Edit post" screen. Enter a two or three sentence summary of the post. Your visitors will probably read this excerpt as a description of the post on certain pages of your site. Therefore try to get in their heads and figure out what would make them click through to read the post? Enter that as the excerpt.

OK, everything is entered. Click the **Publish** button to make your post live on your site.

Post Formats

Some Wordpress themes provide you with a number of "templates" to style each post you create. The Twenty Fourteen theme has several. You'll find them listed in the **Format** section of the **Edit Page** screen:

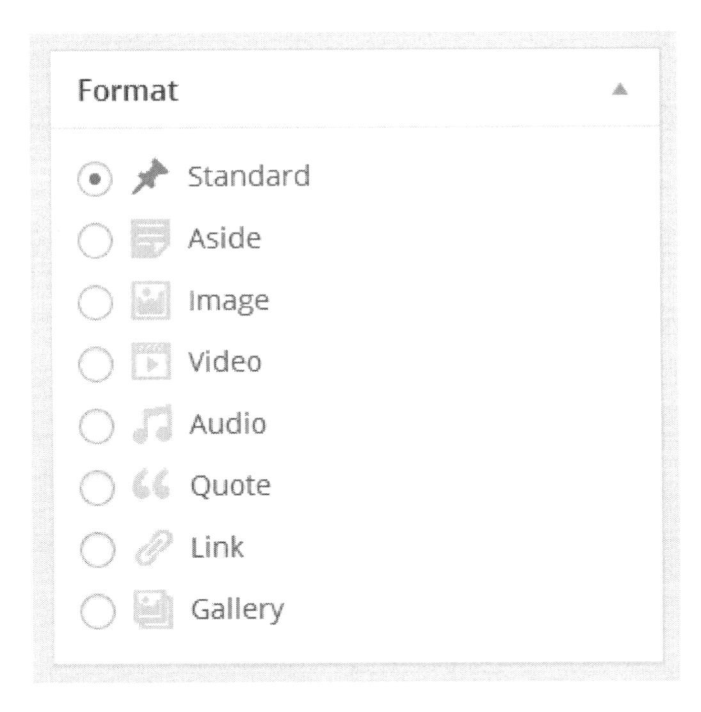

The default format is "Standard" and this is what you should use for most posts on your site. If you select one of the other formats, the layout of that post will change. Each format is designed for a specific purpose, some of which are fairly explanatory because of the name of the format. However, since all themes are different, the formats you see above will not be the same in all themes. Therefore I won't go through each of these.

What I recommend you do is to create a post, choose **Standard** format and publish it. Then go and look to see what your post looks like. Then go back to the **Edit Post** screen, select a different format and update your post. Go and see what it looks like now. Repeat with all formats for your theme, so you can get a better understanding of what each format looks like, and could be used for.

After exploring these formats, don't forget to go back and change it to "Standard" if that is what you want. Always remember to "Update" your posts after any editing.

What to do next?

You can now go off and start writing posts for your website. However, as you do, keep an eye on what is happening with your website. For example, the latest posts are displayed on my homepage, with the latest one at the top of the homepage. I actually prefer to have a more "static" homepage, without displaying my latest posts like this, so I'll show you how to do that soon. However, look around your homepage. In the left sidebar, you will see a "Recent Posts" section, which lists your latest posts:

RECENT POSTS

Recommended Web Hosts and Registrars

There is only one post on my site right now, so only one listed, but this "widget" will list more. We'll see how this is set up later when we look at widgets.

If you click a link in the recent posts list, it will take you to the "post page" on your site, where you will find the full content of your post, and a comment form at the bottom. Remember you can turn comments off on a page by page, or post by post level if you want to. You can even turn all comments off if you wish, but I don't recommend you do that, and we'll discuss why later.

Also in the sidebar is an **Archives** widget. This widget lists all months when posts were published. This is not something I display on my own sites, so I will remove this later. However, click a month in your archive list and you'll be taken to a page on your site that lists all posts made in that month.

Remember earlier in the book, we mentioned RSS feeds? Well Wordpress even creates an RSS feed of each date archive. You can see the contents of the feed by typing /feed on the end of the date archive URL:

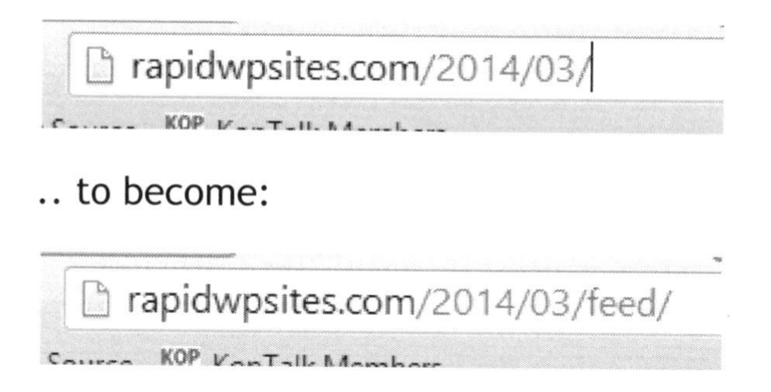

.. to become:

The browser will display the contents of the RSS feed:

This XML file does not appear to have any style information associated with it. The document tree is


```
▼<rss xmlns:content="http://purl.org/rss/1.0/modules/content/" xmlns:wfw="http://wellformed
 xmlns:atom="http://www.w3.org/2005/Atom" xmlns:sy="http://purl.org/rss/1.0/modules/syndica
 version="2.0">
 ▼<channel>
    <title>Rapid WP Sites » 2014 » March</title>
    <atom:link href="http://rapidwpsites.com/2014/03/feed/" rel="self" type="application/rs
    <link>http://rapidwpsites.com</link>
    <description>Tutorials, resources and help with Wordpress</description>
    <lastBuildDate>Tue, 25 Mar 2014 15:57:05 +0000</lastBuildDate>
    <language>en-US</language>
    <sy:updatePeriod>hourly</sy:updatePeriod>
    <sy:updateFrequency>1</sy:updateFrequency>
    <generator>http://wordpress.org/?v=3.8.1</generator>
  ▼<item>
      <title>Recommended Web Hosts and Registrars</title>
    ▼<link>
        http://rapidwpsites.com/tutorials/recommended-web-hosts-and-registrars/
      </link>
    ▼<comments>
        http://rapidwpsites.com/tutorials/recommended-web-hosts-and-registrars/#comments
      </comments>
```


OK, back to the sidebar of the site.

You will also notice there is a widget that lists the categories. Since I only have a post in the “Tutorials” category, that is the only one currently listed by this widget:

This widget only displays categories that contain posts. As I add posts to other categories, those categories will appear in this widget as well .

If I click on the “Tutorials” category, I am taken to the category page for “Tutorials”, which lists all posts in the Tutorials category.

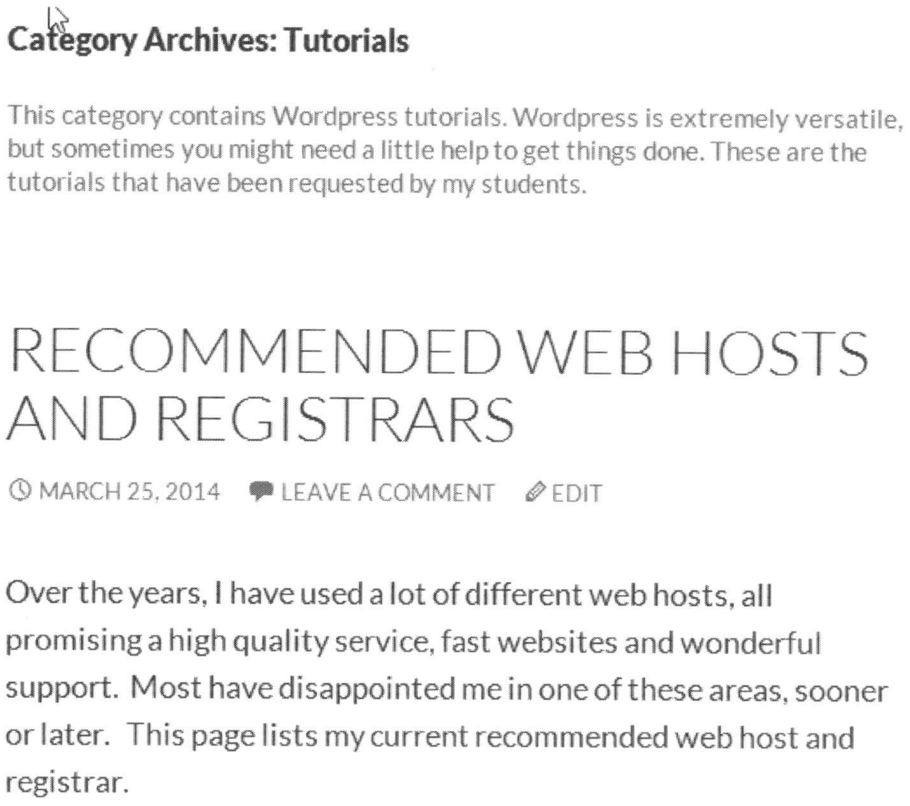

Category Archives: Tutorials

This category contains Wordpress tutorials. Wordpress is extremely versatile, but sometimes you might need a little help to get things done. These are the tutorials that have been requested by my students.

RECOMMENDED WEB HOSTS AND REGISTRARS

MARCH 25, 2014 LEAVE A COMMENT EDIT

Over the years, I have used a lot of different web hosts, all promising a high quality service, fast websites and wonderful support. Most have disappointed me in one of these areas, sooner or later. This page lists my current recommended web host and registrar.

Note that at the top of the category page, this Twenty Fourteen Wordpress theme adds the category description. That is something this theme does, but be aware that not all themes will do this.

Again, Wordpress creates an RSS feed for every category you create. You can find it by adding /feed to the end of the category page URL, just like you did for the archives page.

All of the items in the sidebar are controlled by widgets, and you have total control over what you want and what you don't want displayed in the sidebar. Some themes even allow you to add widgets to other areas of the web page, like the footer.

Let's look at widgets in more detail.

Widgets

From the **Appearance** menu in the left sidebar, select **Widgets**.

Think of widgets as features you can add to your website. We looked at a few sidebar widgets towards the end of the previous chapter (recent posts, archives, categories etc).

In the Widgets section of the Dashboard, you can see a list of all available widgets, as well as the places you can put them on your website.

The Twenty Fourteen theme gives you three places on your site where you can insert widgets:

1. Primary Sidebar
2. Content Sidebar
3. Footer Widget Area

We will look at these in a moment. First, when we looked at the website so far, we saw a number of widgets in the "Primary Sidebar". That is, the sidebar on the left.

Each widget we saw on the site corresponds to a widget currently in the Primary Sidebar section of the widget screen:

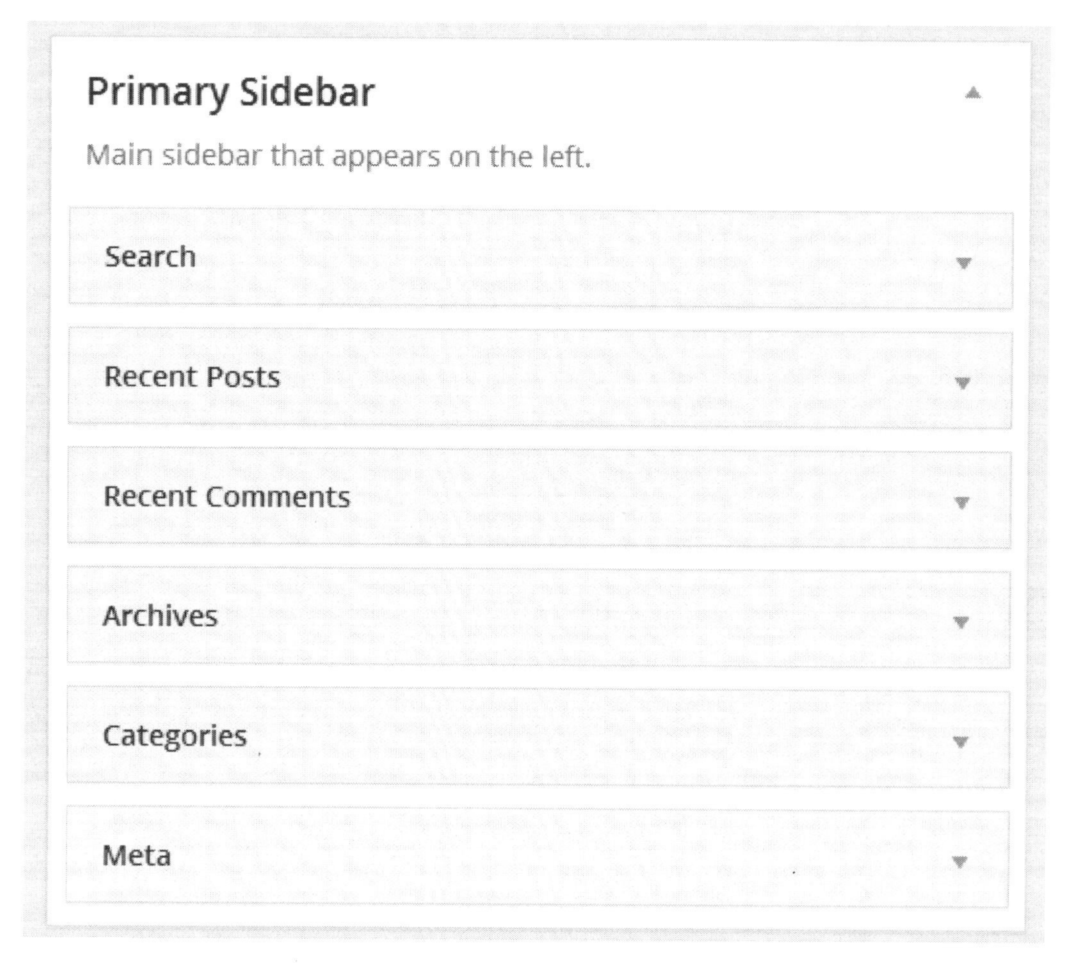

So, in the sidebar, we have the following widgets:

- Search
- Recent post
- Recent comments
- Archives
- Categories
- Meta

If you go and look at your website, you will see all of these widgets, from the search box at the top, to the "Meta" widget at the bottom.

Each of the widgets have a number of options. These can be accessed by clicking the down arrow on the right of the widget.

For example, here are the options for the Search box:

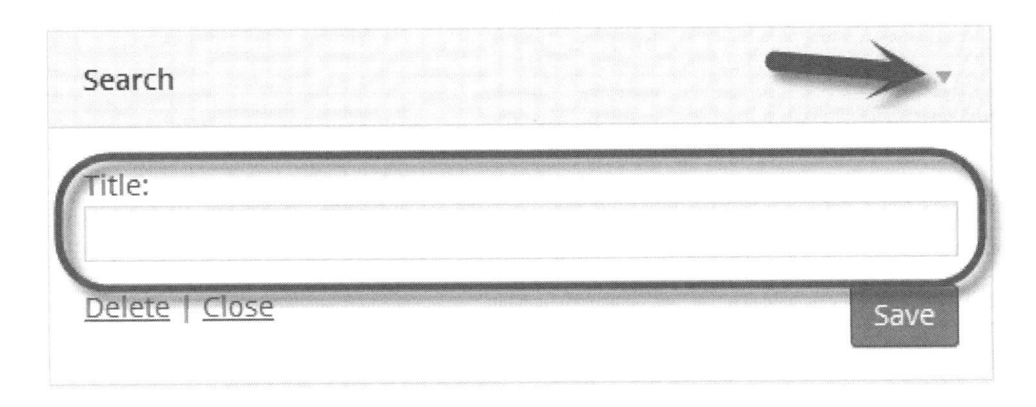

OK, so the only option is to give it a title. At the moment, there isn't a title and this is how it looks on my site:

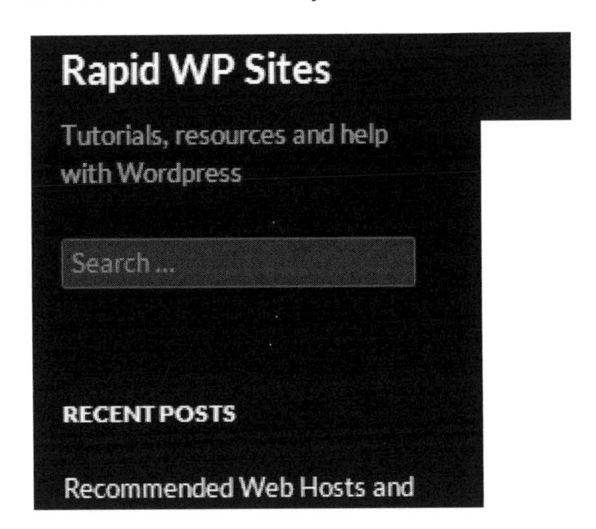

Since the search box has the word "Search" inside, there really isn't a need to give this widget a title. However, feel free to experiment with your own site widgets.

The Recent Posts widget has a couple of options:

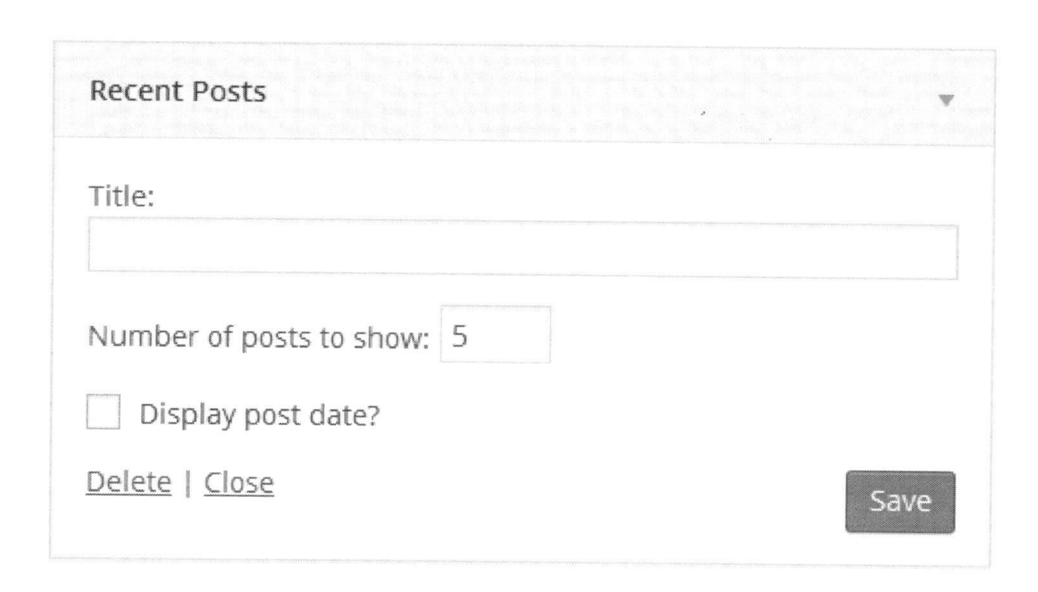

Again, there is no title specified, yet if we look at the site we see this:

What? There is a title...

If you leave the title blank for a widget, Wordpress will use the default title for that widget, in this case "Recent Posts". In the case of the Search widget, there was no default title.

If you want to change that title to something else, you can enter a title into your widget options:

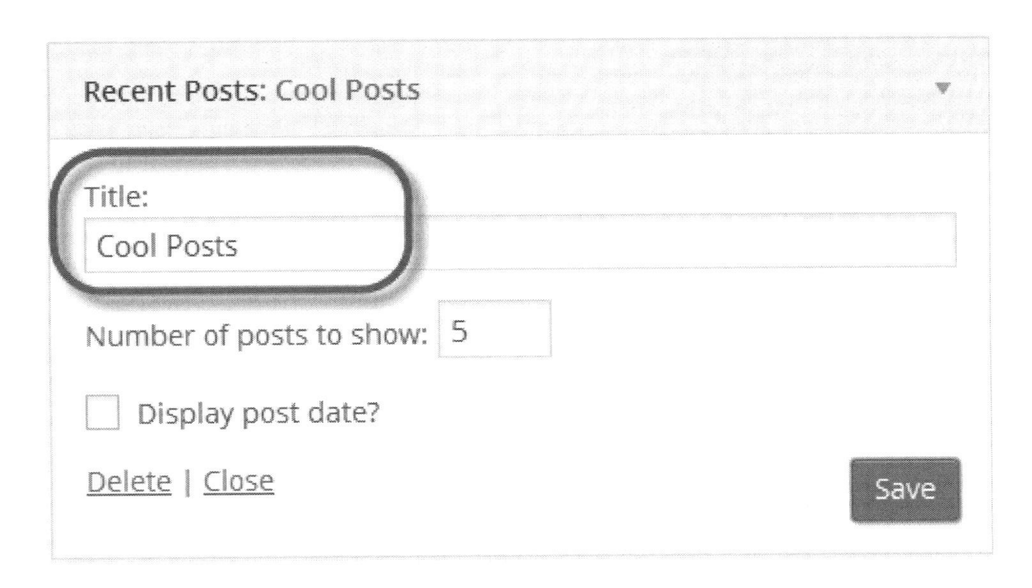

Here is what this looks like on my site:

This widget also lets you choose how many recent posts to display and you can even get the widget to display the dates of each post if you want.

I will leave you to explore the other sidebar widgets that were installed by default. Open the options and look at how you can configure each widget. Feel free to change settings and see how they affect the display of the widget on the site.

For my site, I don't want recent comments, archives or the Meta widget. Deleting a widget is easy. Open the options for the widget, then click the Delete link.

After deleting those, my sidebar looks a lot cleaner:

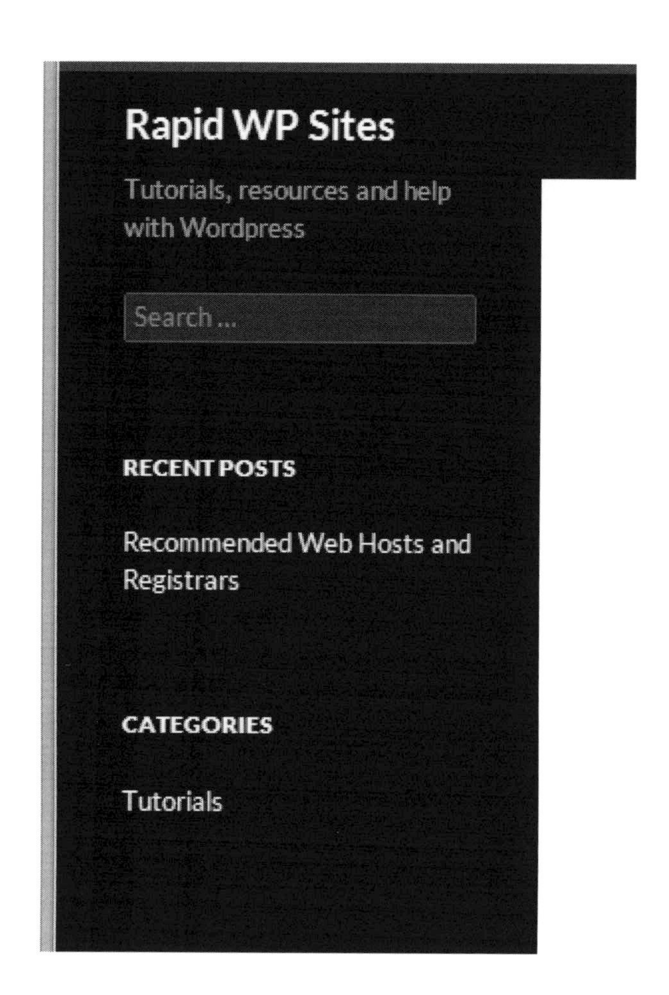

Other widget areas

OK, so we've covered the primary sidebar. However, the Twenty Fourteen theme also allows us to place widgets in the "Content Sidebar" and the "Footer Widget Area". Again, different themes will allow widgets in different areas, so there is little point in going over these widget areas in any detail. The best thing you can do is to put a widget into a widgetized area and see where it appears on your site.

In Twenty Fourteen. the Content Sidebar is basically a sidebar on the right hand side of the theme:

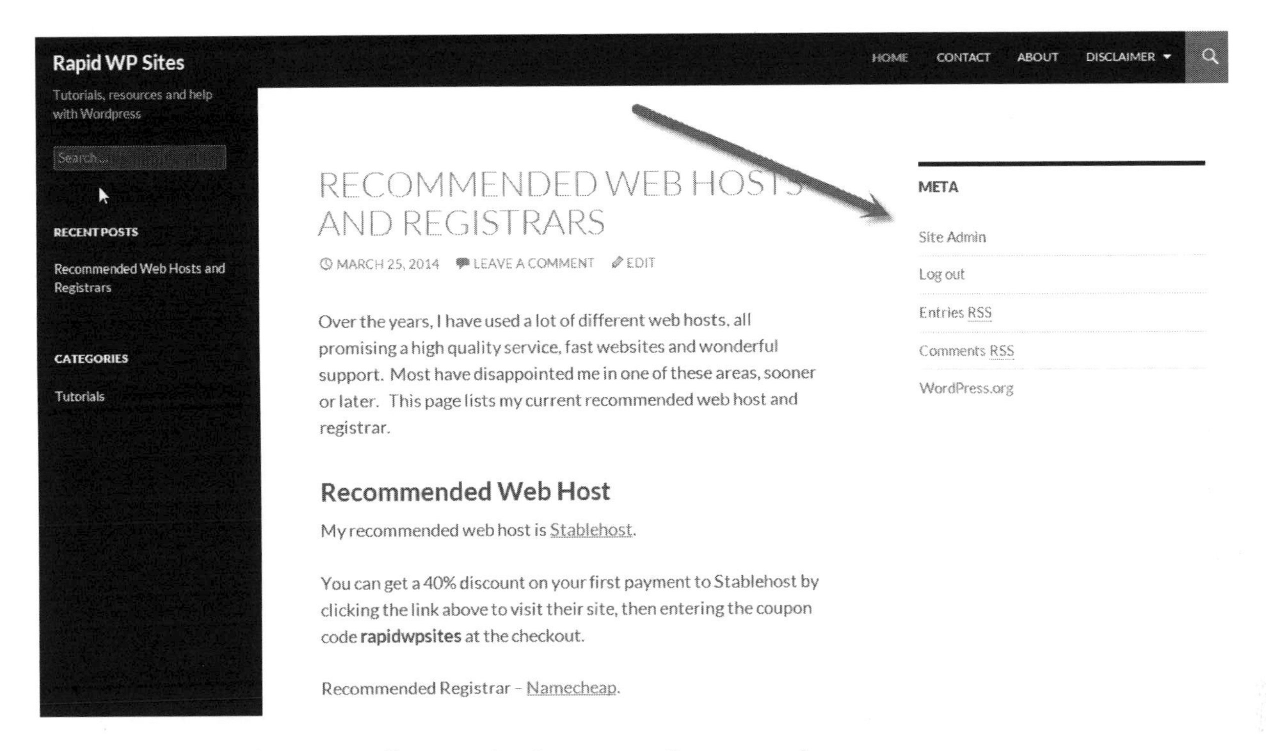
Rapid WP Sites
Tutorials, resources and help with Wordpress
HOME
CONTACT
ABOUT
DISCLAIMER
Search ...
RECENT POSTS
Recommended Web Hosts and Registrars
CATEGORIES
Tutorials
RECOMMENDED WEB HOSTS AND REGISTRARS
MARCH 25, 2014
LEAVE A COMMENT
EDIT
Over the years, I have used a lot of different web hosts, all promising a high quality service, fast websites and wonderful support. Most have disappointed me in one of these areas, sooner or later. This page lists my current recommended web host and registrar.
Recommended Web Host
My recommended web host is Stablehost.
You can get a 40% discount on your first payment to Stablehost by clicking the link above to visit their site, then entering the coupon code rapidwpsites at the checkout.
Recommended Registrar - Namecheap.
META
Site Admin
Log out
Entries RSS
Comments RSS
WordPress.org

The “footer widget area” is at the bottom of your web pages:

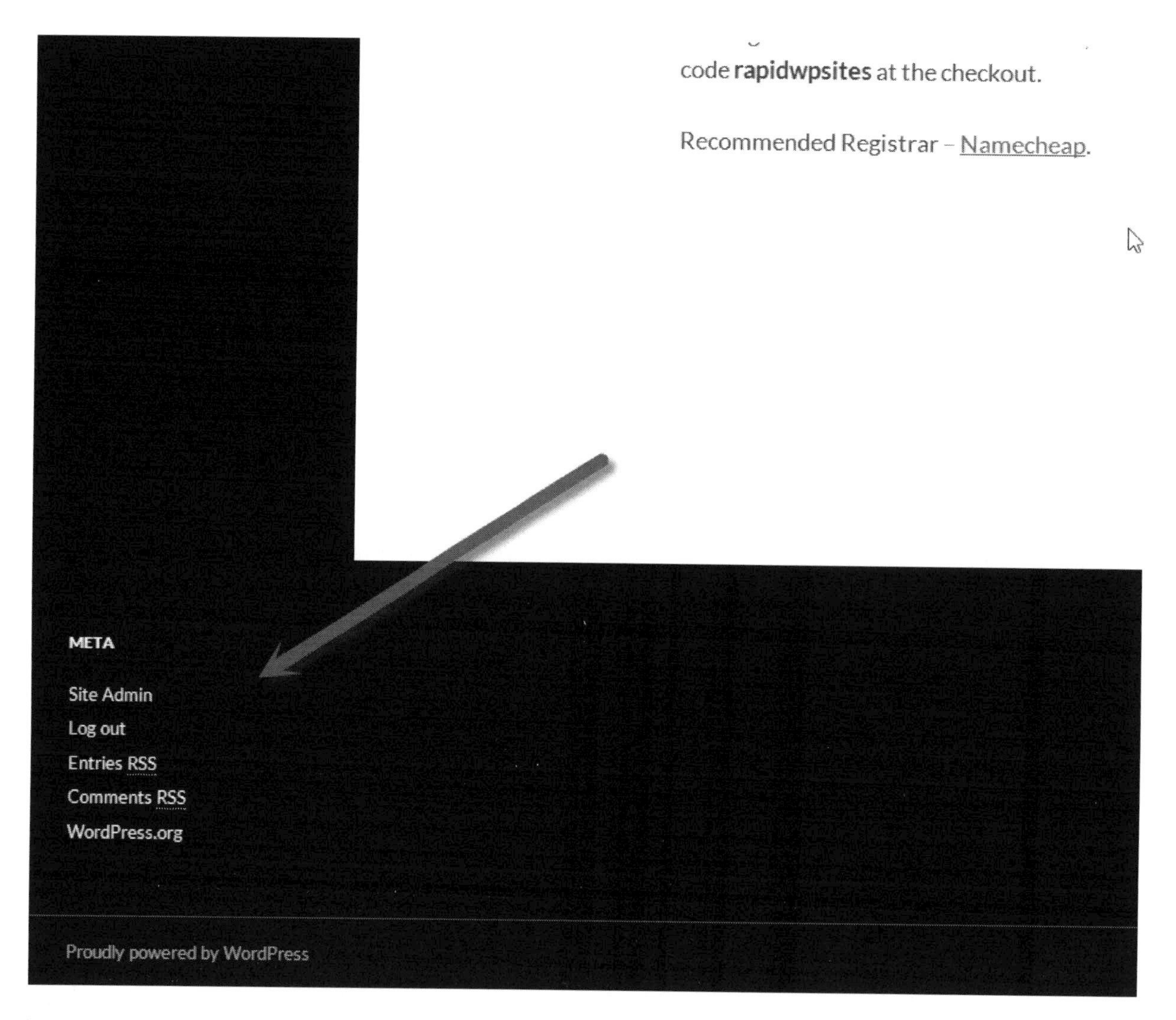

It is wise to remember that when you add widgets to one of these areas, it will appear on all posts / pages on your site.

There are ways to only include certain widgets in specific categories, posts or pages, but you'll need a Wordpress plugin to achieve that. The one I use is called Dynamic Widgets, and you can find out more about that later in the book.

Other available widgets

Wordpress installs a basic stock of widgets for you to use, and you can experiment with those to see what they do. More widgets are also available online if you need extra functionality. We'll see some as we develop the "Rapid WP Sites" website.

The Homepage - A special case

By default, Wordpress will show your recent posts on the homepage. I personally do not like this, and want to have a homepage that I write from scratch, so I can help my visitors. We can do this quite easily by telling Wordpress to use a specific page as the homepage.

Let's create a "static" homepage for the site. First we need to create a Wordpress page to use as our Homepage.

Go and click on the **Add New** item in the **Pages** sidebar menu.

I'll give my page a title that I think fits the website (though this may change as I develop the site):

Now it's time to enter a little content for the homepage.

The content I write for my homepage today will change. At the moment, the site has almost no visitor-focused content, so I'll just write something that will explain what the site will be when it's finished. I can then come back to this page at a later date to update the homepage.

This is all I am adding now:

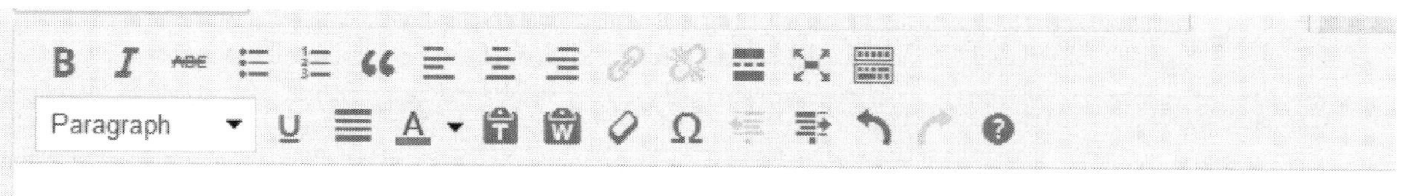

Rapid WP Sites is a website set up to accompany my book "Rapid Wordpress Websites", available on Amazon Kindle and as a paperback really soon...

Not only does this site act as a demonstration site that was built in the book, but it also serves as a further source of education for those wanting to take their Wordpress skills to the next level.

The site will have Wordpress tutorials, articles on themes and plugins, and a lot more.

After clicking the **Publish** button to make it live, my homepage still looks the same. It still lists the most recent posts...

Don't panic. That's simply because we have not told Wordpress to use the page we just created as a homepage.

To do that, go to the **Reading** settings inside the **Settings** menu in the left sidebar.

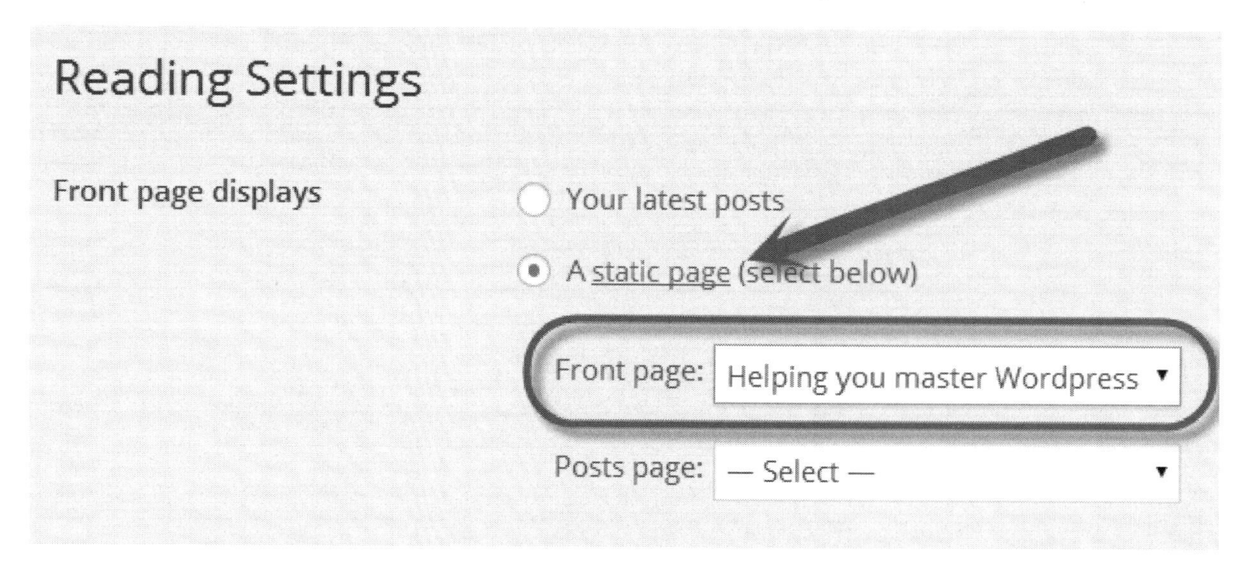

Select "A static page" from the **Front page displays** section and then choose your newly created pages from the **Front Page** drop down box.

Click the **Save Changes** button to finish.

If you now visit the homepage of your site, you'll no longer see your most recent posts in the main area of the homepage. Instead, you will find the Wordpress page you just created:

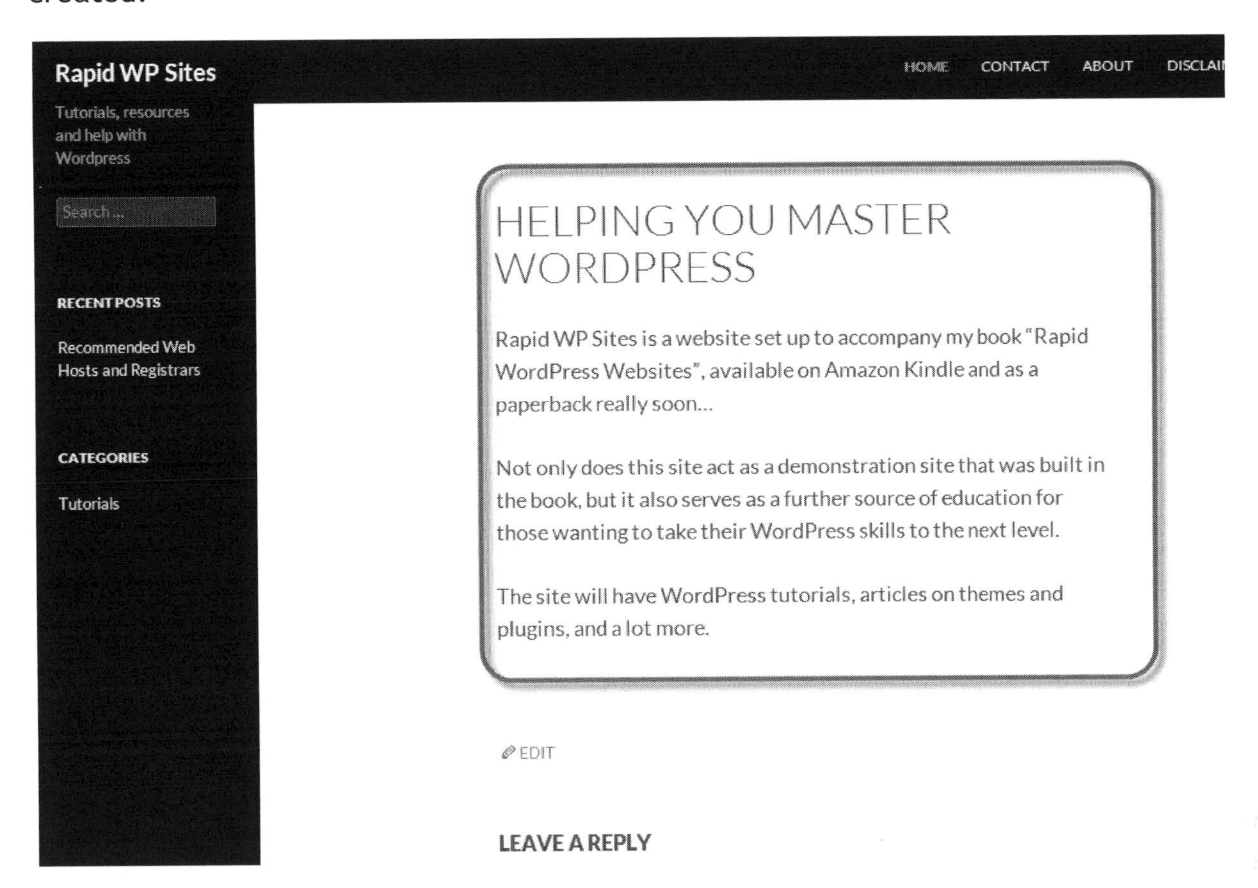

We will have a comment box at the bottom by default, so if you don't want that, switch it off in the Edit Page screen like we did for the other pages on our site.

OK; our site is starting to take shape.

You might not like the overall look and feel of the site, but later in the book I'll show you how to change that, any time you like, in seconds, for an almost unlimited variety of styles.

For now, we need to concentrate on adding the posts to the site. For me, that means writing some more posts for the "tutorials" category, as well as the "plugins" and "themes" categories. While I am working on that, there are a few things we should discuss.

Allowing Comments

I love getting comments from real people wanting to engage me on the site, or add their own tips, ideas or thoughts to the post. However, comments are also a major source of frustration because spammers can flood your inbox with hundreds of automated spam comments. Because of this, a lot of webmasters turn them off. You should not turn them off because real visitors like to comment on your posts. Just as importantly, the search engines love to see websites that are actively engaging its visitors.

So what is the problem with spammers and how can we stop them?

Well, if you don't already know, you soon will. Spammers see comments on other people's websites as a way to make their own web pages rank better. You see, when a comment is approved, it links back to the website that was entered into the comment form.

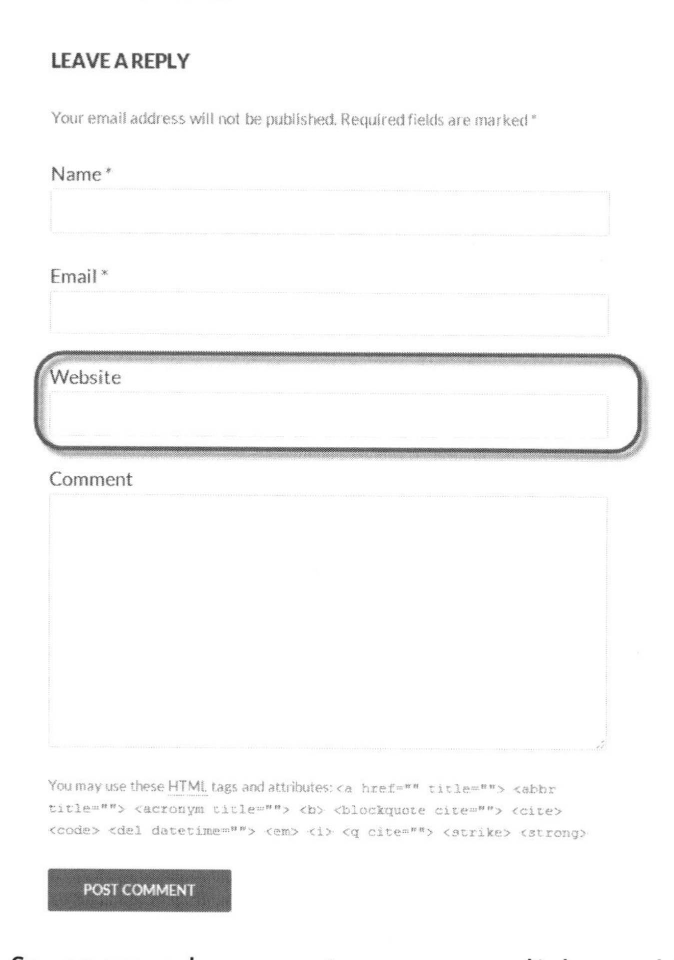

So, approved comments are seen as links, and links help boost your rankings in Google!

Because of the problems with spammers, we have already set up Wordpress so that all comments need to be manually approved. There are also plugins you can install to help cut down on spam comments. One popular plugin is called GrowMap.

Let's install and configure it.

Click **Add New** from the **Plugins** menu in the left sidebar, and in the search box, type growmap.

Name	Version	Rating	Description
Growmap Anti Spambot Plugin Details | Install Now	1.5.5	★★★★☆	Upgrade to CommentLuv Pro For More This plugin will add a client side gener users to confirm that they are not a sp It is a lot less trouble to click a box thar genereated via client side javascript th automated spam bots. A check is mad... By Andy Bailey.

Install the "Growmap Anti Spambot Plugin", and activate it.

Once activated, you'll find the settings for the plugin labeled as **G.A.S.P.** in the **Settings** menu of the left sidebar.

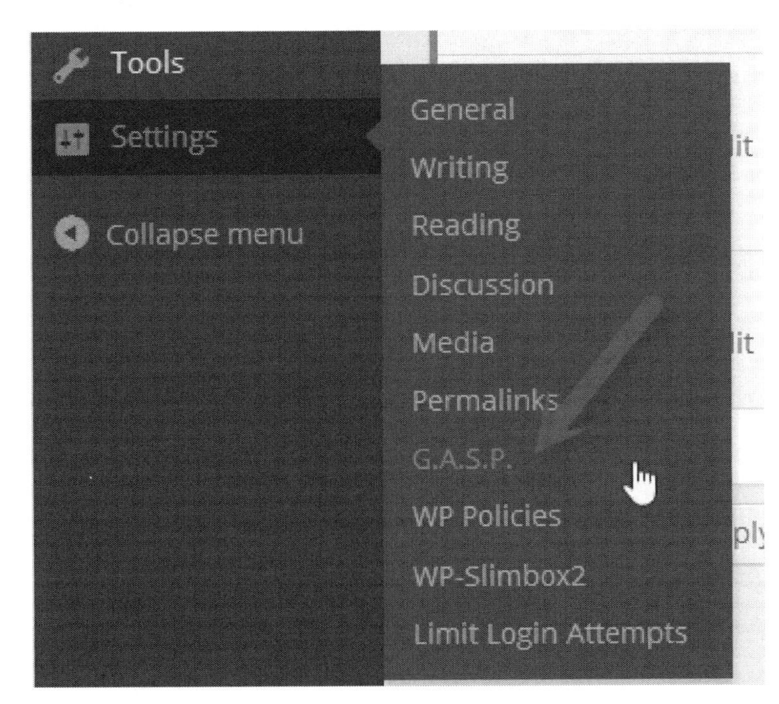

Go to the settings and make the following changes:

.. and then a little further down:

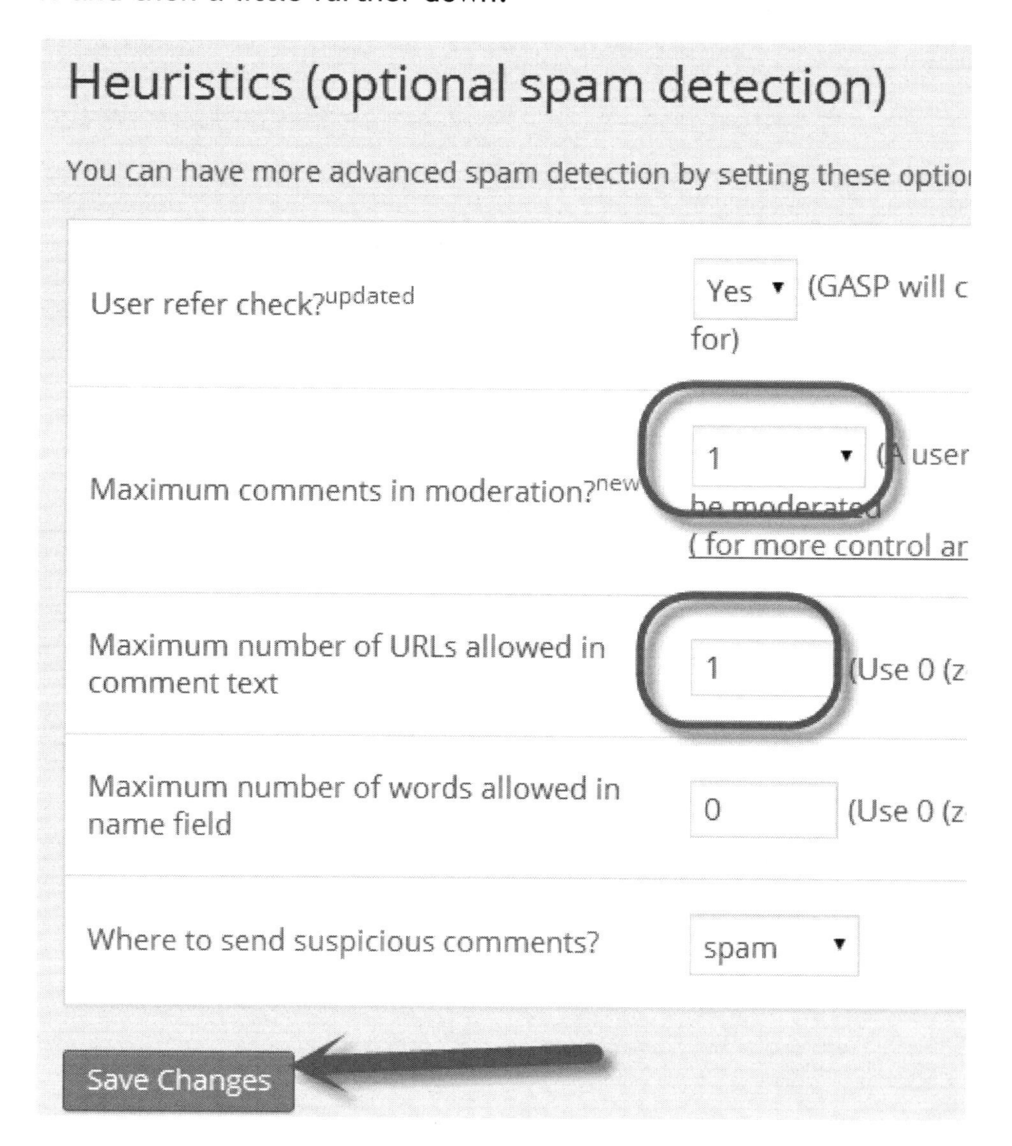

Finally save changes and you are done.

This plugin is good at protecting against automated software bots trying to posts pre-written spam to your site. However, you will probably still end up getting a lot of spam comments. If you do, you can find a more effective anti-spam plugin later in this book.

Moderating Comments

We have already seen the comments screen when we looked at the demo comment installed by Wordpress. Therefore you should already have a pretty good idea of how this all works.

When someone comes to your site, and leaves a comment, it is checked against our blacklist (we set that up earlier). If the comment contains a word or phrase in the blacklist, it is sent to the spam folder. If it passes the checks, and also passes the checks by the Growmap plugin, the comment is added to the "Pending" list. At this point, Wordpress sends an email to your admin email address telling you there is a comment to moderate. That email is useful because it contains links to approve, trash or spam the comment.

```
A new comment on the post "Recommended Web Hosts and Registrars" is waiting for your approval
http://rapidwpsites.com/tutorials/recommended-web-hosts-and-registrars/

Author : My Web Host (IP: 88.18.143.85 , 85.Red-88-18-143.staticIP.rima-tde.net)
E-mail : andy@mywebhost.com
URL    : http://mywebhost.com
Whois  : http://whois.arin.net/rest/ip/88.18.143.85
Comment:
Give me a link back.

Approve it: http://rapidwpsites.com/wp-admin/comment.php?action=approve&c=3
Trash it: http://rapidwpsites.com/wp-admin/comment.php?action=trash&c=3
Spam it: http://rapidwpsites.com/wp-admin/comment.php?action=spam&c=3
Currently 1 comment is waiting for approval. Please visit the moderation panel:
http://rapidwpsites.com/wp-admin/edit-comments.php?comment_status=moderated
```

You may or may not use this email to moderate comments, that is up to you. However, if you login to your Dashboard and there are comments waiting, you will see a visual indicator of comments awaiting moderation:

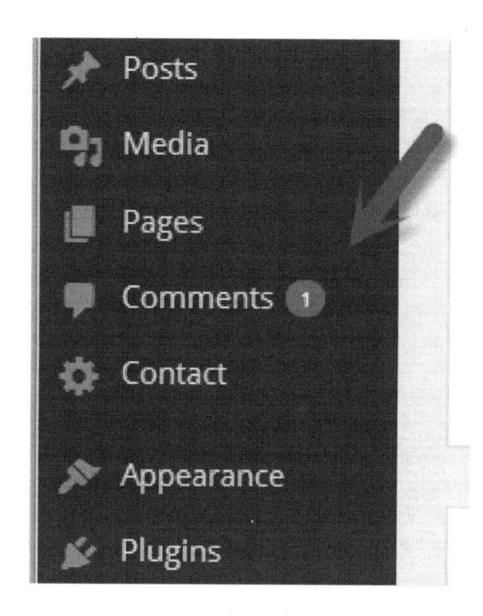

Clicking on the **Comments** menu item takes you to the moderation screen.

Move your mouse into comment and a menu appears:

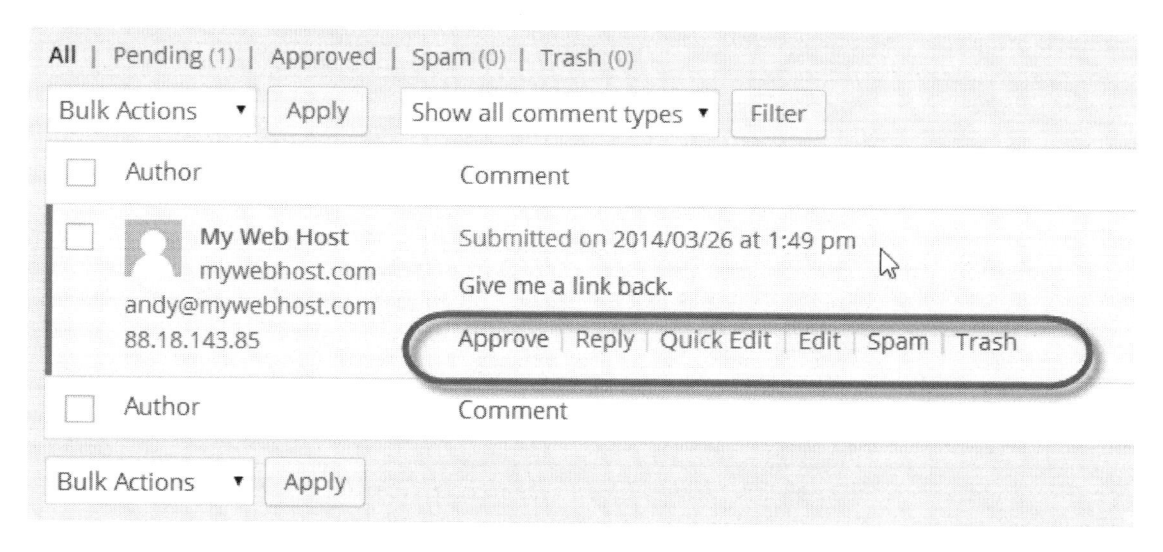

From there, you can approve the comment, or send it to spam or trash.

My advice is to send all spam comments immediately to trash when moderating.

Also, I highly recommend that you are very strict about approving comments. If you do not know the commenter (ie they are not a friend or a frequent visitor you know of), then never approve a comment that does not add to the conversation on the post they are commenting on.

For example, on my web hosting post, I would trash all of the following comments:

"Love the site, great work!"

"What theme are you using, it looks great".

"I love this site"

"Fantastic article. I will send my friend over to read it".

"I think you have a problem with browser compatibility".

Incidentally, these are all very common spam comments, whose sole purpose is to get a link back to a website. Quite often, spam comments try to flatter you into approving them.

Do you see how none of these are actually about web hosting? These comments could have been made on ANY post. That is often the sign of a spammer at work.

I tend to only approve comments that add to the "discussion" started by the post. I'd also approve a comment that was obviously written by someone who had read the post and wanted help or advice related to the post. Comments are there for you to interact, help and discuss with your audience. Any comment that does not add to the conversation should be trashed.

When you have comments in the trash, or spam folders, you will eventually need to go in and empty the trash (or empty the spam folder). Just click on the tab (in the screenshot below I have clicked onto the **Trash** tab):

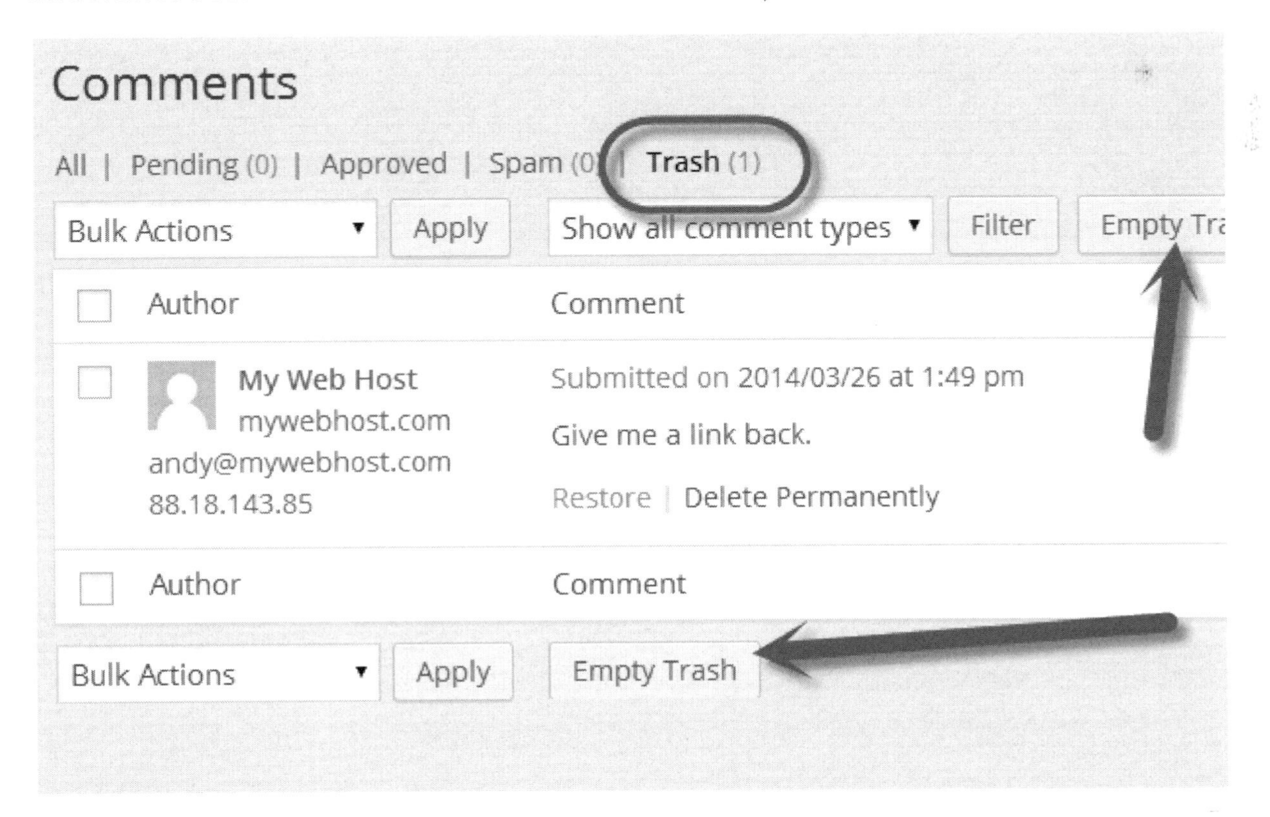

Then click the Empty Trash button.

On the spam screen there is an "Empty Spam" button.

So what is the difference between spam and trash?

Well, there isn't a lot of difference. Wordpress and many anti-spam plugins will send suspicious comments to the spam folder as a place to hold them until you moderate them. Everything in the spam folder will be suspicious, so you can have a quick glance down and just click the "empty spam" button if you don't see anything worth approving.

If there is anything worth approving, you can move your mouse over the comment, and click the "Not Spam" link.

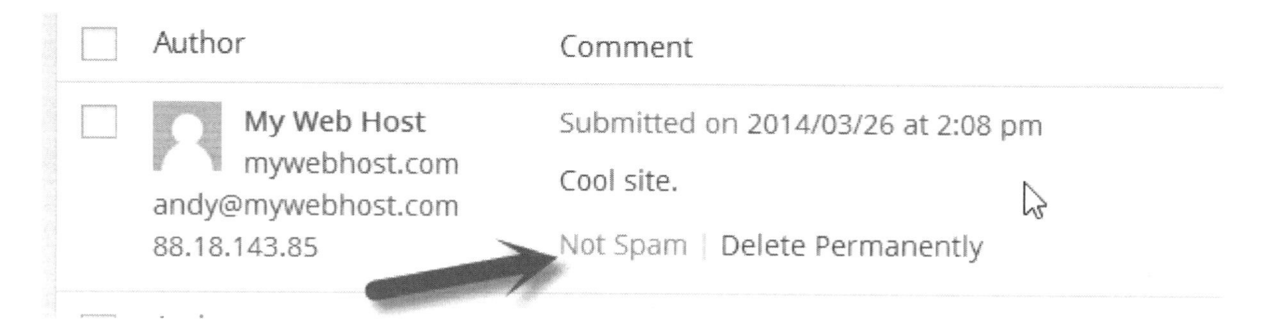

That will send it to the Pending tab.

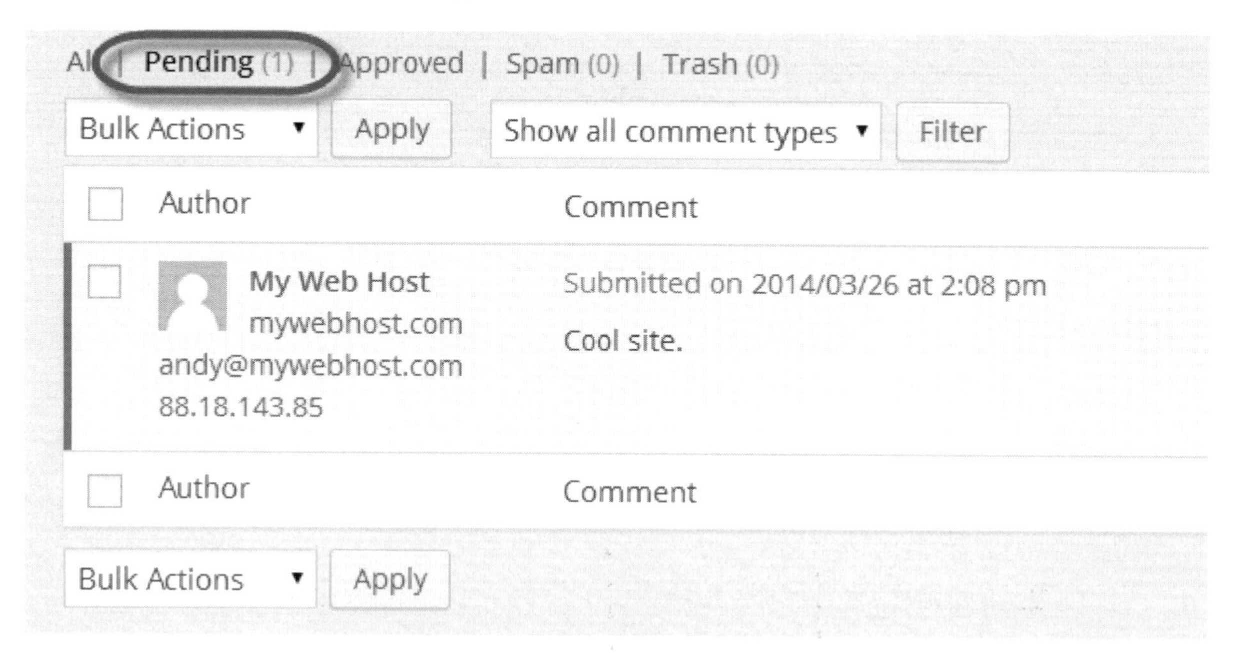

From there, you can approve the comment if you want.

Social Sharing?

You put a lot of effort into your website, so wouldn't it be nice to give your visitors an easy way for them to share your content with their friends?

Social sharing plugins make this easy.

There are a huge number of different social sharing plugins to choose from. We'll install a popular one here.

Click **Add New** from the Plugins sidebar menu.

Search for **Fast & Easy social share.**

Find and install this one:

Name	Version	Rating	Description
Fast & Easy Social Sharing Details | Installed	1.0.2	★★★★★	A simple and fast social media sharing plugin. The share buttons are loaded as fonts thus load fast and can scale as large as you want them to be. No JavaScript is loaded from any of the social networks. Only two requests are being made, one for the fonts and another for the stylesheet, that's it. For the time being, the icons are displayed only on posts, not pages or your homepage. Future versio... By Michael Tieso.

You'll find the plugin adds a menu to the **Settings** menu:

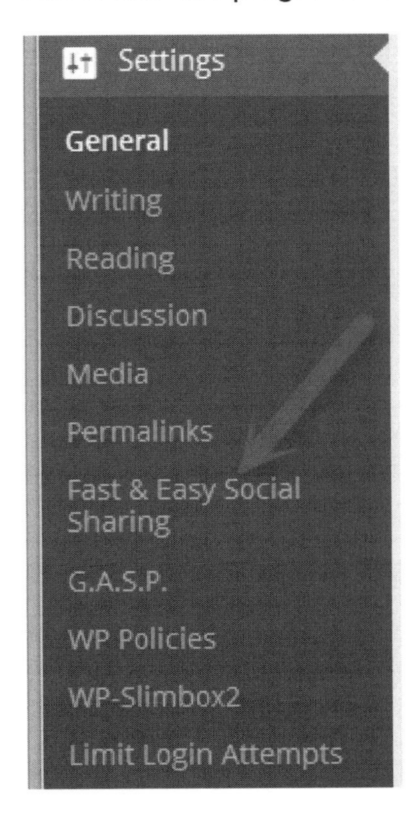

Click on the **Fast & Easy Social Sharing settings** link.

The only option I want you to change is this one:

Font Size of Icons

If you have a Twitter handle, enter that as well.

Click the **Save Changes** button.

At the bottom of every post, you will now have social sharing icons.

or later. This page lists my current recommended web host and registrar.

Recommended Web Host

My recommended web host is Stablehost.

You can get a 40% discount on your first payment to Stablehost by clicking the link above to visit their site, then entering the coupon code **rapidwpsites** at the checkout.

Recommended Registrar – Namecheap.

Tell your friends about this post:

Your visitors can click these buttons to share your post on Facebook, Twitter, Pinterest, Google Plus, etc. This in turn can bring more traffic to your site from these social networks.

The options for this plugin are a little limited, and the plugin currently only allows the sharing buttons on posts (not on homepage or pages), and only below the content. However, the plugin buttons look great and load fast, without slowing the site down. The developer is actively working on this plugin, so I do expect to see more options added to it soon.

If you want to check out some other social sharing plugins, see the plugins section of the RapidWPSites.com website.

Website Navigation

Someone landing on your website for the first time will have no idea what content is on your site or how to find it. It is therefore vital that you have good website navigation.

On sites I build, I make sure the following navigation is in place:

1. A homepage that tries to help the visitor find what they want. That can literally mean writing out instructions, using graphics, or just making the sidebar and menu navigation speak for itself.
2. A search box. This is already installed on the site as a widget. The default search box that comes with Wordpress is poor. A better option is to add a custom Google search box which offers far more relevant search results from your site. If you want to see how this is done, you can find the "Adding a Google search box" tutorial on the RapidWPSites.com website.
3. A Main menu offering contact, about and other "legal" pages. This does not always need to be in the header area of your site. I often put this type of menu in the footer widget area.
4. A recent posts widget in the sidebar of my site. Visitors can quickly see the recent articles I have written, and use those as a starting point for investigating my site.
5. Every post on my site will have a related posts section, which lists other posts that I think a visitor may be interested in.

The only one on that list we have not considered so far is the related posts plugin. Let's install and configure that now.

Select **Add New** from the **Plugins** menu.

In the search box, search for YARPP.

This is the one you need to find, install and activate:

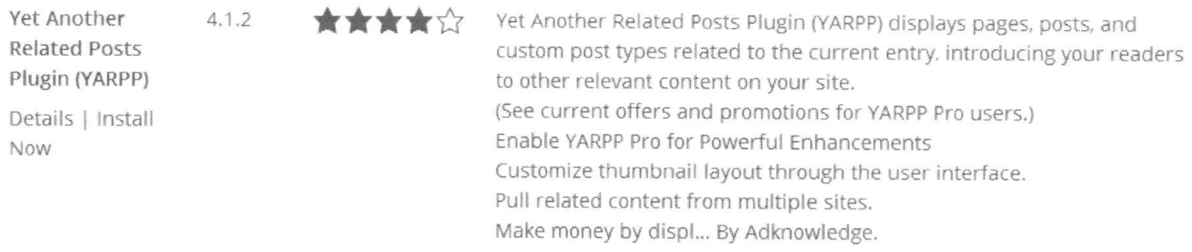

Yet Another Related Posts Plugin (YARPP)

Details | Install Now

4.1.2

★★★★☆

Yet Another Related Posts Plugin (YARPP) displays pages, posts, and custom post types related to the current entry, introducing your readers to other relevant content on your site.
(See current offers and promotions for YARPP Pro users.)
Enable YARPP Pro for Powerful Enhancements
Customize thumbnail layout through the user interface.
Pull related content from multiple sites.
Make money by displ... By Adknowledge.

You will now have a new menu in the Settings:

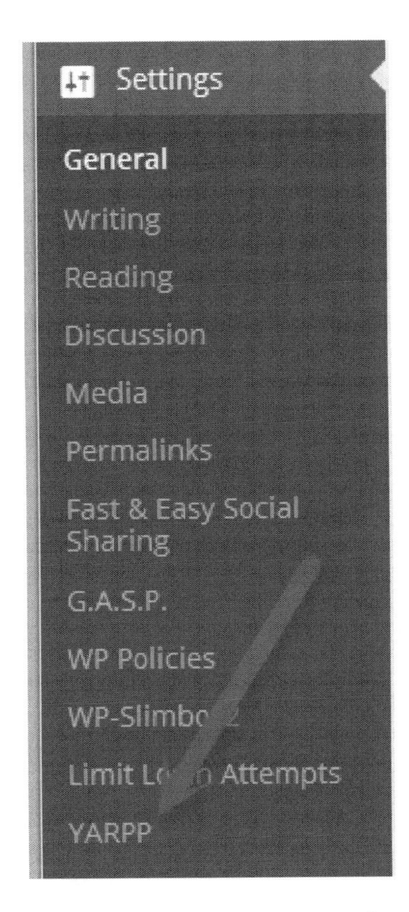

Click on YARPP to visit the plugin settings.

The only settings I want you to change are the following:

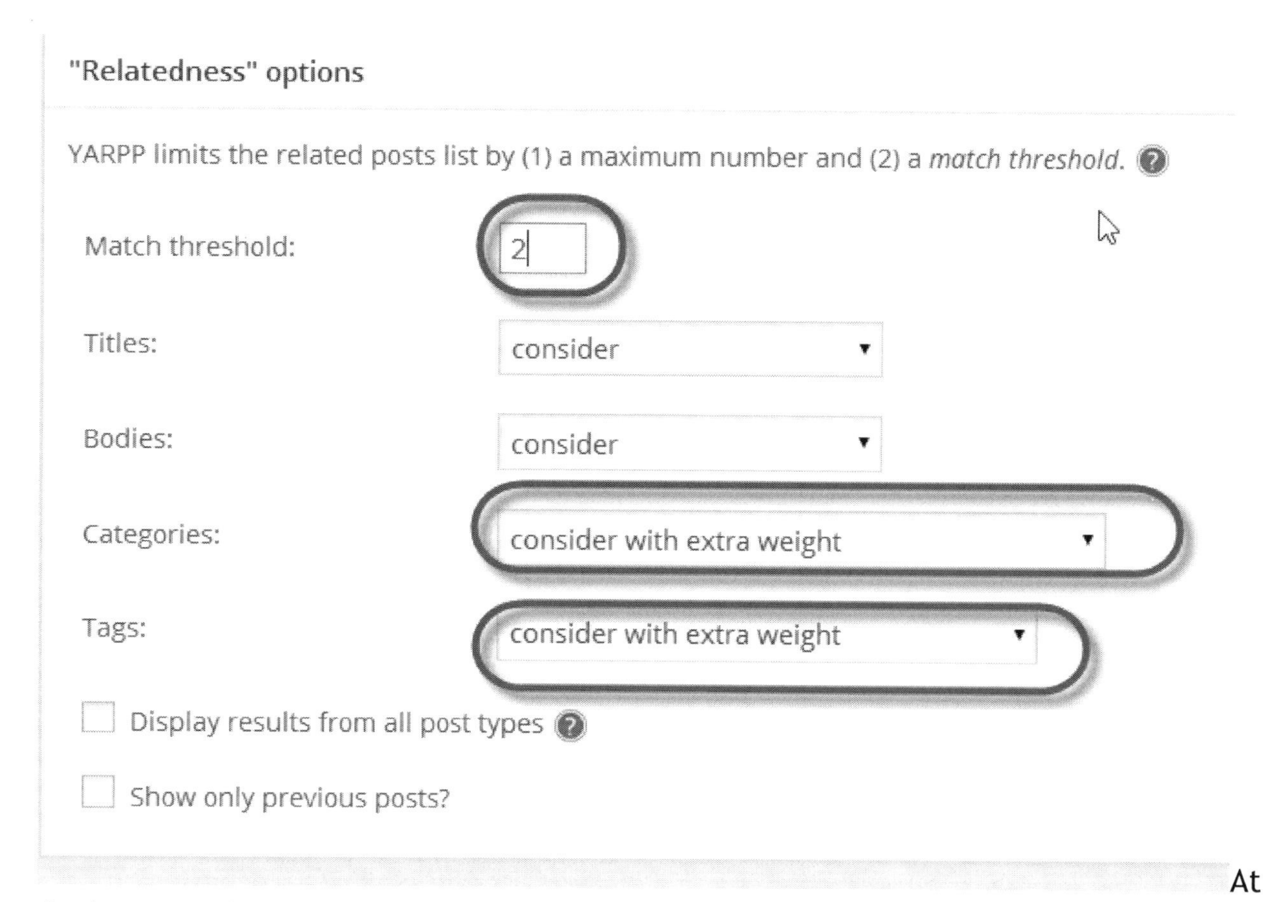

At the bottom of the options screen, click the Save Changes button.

We have set this up so that the plugin will give greater weight to posts in the same category, or use a common tag. This should ensure that the related posts section at the end of every post on our site, displays the most relevant posts. This in turn will encourage our visitors to stay on our site, exploring more.

That's it. Now, for any post on your site, if this plugin finds posts that are related, it will include them in a related posts section at the end of the post content. If no related posts are found, you just see this:

Recommended Web Host

My recommended web host is Stablehost.

You can get a 40% discount on your first payment to Stablehost by clicking the link above to visit their site, then entering the coupon code **rapidwpsites** at the checkout.

Recommended Registrar – Namecheap.

Tell your friends about this post:

No related posts.

This message is controlled by the settings screen here:

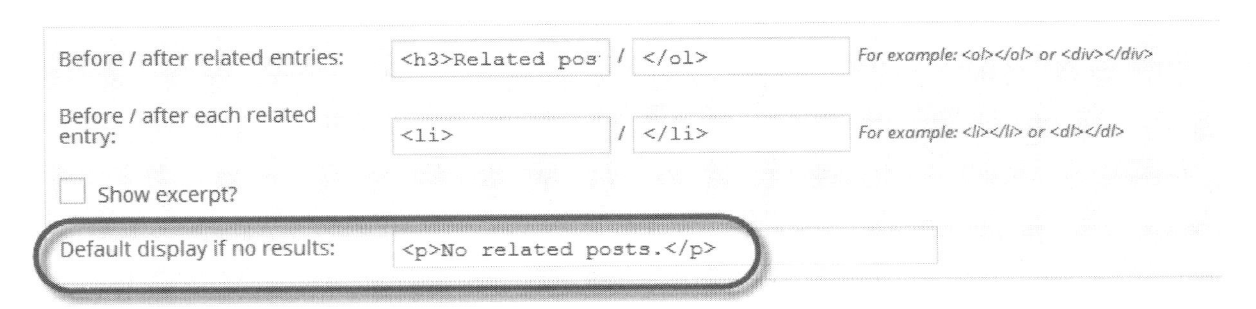

By all means, play around with the settings of this plugin once you have a number of posts on your site. This plugin has a lot of possible customizations, and I will cover some of them in a tutorial on RapidWPSites.com for those that are interested.

Keeping Wordpress Updated & Secure

Wordpress is updated frequently (every few months) and achieve two major things:

1. Add new features.
2. Fix bugs in older version.

While some bugs are inconvenient but harmless (e.g. a feature not quite working as it should), others cause security problems for your site. Very occasionally a bug is found that could allow hackers to get into your website, through a "back door". These types of bugs need to be fixed as soon as possible, and are usually fixed within hours of being found.

Fortunately, these bugs are rare, BUT, it does mean that you should always keep Wordpress updated to the latest version.

When you installed your site, you may have had the option to enable an auto-upgrade script. Here is a screenshot from earlier in the book:

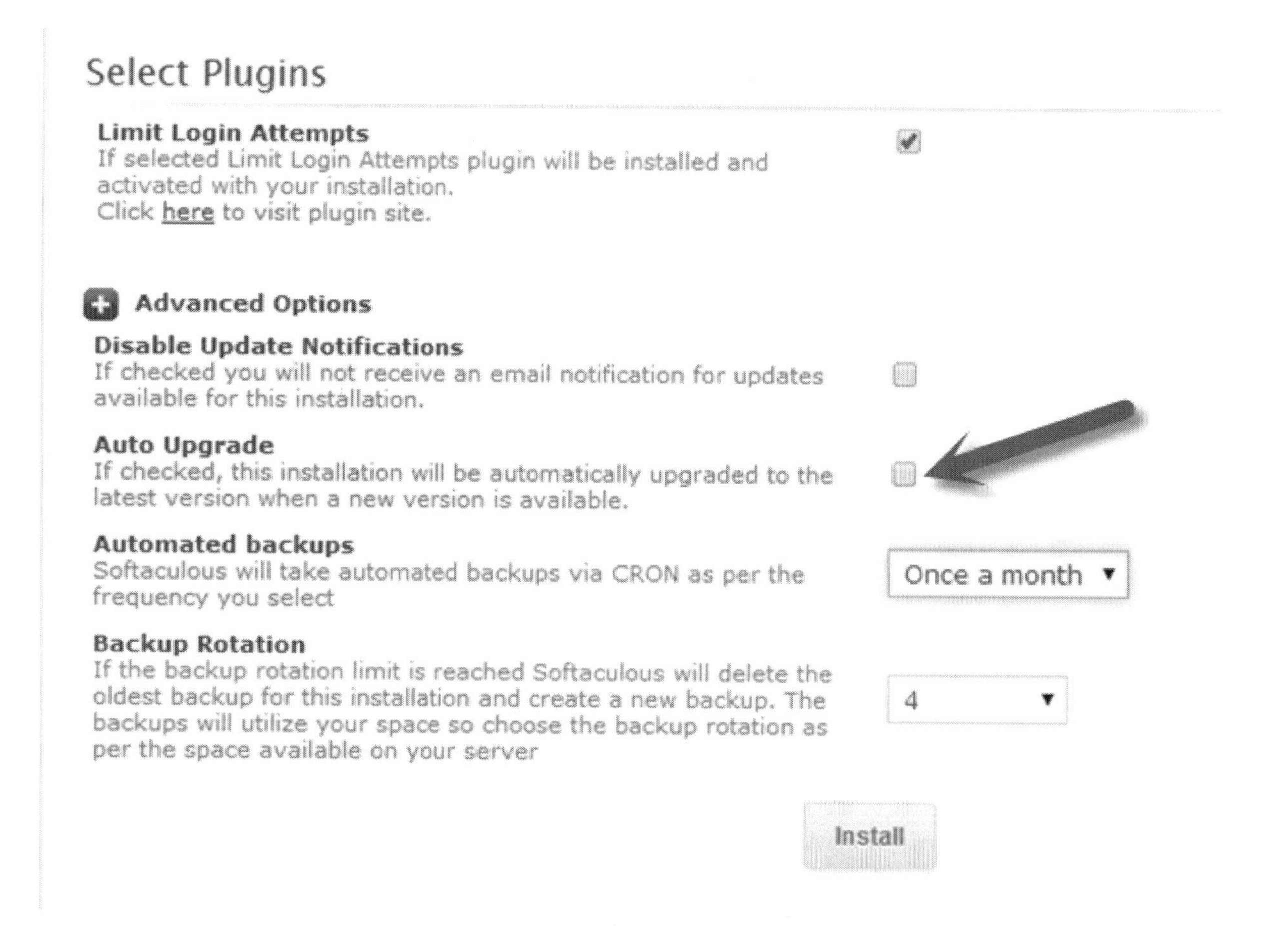

By checking that box, whenever a new version of Wordpress is released, your copy would automatically be updated.

I personally do not use that option, for one simple reason.

Upgrades can sometimes cause problems with plugins I use. If Wordpress was automatically updated, and a plugin was no longer compatible, then at best the plugin would stop working, at worst it would break my site completely.

I therefore choose to upgrade manually, and usually leave it 3-4 days to make sure no one is reporting problems with the latest version.

Upgrading manually is very easy.

When you log in to the Dashboard, there is an **Updates** item in the **Dashboard** menu.

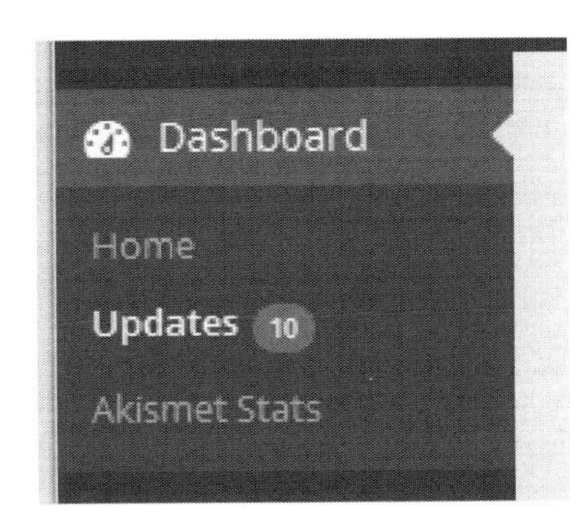
Dashboard
Home
Updates 10
Akismet Stats

This will notify when there are updates available, much like the notification we saw earlier with comments to moderate. You can then click through to the **Updates** area, and update the files.

The "Updates" area lists all available updates for Wordpress itself, and plugins.

When a Wordpress upgrade is available, you'll see something like this:

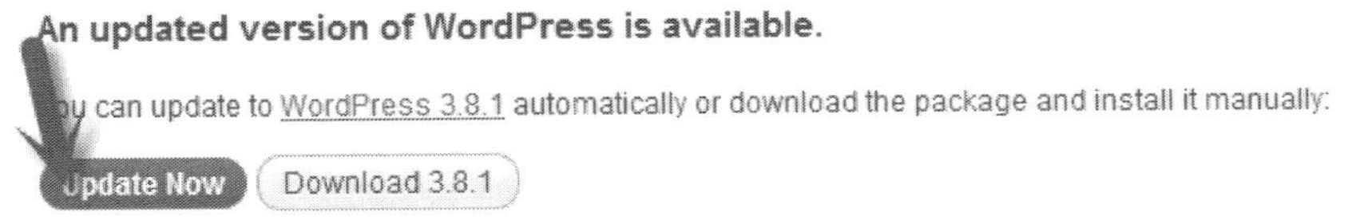
An updated version of WordPress is available.
u can update to WordPress 3.8.1 automatically or download the package and install it manually:
Update Now
Download 3.8.1
While your site is being updated, it will be in maintenance mode. As soon as your updates are complete, your site will return to normal.

Just click the **Update Now** button and the upgrade will proceed automatically on its own. You may have to click a button or two to "upgrade the database" or some other task, but that's as technical as it gets. Just follow the instructions on screen and you'll be fine.

If there are plugins to update, you'll see something like this:

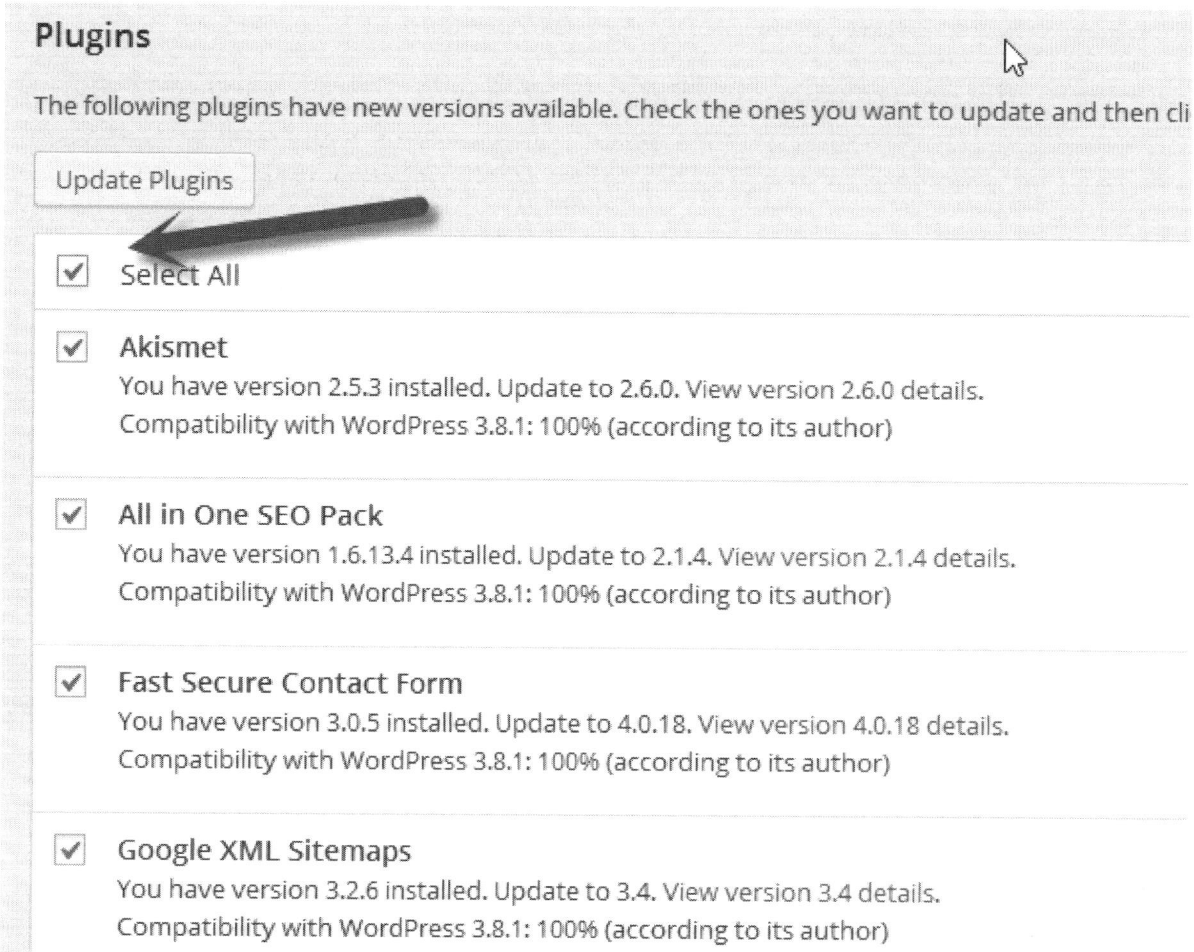

Plugins

The following plugins have new versions available. Check the ones you want to update and then cli

Update Plugins

Select All

Akismet
You have version 2.5.3 installed. Update to 2.6.0. View version 2.6.0 details.
Compatibility with WordPress 3.8.1: 100% (according to its author)

All in One SEO Pack
You have version 1.6.13.4 installed. Update to 2.1.4. View version 2.1.4 details.
Compatibility with WordPress 3.8.1: 100% (according to its author)

Fast Secure Contact Form
You have version 3.0.5 installed. Update to 4.0.18. View version 4.0.18 details.
Compatibility with WordPress 3.8.1: 100% (according to its author)

Google XML Sitemaps
You have version 3.2.6 installed. Update to 3.4. View version 3.4 details.
Compatibility with WordPress 3.8.1: 100% (according to its author)

You can check one or more plugins to update, or click the **Select All** check box, which selects all plugins for updating. Then, simply click the **Update Plugins** button, and Wordpress does the rest for you.

Backing up the Site

Backing up anything on a computer should be a priority. While good web hosts do keep backups for you, if your site gets infected with any kind of malicious code, and you don't find out about it for a while, all of your backups can be infected, and therefore not much use.

I always recommend you have some kind of backup plan, and fortunately, there is a great plugin that can help.

Click the **Add New** item in the **Plugins** menu.

Search for WP-DBManager.

Find, install and activate this plugin:

Name	Version	Rating	Description
WP-DBManager Details | Install Now	2.65	★★★★☆	Allows you to optimize database, repair database, backup database, restore database, delete backup database , drop/empty tables and run selected queries. Supports automatic scheduling of backing up, optimizing and repairing of database. Previous Versions WP-DBManager 2.40 For WordPress 2.7.x WP-DBManager 2.31 For WordPress 2.1.x To 2.6.x WP-DBManager 2.05 For WordPress 2.0.x WP-DBManager 1.00 F... By Lester 'GaMerZ' Chan.

It will create a new "Database" menu in the sidebar:

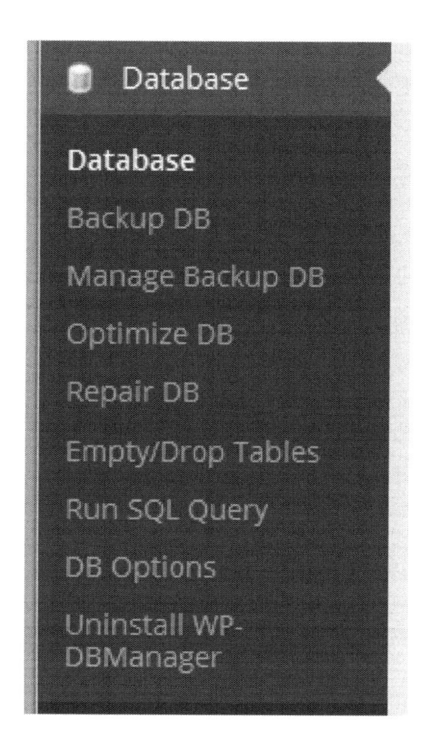

Click on **DB Options:**

At the top of this screen, you need to check the **Paths** to make sure they are entered correctly.

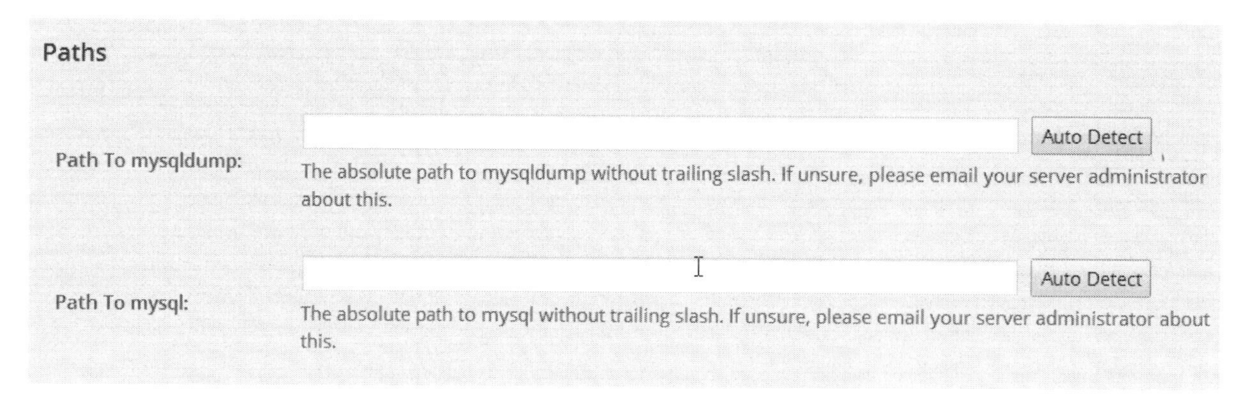

Both of mine are blank, and the **Auto Detect** button does not work.

If you are using the same web host as I am, enter **mysqldump** in the top box, and **mysql** in the lower one:

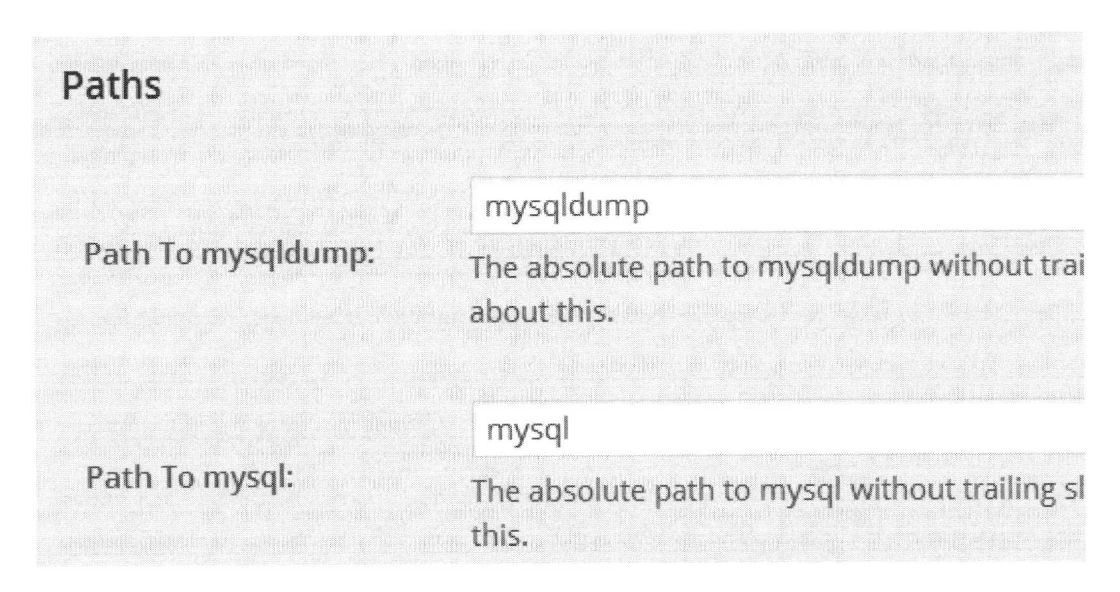

Now scroll right to the bottom and click the **Save Changes** button.

You should now see this:

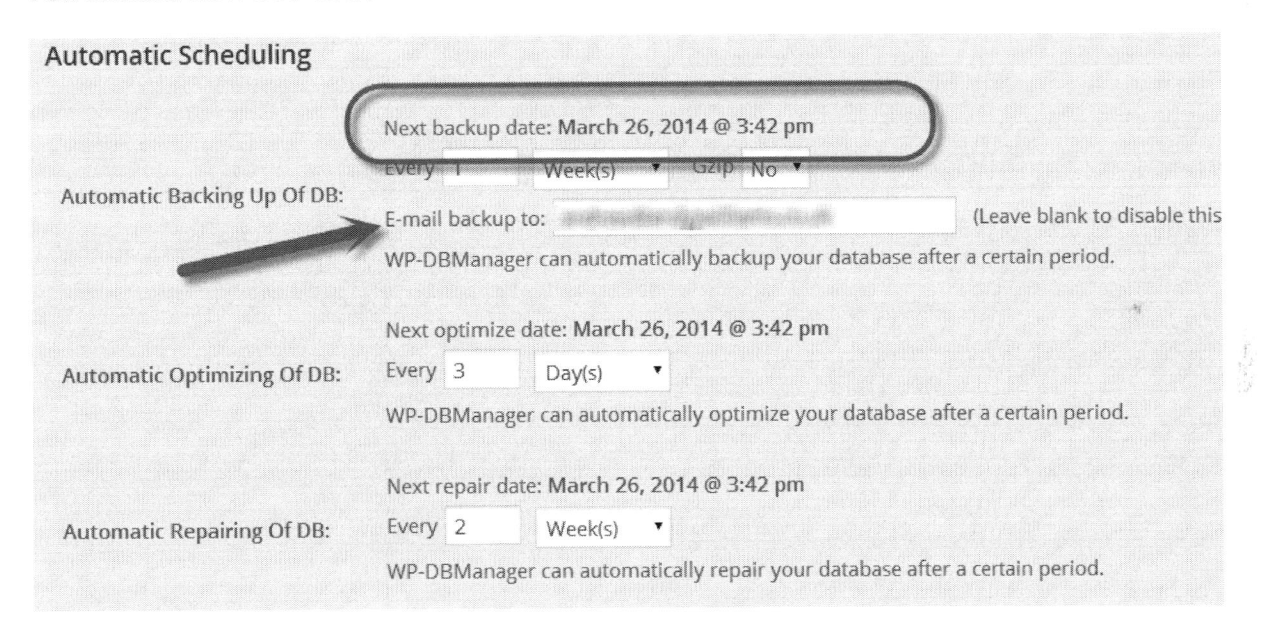

In addition to scheduling the next automated backup, a backup should have been sent to the email address in the **E-mail backup to:** box shown in the screenshot above.

Go and check your email for the backup.

You need to check whether or not the backup contained any data.

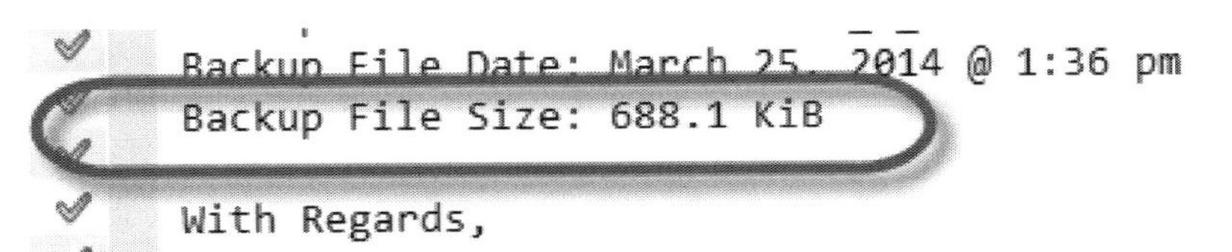

The "Backup file size" listed in the email should not be zero. If it is, then the backup was not successful.

The most common cause for a backup failure, is the two paths we fixed above, not being correct. If necessary, contact your web host and ask for the path to the **mysql dump** and **mysql** for your site. You can then enter these and resave your settings.

Now, you'll also notice that there is a warning message at the top of your Dashboard now.

Your backup folder MIGHT be visible to the public

To correct this issue, move the **.htaccess** file from **wp-content/plugins/wp-dbmanager** to

We need to move a file on the server, and for this, we need to login to our cPanel (if you know how to use FTP, then use that instead).

Once in your cPanel, find the **Files** section and click on **File Manager**:

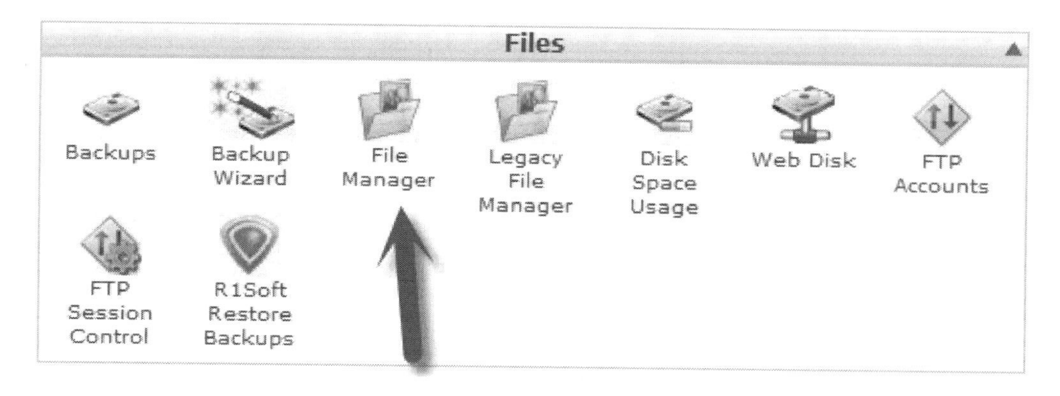

You will see a popup:

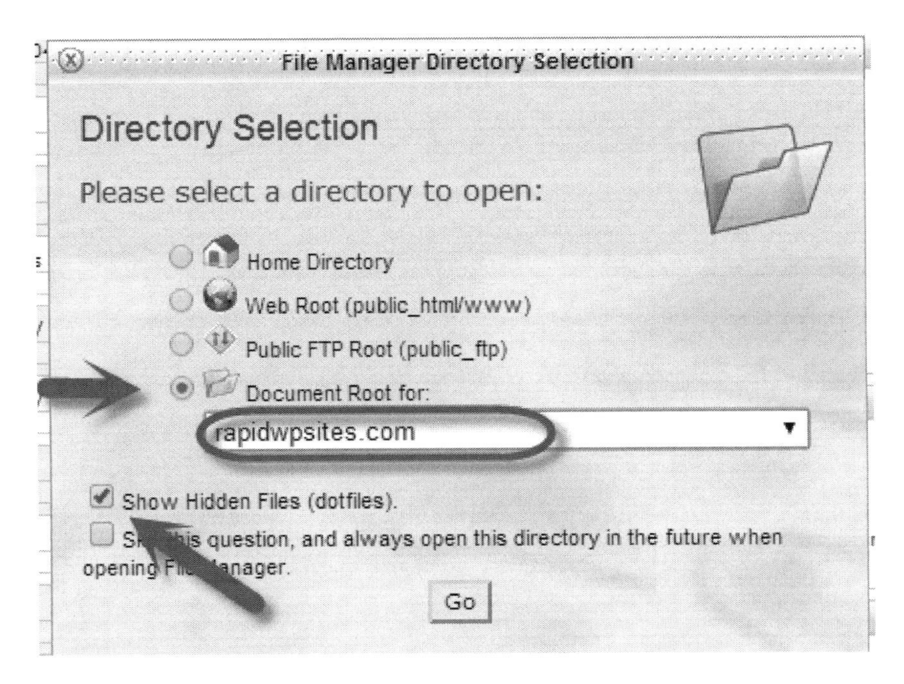

Select **Document Root for:** and choose your domain from the list.

Make sure **Show Hidden Files** is checked.

Click the **Go** button and the file manager will open in a new window.

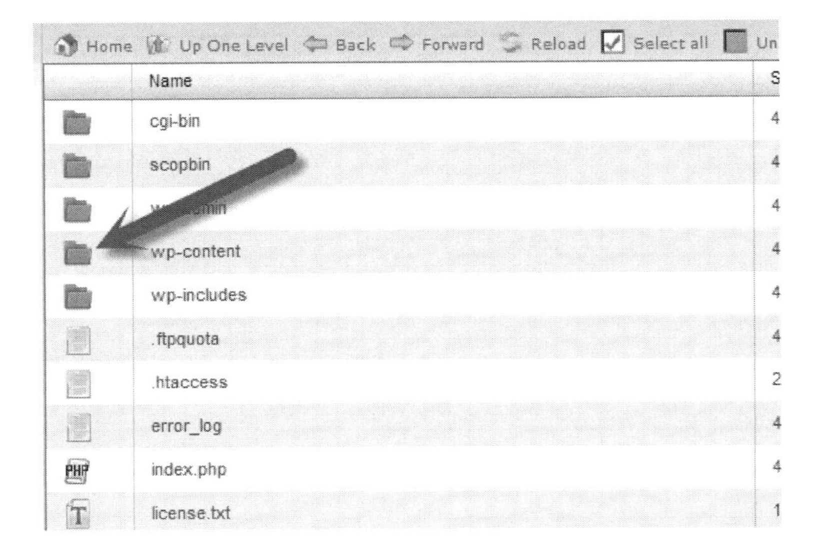

Double-click on the little folder icon next to **wp-content**.

Now double-click on the little folder icon next to **plugins**.

Now double-click on the folder icon next to **wp-dbmanager**.

You will see a file there called htaccess.txt.

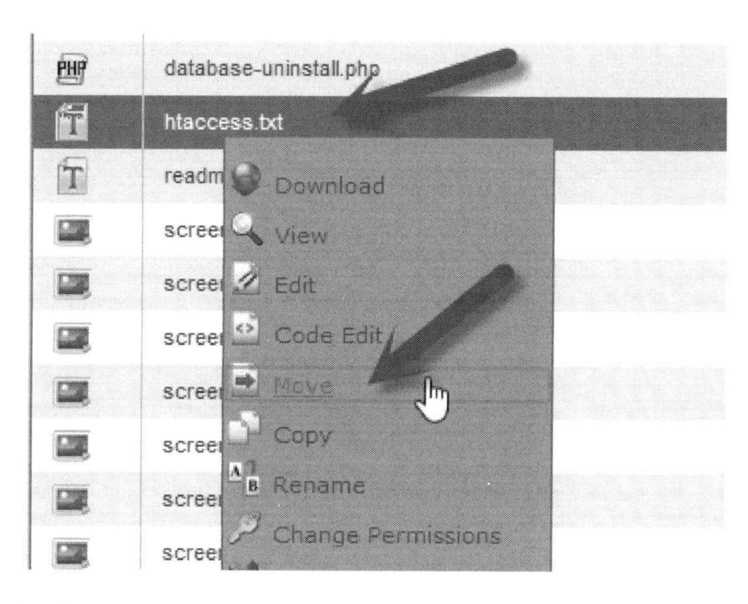

Right-click on htaccess.txt and select **Move**.

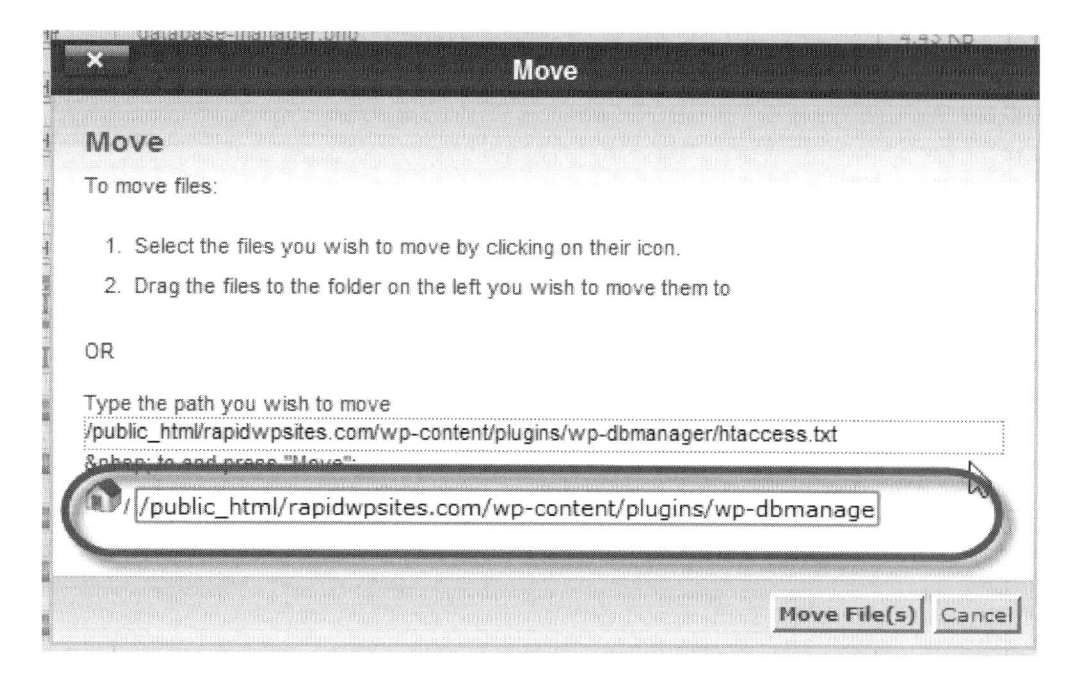

We need to edit the path highlighted in the screenshot above.

Basically, we need to delete everything after "**plugin/**" (start deleting from wp-dbmanager….) to the end of the line, and replace it with **backup-db**.

So my new path is:

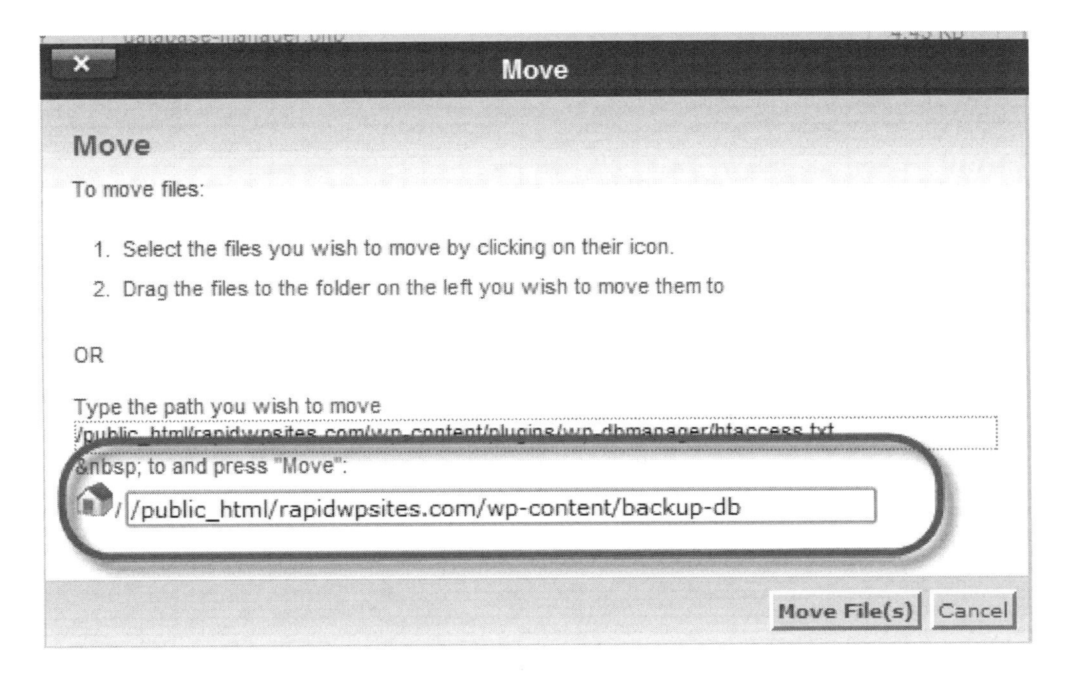

Yours WILL NOT be identical to mine.

However, yours should end with /wp-content/backup-db, just as mine does. Now click the **Move File(s)** button.

The htaccess.txt file will disappear from your file manager window. We need to find it.

Click the **Up One Level** button in the toolbar:

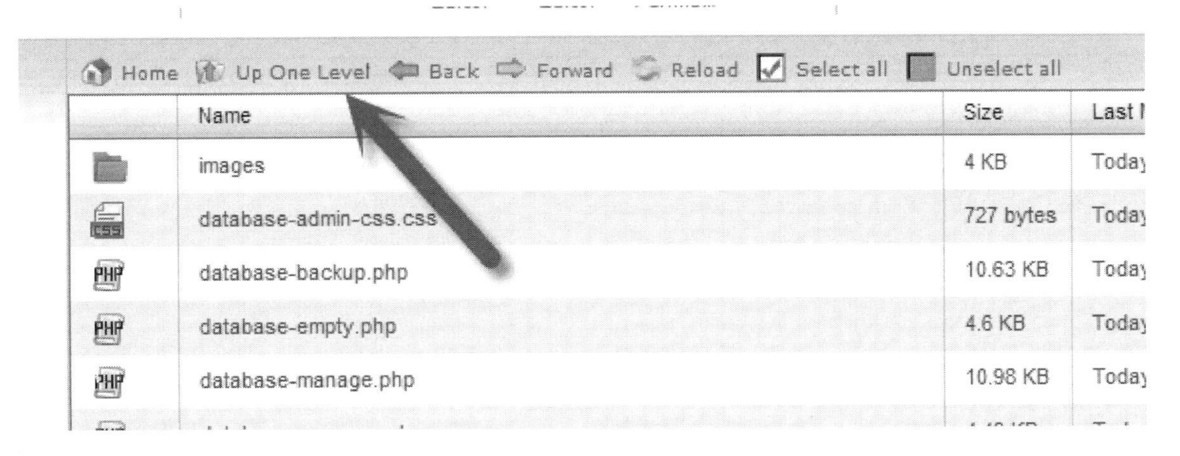

Then click it again.

You should now see the folder labeled **backup-db.**

Double-click the folder icon next to the backup-db folder to open it.

You will now see the htaccess.txt file.

The final thing we need to do is rename the file. Click on htaccess.txt to highlight it.

Now in the toolbar at the very top of the File Manager is a **Rename** button. Click it.

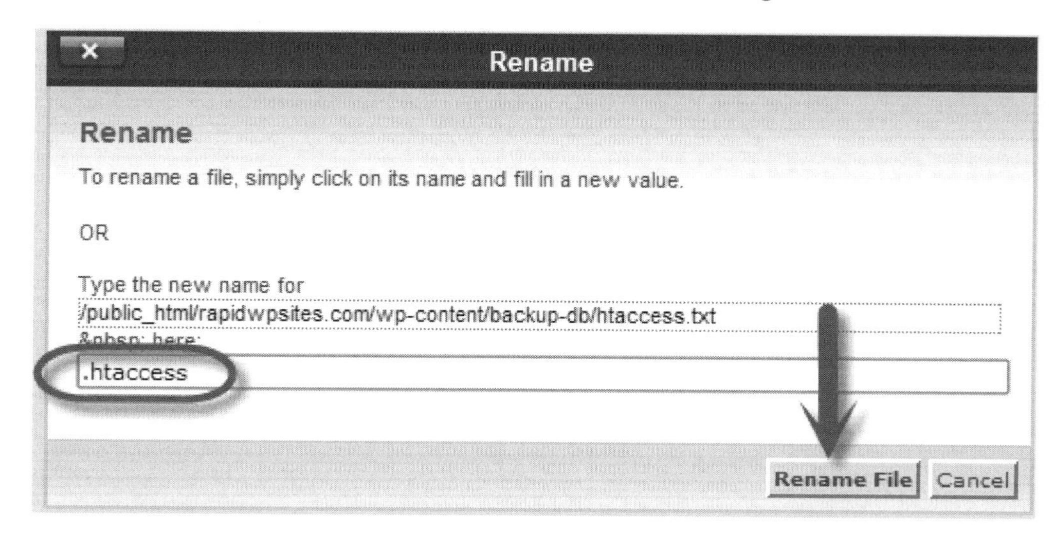

You need to rename htaccess.txt so that it is now called .htaccess

Finally, click the **Rename File** button.

The File Manager screen will refresh and you should now see the .htaccess file listed, together with any backups of your site that have been done already.

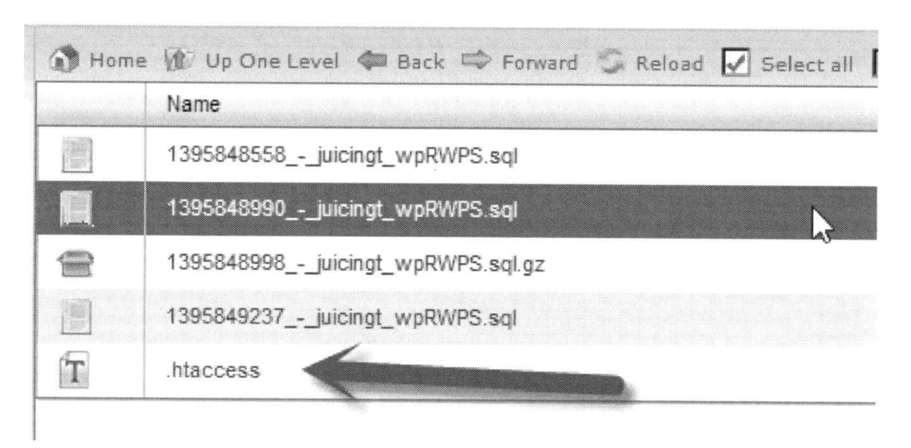

Go back into your Dashboard, where you saw the original warning and refresh the screen. The warning should now have disappeared.

This plugin will create automatic backups and email them to you every week. That's a great start. If you ever do need to restore a backup, you can check out the documentation for the WP-DBManager plugin. I'll also create a tutorial on the RapidWPSites.com website.

Changing the Look & Feel of the site

By now you should have a fully functioning website and know how to add more content to the site. However, you might not like the look of your site. Maybe the colors, the fonts, or the layout don't look right to you. That is where themes come in.

Wordpress was created to be modular in nature, so that developers could create add-ons. We've seen some of these in the form of plugins and widgets, but another major way you can customize your site is by changing the theme of your site.

Think of themes a little like skins. You can add a new skin over the top, which changes the look and feel, but doesn't touch your underlying data (content, installed plugins, etc).

The quickest way to experience themes is to look at the ones Wordpress installed on your server when you installed Wordpress.

Go to the **Themes** item in the **Appearance** menu in your Dashboard.

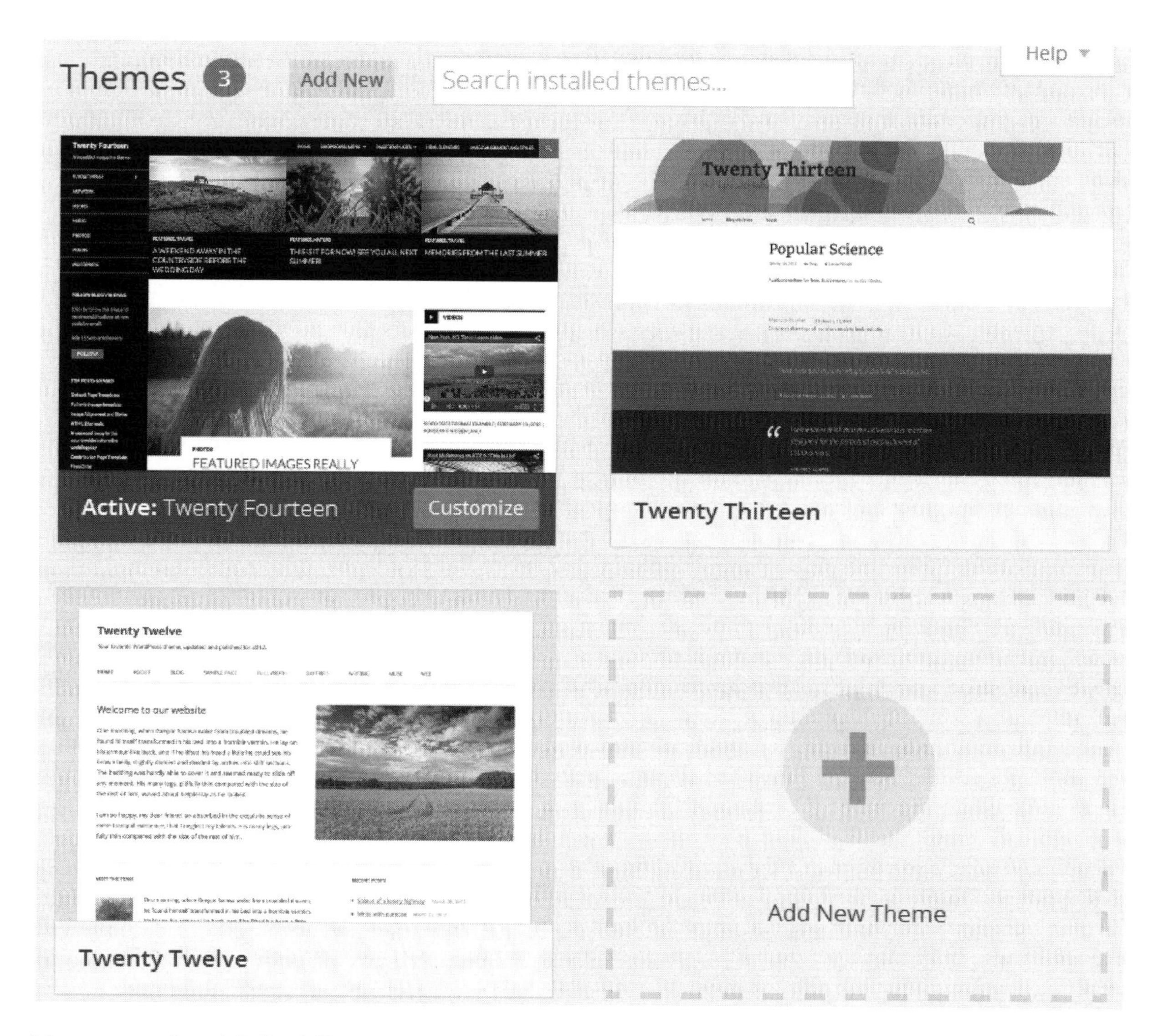

Here you should find Twenty Twelve (released in 2012), Twenty Thirteen (released in 2013) and Twenty Fourteen (released in 2014).

The one we have been using in this book so far is the Twenty Fourteen theme, and with it, my site looks like this:

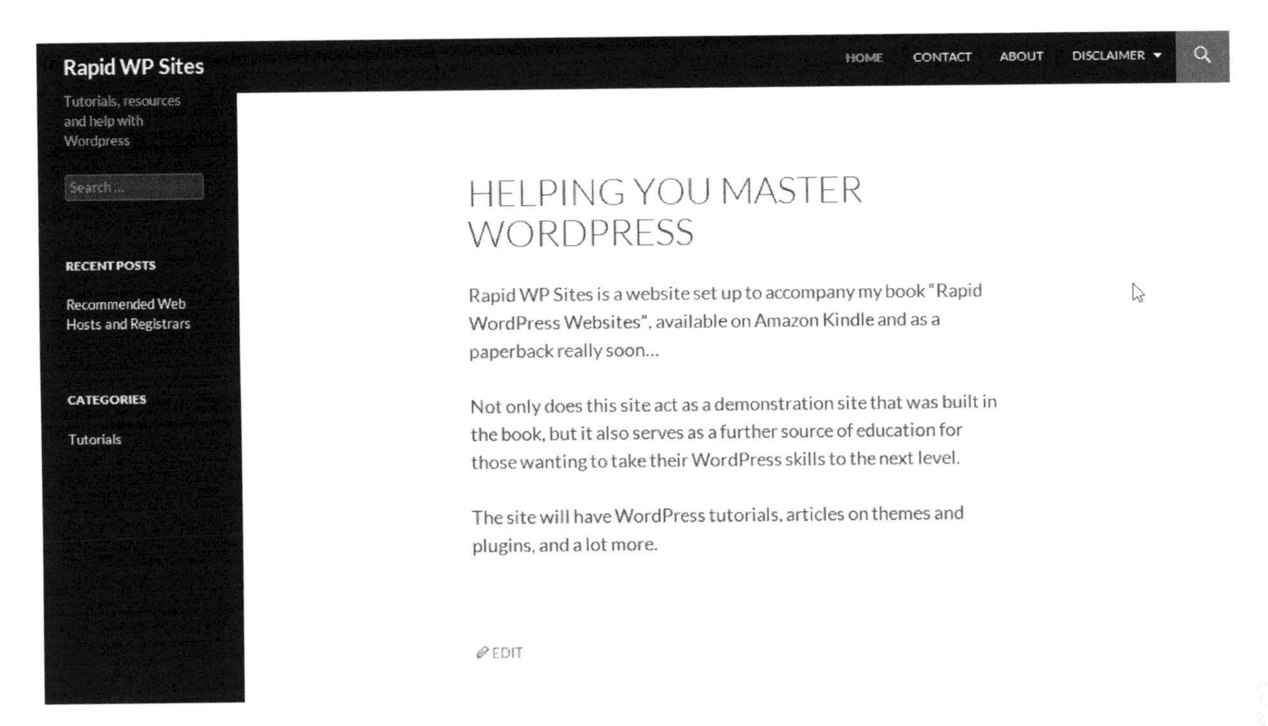

I can change the theme to one of the other installed themes, quickly and easily.

Let's try the Twenty Thirteen theme.

When you move your mouse over the image, it changes to include two buttons. A **Live Preview** button allows you to see what the theme would look like IF you activated it.

I am going to go ahead and just click on the **Activate** button.

If I now visit my homepage, this is how it looks:

Helping you master WordPress

Rapid WP Sites is a website set up to accompany my book "Rapid WordPress Websites", available on Amazon Kindle and as a paperback really soon...

Not only does this site act as a demonstration site that was built in the book, but it also serves as a further source of education for those wanting to take their WordPress skills to the next level.

The site will have WordPress tutorials, articles on themes and plugins, and a lot more.

Edit

That's very different, but my content is still there! It's only the layout and appearance that has changed. The left sidebar from the Twenty Fourteen theme is not showing, and the widgets I had in that sidebar are now in the site footer:

Not only does this site act as a demonstration site that was built in the book, but it also serves as a further source of education for those wanting to take their WordPress skills to the next level.

The site will have WordPress tutorials, articles on themes and plugins, and a lot more.

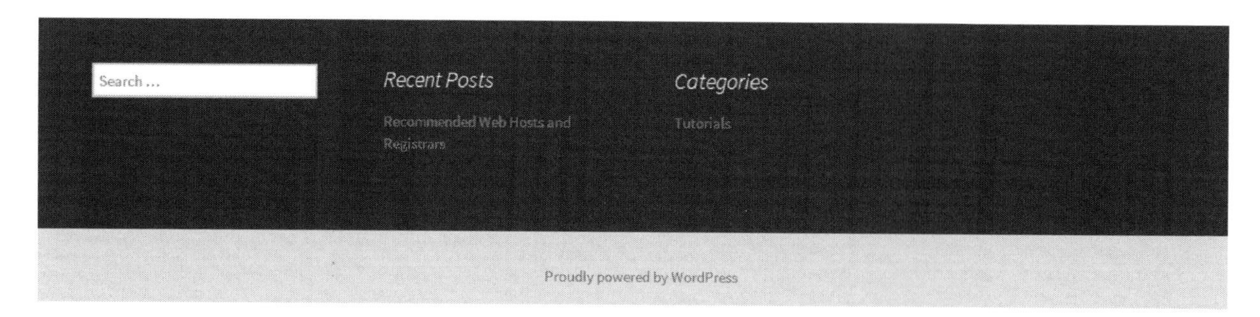

Note that when you switch between themes, you may need to move your widgets around after the switch, or even re-add them. This is because all themes are different and have different widget areas, with different names. Wordpress does its best when you switch themes, but often doesn't get it quite right.

If I visit the Widgets screen in the Dashboard, I can see that the widget areas in the Twenty Thirteen theme are different:

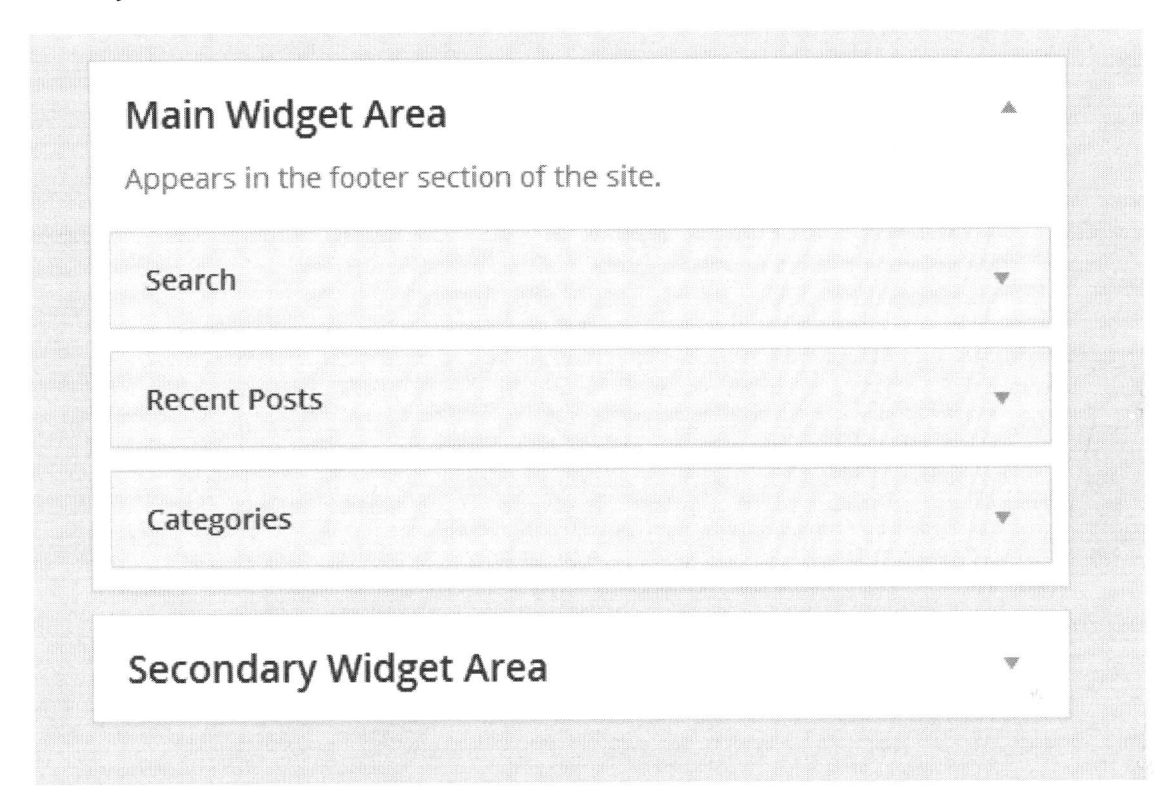

This is something you need to get use to. Different themes have different areas designed to accept widgets. This theme has just two. The **Main Widget Area** looks like the footer, and if I add a widget to the **Secondary Widget Area**, I see that is actually a right sidebar:

Helping you master WordPress

Rapid WP Sites is a website set up to accompany my book "Rapid WordPress Websites", available on Amazon Kindle and as a paperback really soon...

Not only does this site act as a demonstration site that was built in the book, but it also serves as a further source of education for those wanting to take their WordPress skills to the next level.

The site will have WordPress tutorials, articles on themes and plugins, and a lot more.

Edit

Meta

Site Admin

Log out

Entries RSS

Comments RSS

WordPress.org

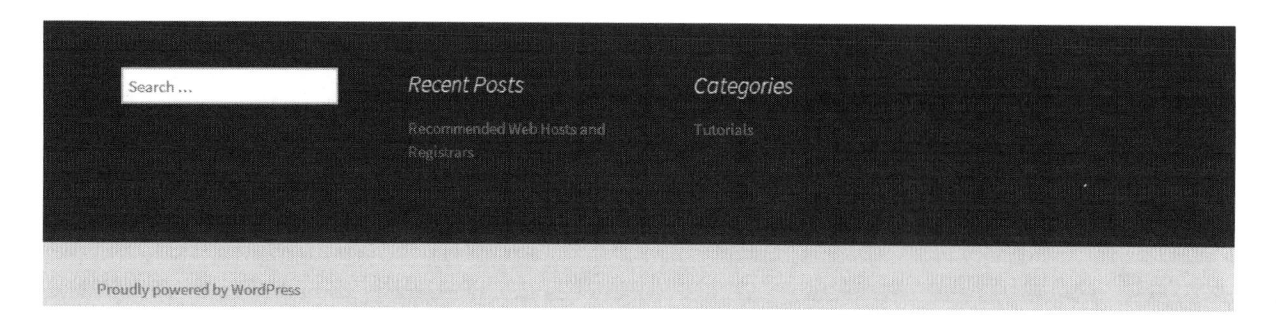

OK, so let's change the theme again. This time we'll activate the **Twenty Twelve** theme.

This is what my site now looks like:

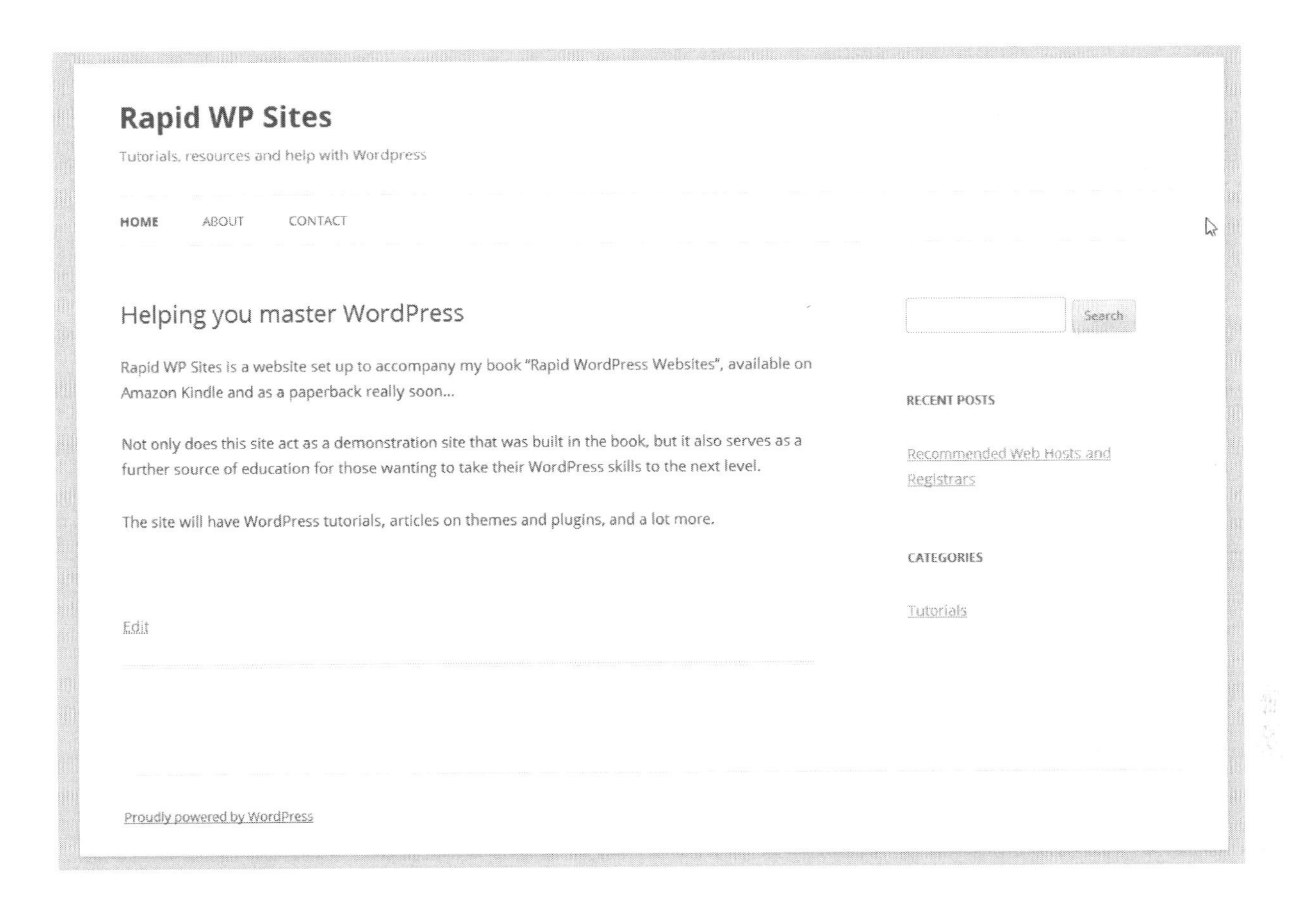

The sidebar is back, and on the right.

Checking the widgets settings, I can see that this theme has three areas where I can add widgets:

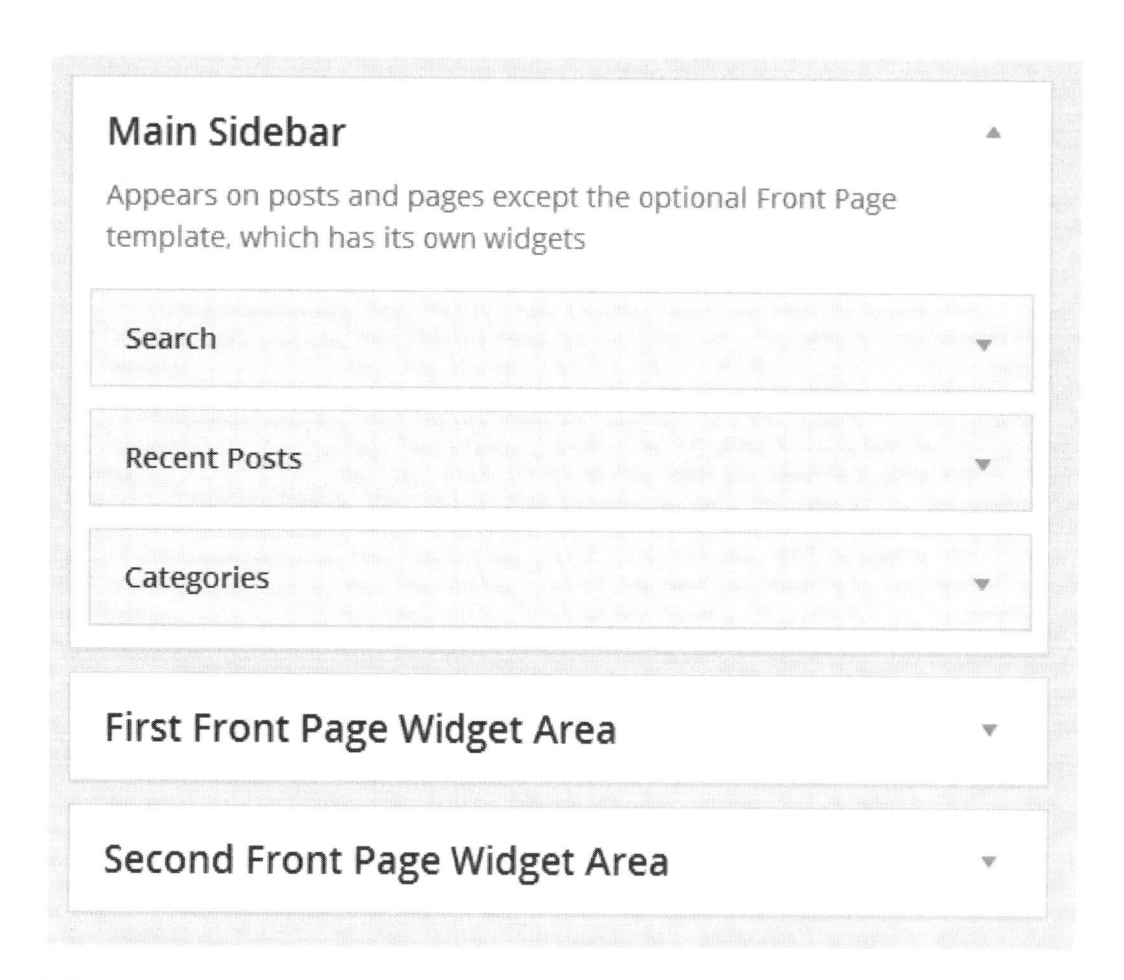

With any theme you want to use, you need to check to see where you can add widgets. Another thing to check is how many menus it can accommodate, and where these menus are located.

This Twenty Twelve theme allows just one menu, located at the top, under the header logo (see screenshot of the site with this theme active):

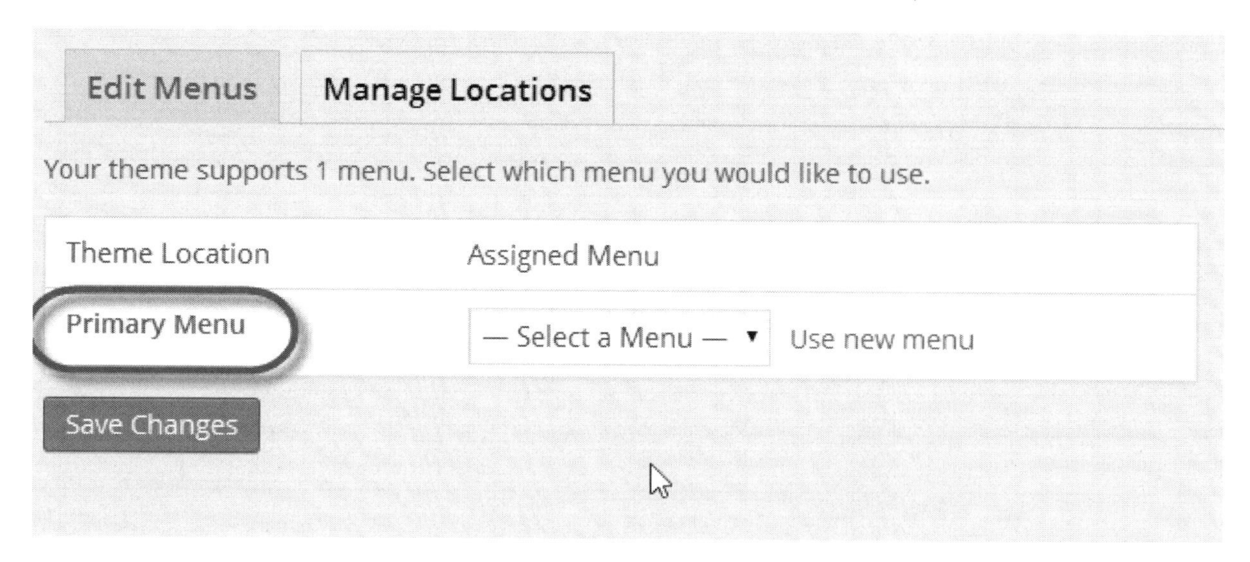

The Twenty Thirteen theme also only allows one menu.

The Twenty Fourteen theme, however, allows two:

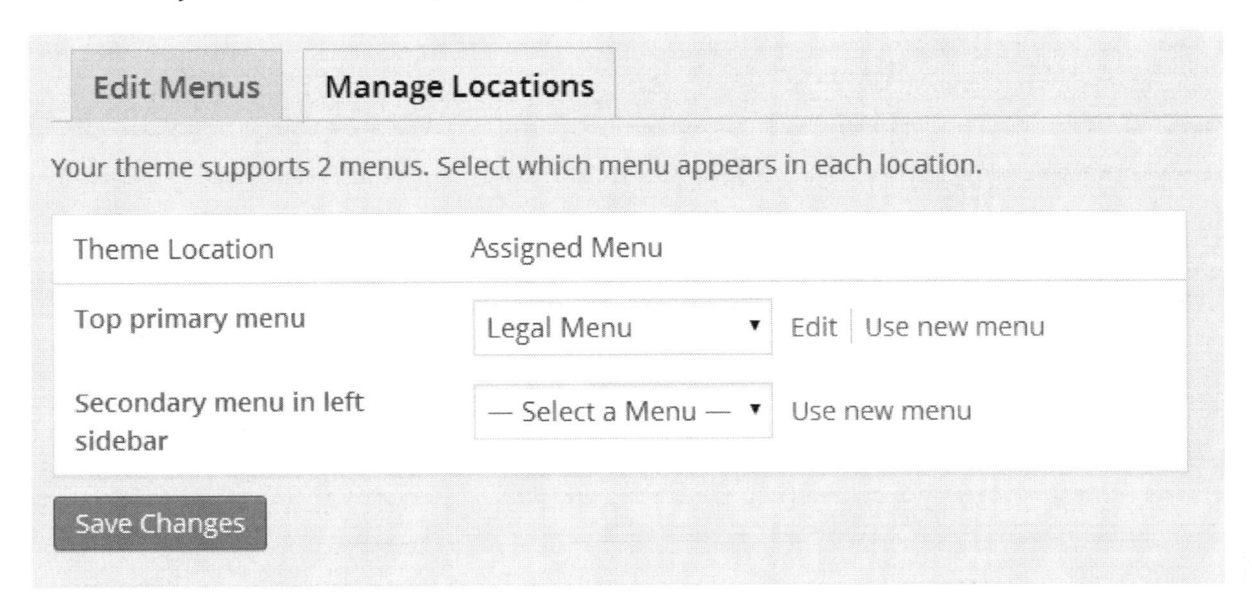

As we already know, one is at the top, the other is in the left sidebar, though, as I said before, we could add a menu to any sidebar (or any area that accepts a widget) with a **Custom Menu** widget.

Customizing a theme

Wordpress has a simple point and click interface to help you customize your active theme. However, the customizations that are available to you are dictated by the theme itself, and what its developers made available to you. Some themes have very few customizations, while others will offer you pages and pages of custom settings.

The three themes that come with Wordpress do not allow much in the way of customization.

There are a couple of ways you can get to the Customize screen. The first is by clicking the **Customize** button on the thumbnail of the active theme in the Themes screen:

The second method is by using the sidebar menu of the Dashboard, where you will find **Customize** in the **Appearance** menu:

Both of these options will open up the "customize" screen. Here is the customize screen for the Twenty Fourteen theme:

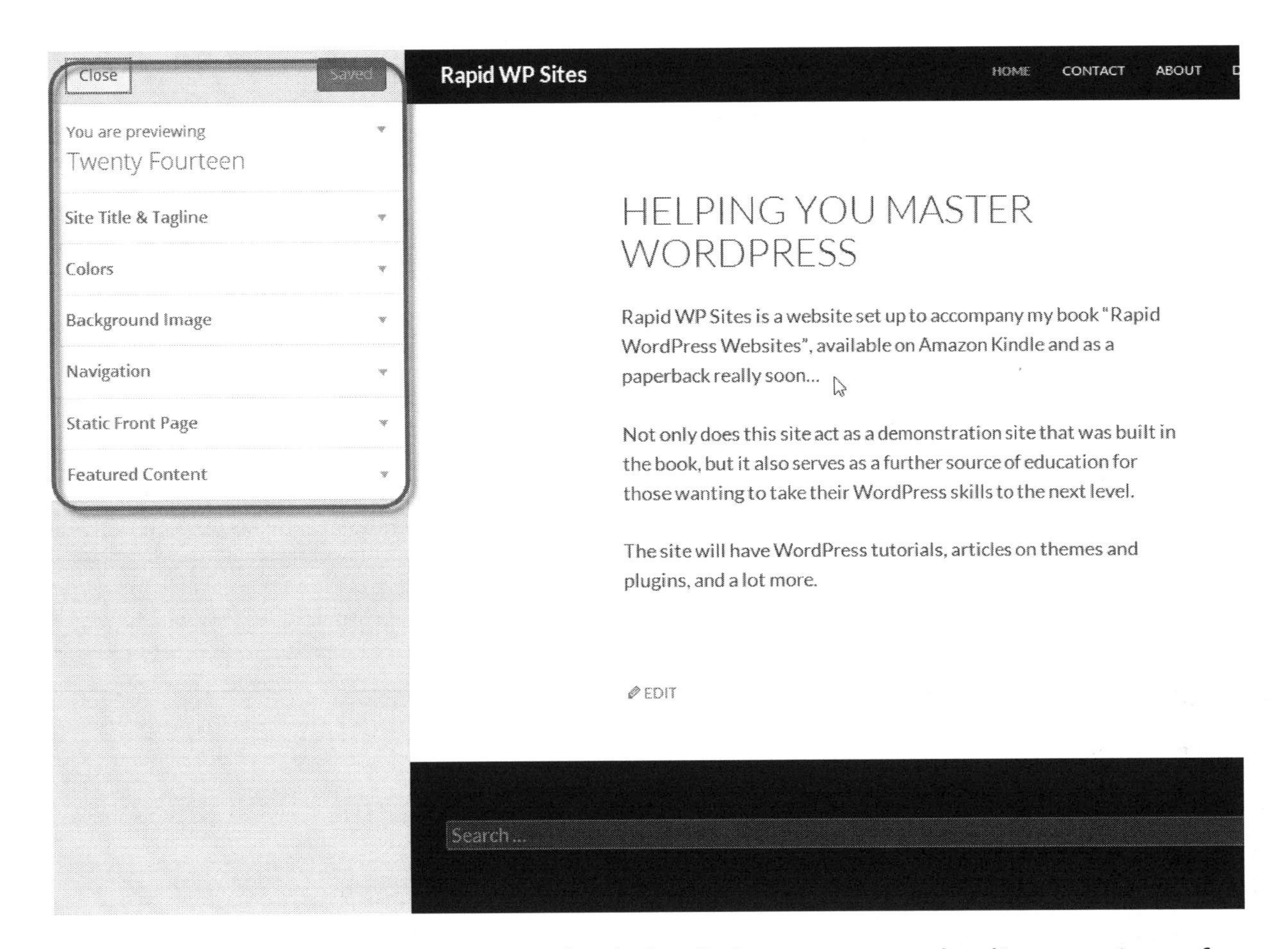

The customization options are on the left of the screen, and a live preview of your site on the right. This allows you to tweak you theme and immediately see the effects of those tweaks in the live preview.

Many of the customizations available here, are also accessible via the standard sidebar menus in Wordpress (mainly through the **Settings** menu).

Remember that these customization options are specific to the theme you are using. You may see different options with your theme. I am showing you the options for the Twenty Fourteen theme.

The options are grouped into related items. To open these groups you just click on the little arrow to the right of the group name.

Site Title & Tagline

This is where you can change the site name and tagline for your site.

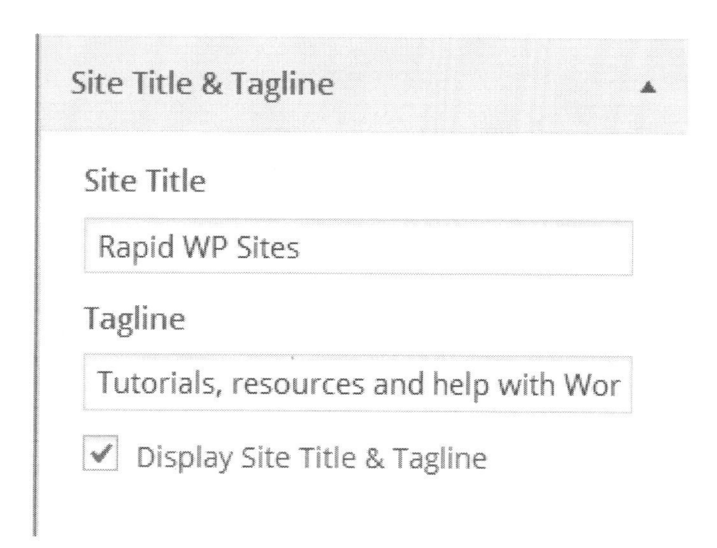

By default, site title and tagline are displayed at the top of every page, though you can turn them off in these settings, for example, if you wanted to use an image header instead. We'll look how we can do that later in this chapter.

Colors

This is where you can change the color of the title text, and also the background color. The background color is not the color used behind the text of your posts and pages. It is the color used to the right or left of your site on wide screens:

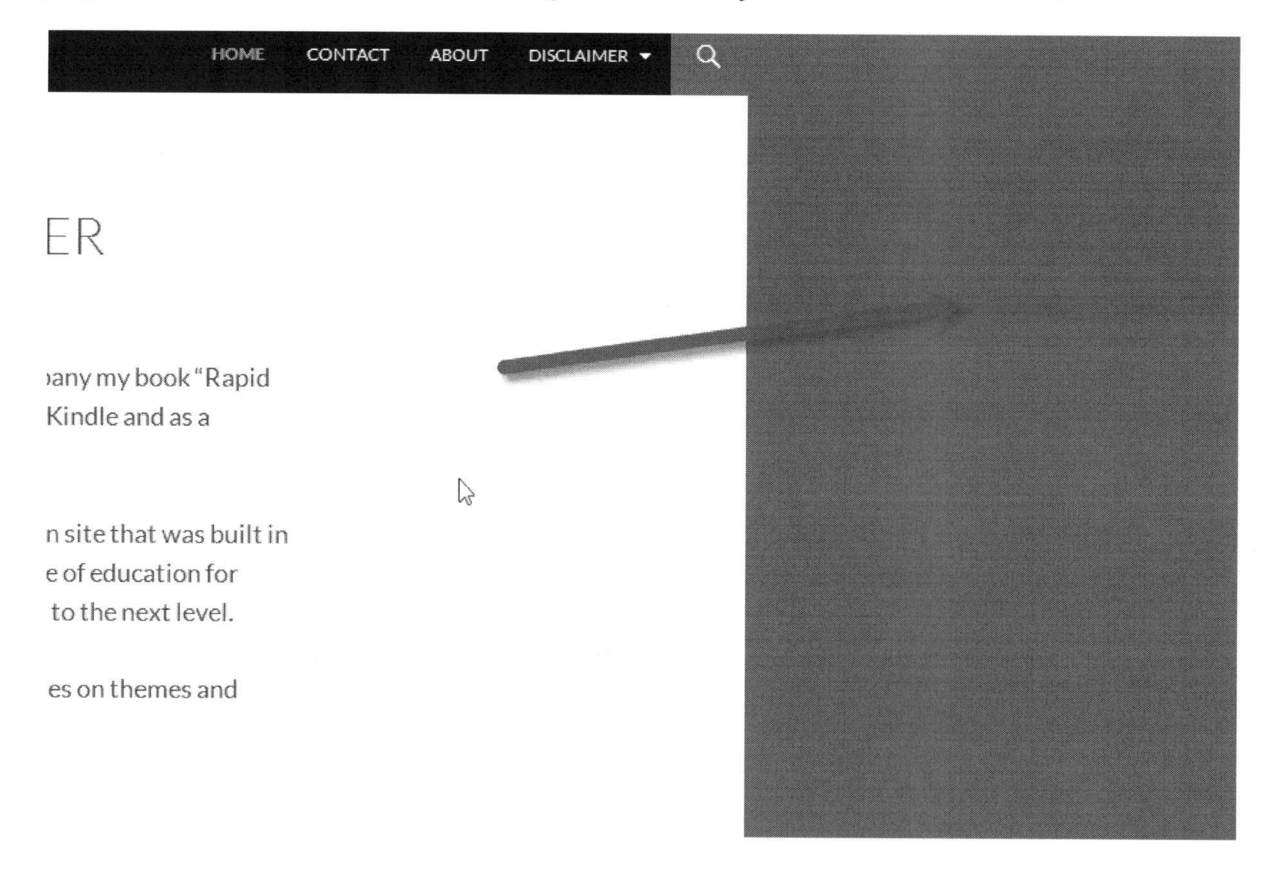

Background image

A background image is an image that is displayed in the same area of the screen as the background color. If a background image is selected, the color won't be used.

Navigation

This is where you can select the menus to use in your theme. As you select them, you should see them appear in the preview on the right.

Static Front Page

In these options, you can choose to display your latest posts, or a static "Page" as your homepage. You can also define a **Posts page**, which we will look at later in the section called "Another common site structure".

Featured Content

This essentially allows you to stick content to the top of the homepage in either a grid layout or in a slider. Play around with it if you are interested. I won't be covering it in this book (it is specific to the Twenty Fourteen theme).

Adding a header image

The Twenty Fourteen theme uses text to display the site name in the header area of your site. Most themes do by default. However, many people prefer to use an image. You can do this quite easily, but you need to make sure your image is the correct size.

Go to the **Header** settings in the **Appearance** menu.

This screen will tell you what size your image needs to be for the currently active them.

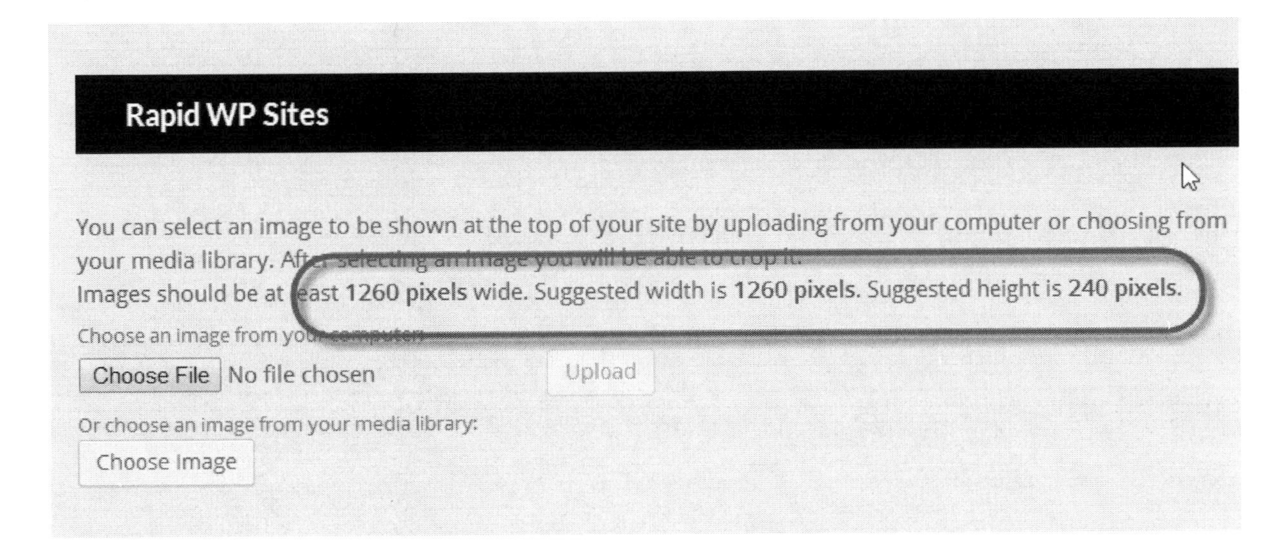

For Twenty Fourteen, it asks for an image width of 1260 pixels, and 240 pixels in height. You can choose the image from your computer via this screen.

Be aware that any image you choose to use for a logo needs to be loaded with the web page. Therefore file size is important and I recommend you keep it below 100 Kb.

If you do choose an image, chances are you want to switch off the text based title and tagline.

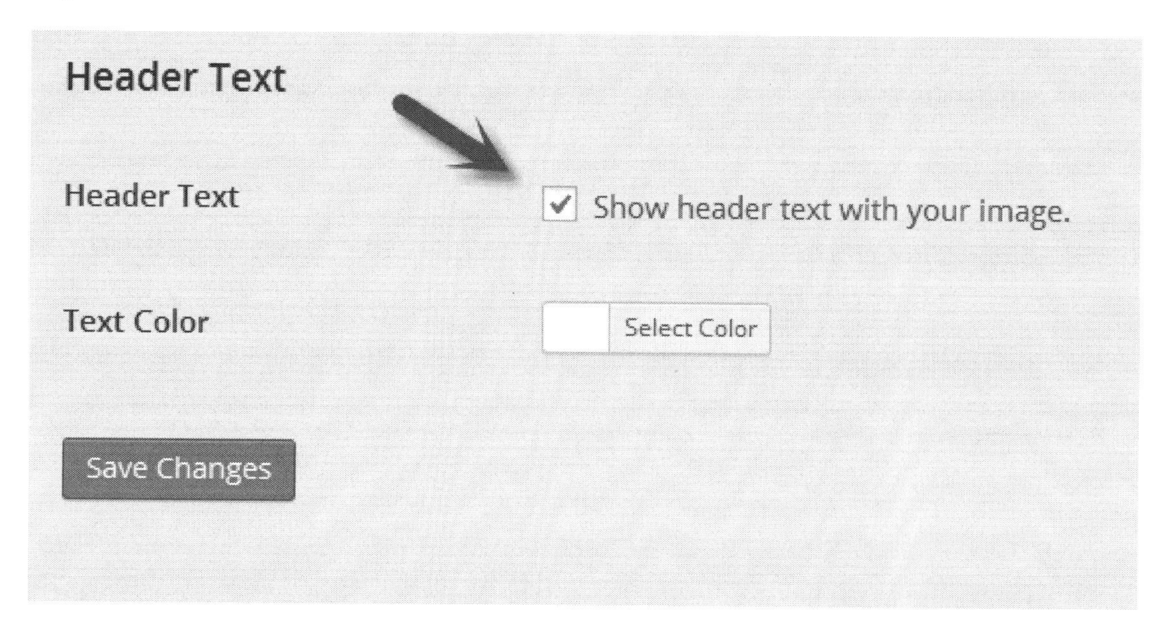

Just uncheck that box to remove the text.

Click the Save Changes when you have finished.

Where to get free themes

Wordpress makes it easy for you to find and install themes for your site.

Click on **Themes** in the **Appearance** menu.

At the top of the Theme page, click the **Add New** button.

You will be taken to an "Install Themes" screen that allows you to search for free themes based on criteria you set. For example, if I wanted to search for a green theme, with a right sidebar and responsive layout (this means it will look good on all screen sizes, including mobile phones), then I'd search like this:

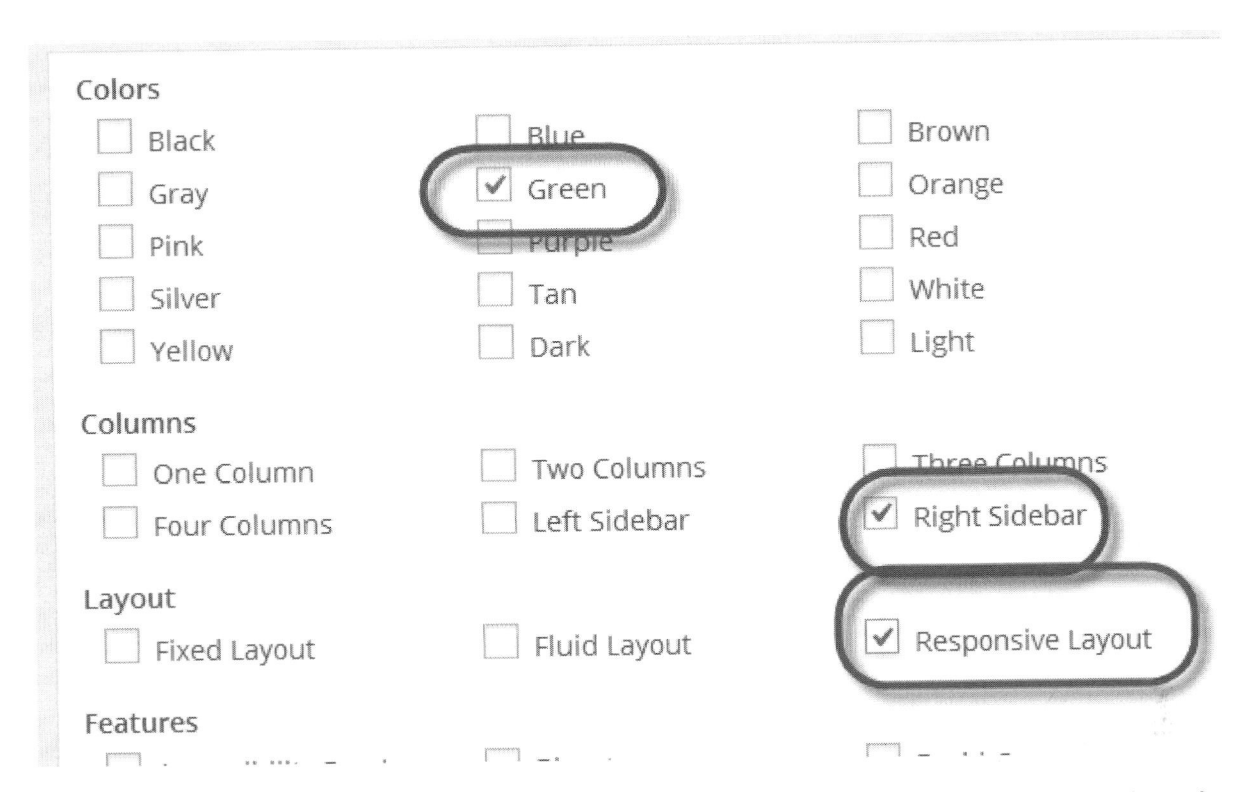

On clicking the **Find Themes** button at the bottom, any matches are displayed and appear in the search results:

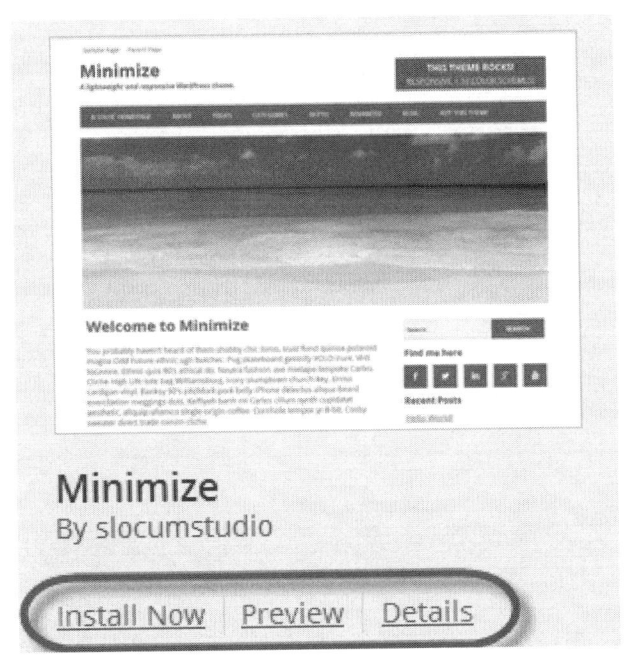

Clicking the **Details** link on a theme thumbnail will give you a little description of the theme.

The **Preview** link will show you a demo web page using that theme.

The **Install Now** link will install the theme into your Dashboard, so you can activate and use the theme.

The biggest problem with a lot of free themes is that they have a link back to the creator's website in the footer. This is really bad from a search engine point of view, and I do not recommend you use any theme that forces this link on your site.

The Wordpress themes we saw earlier do contain links to Wordpress, but that is a little different, since they are a huge authority site, the creators of the theme and creators of your content management system (CMS). Besides, you can remove that link if you want to.

This chapter has looked at changing the appearance of your site using the themes that come pre-installed with Wordpress. We have also looked at a free resource for downloading and installing themes.

The RapidWPSites.com website will showcase a number of my favorite themes and how to install and set them up. Since I may change the theme used on that site periodically, I will always include the name of the current theme in the site footer. I'll also include a link to the site that sells that particular theme.

Another common site structure

The structure of the site created in this book will do for most purposes. Here is a reminder of what we have done:

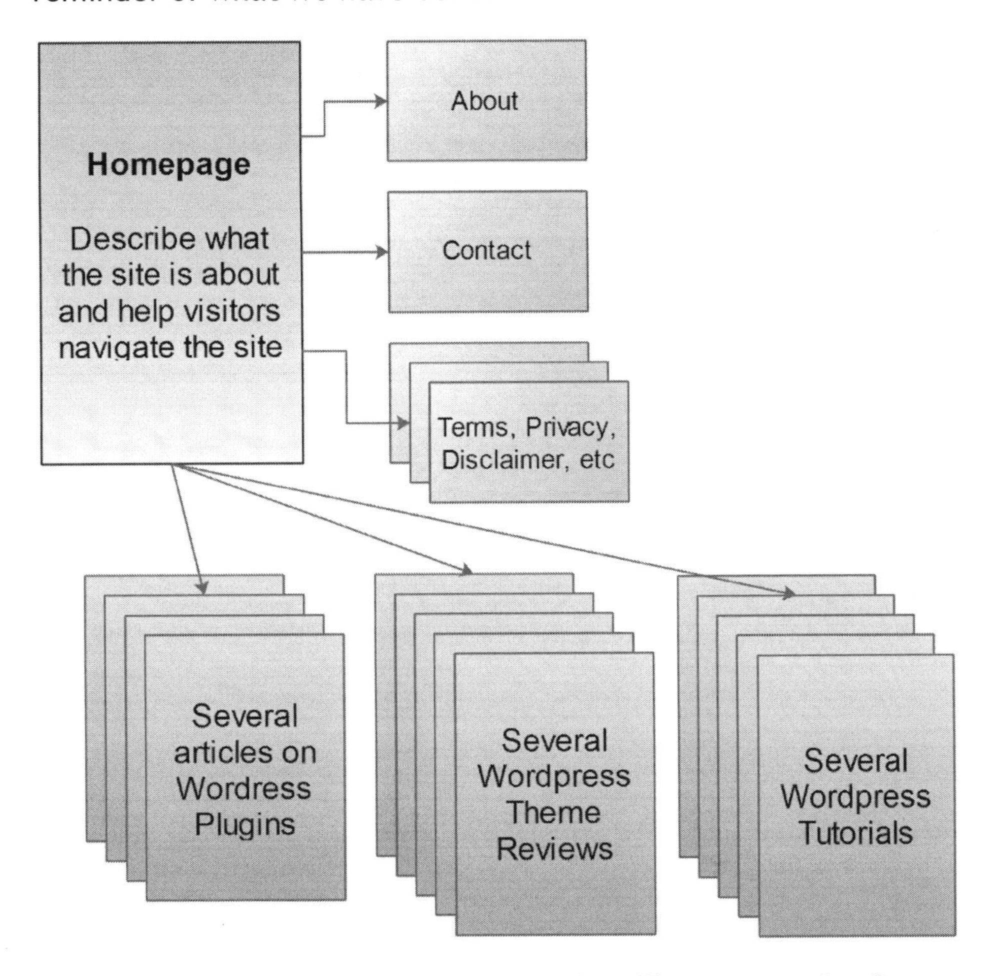

We have a homepage, with several "legal" pages, and a few categories, each with a number of posts.

However, there is another structure that some people prefer, and I want to show you how to set that up. Let's look at a diagram of this structure:

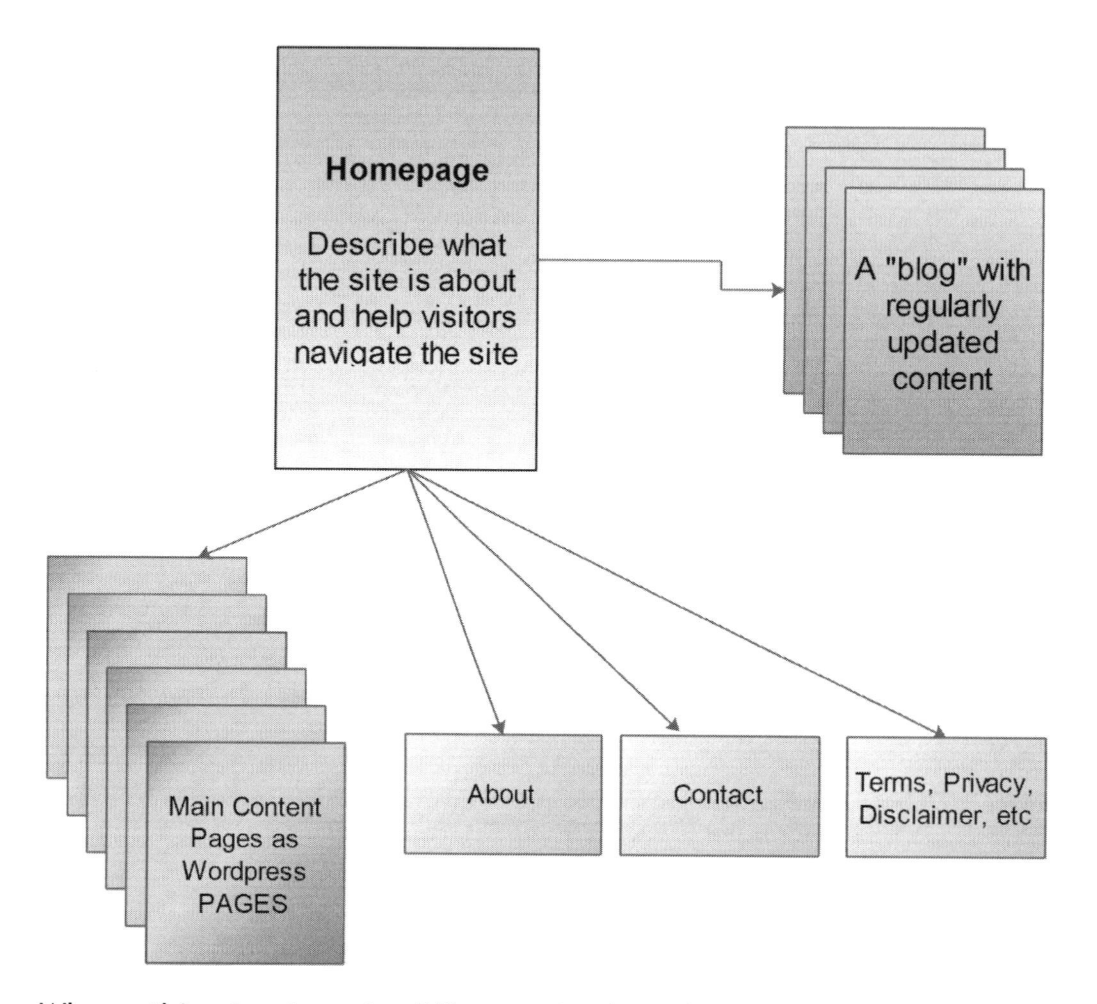

Where this structure is different, is that the main content pages of the site use Wordpress pages, not posts. Wordpress posts are used as a blog "attached" to the main site.

This type of site is typically a small site, with 5 or 6 main "static" pages. The blog is then used for regular updates on any topic relevant to the blog.

Let's look at an example.

If you were an author, a small website could help showcase your books and offer a little more information about you and your interests to your readers. A contact form would allow your readers to have direct contact with you, and comments on posts would allow a two-way dialogue (a unique opportunity for many authors, since most never get to meet the people that buy their books).

You might want to have the following pages on your site:

- About
- Contact

- My Books
- Events

These could all be set up as Wordpress Pages, because they are all fairly independent of one another.

You might then want to have a blog where you can post short stories, interesting anecdotes, interesting background information on stories you are writing, etc. If these were done with posts, your visitors could then leave comments and interact with you and give you feedback on your work.

In this scenario, it makes perfect sense to use Wordpress pages for the small number of static pages on your site, and Wordpress posts for more regular updates, and interacting with your readers.

We already know how to set up pages, so setting up the basic structure of this site is easy. Just create a Wordpress page for each of those 4 pages we mentioned above.

For the blog, you might just like to use one category, or use several. This will depend on what you intend to do with the blog. However you structure the blog, Wordpress makes it easy to showcase your blog postings.

The first step is to create a new Wordpress Page called "Blog" (or whatever you want to call it). Leave the contents of the page empty and publish it.

Now, under the **Settings** menu, click **Reading**.

In the same way we set the homepage to be a static page, we can set a static page to showcase our "posts", which in this case is the author's "blog" section.

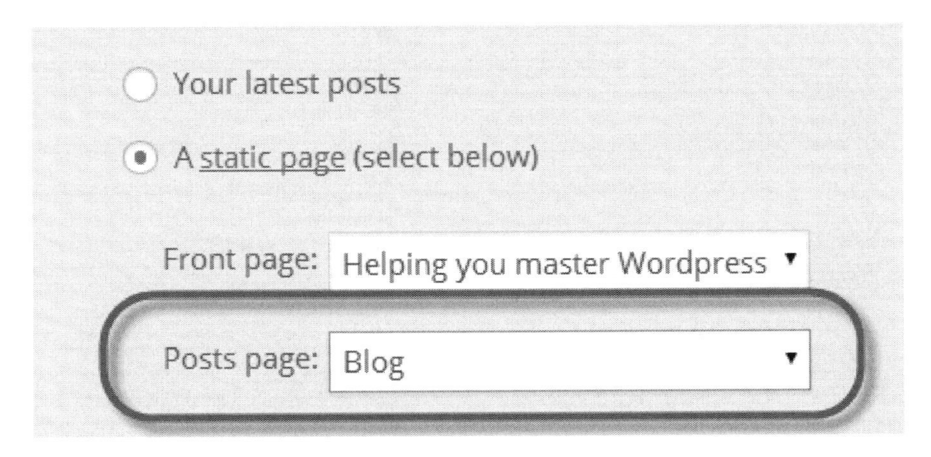

Just select your Blog page from the **Posts page** section of the form, and save changes.

The author could now create the website top navigation menu to include a link to the blog page. Visitors clicking on that would see all of the latest blog posts (from all categories if there is more than one) in chronological order, starting with the most recent.

This is the menu bar from the site of an author I know:

He has used Wordpress pages for his About, Books, Interests, Links, Contact & Disclaimer. He then created a Wordpress Page to host his blog posts, and added all of these pages to the top navigation menu.

Even though one page is dedicated to all blog posts, if you use multiple categories for your posts, you can still use a category widget (if you want to) to help your visitors find specific posts.

NOTE: Anyone can set up a "Blog" page if they want a single location to display all recent posts in chronological order. On a traditional Wordpress site where the latest 10 posts are shown on the homepage, this type of blog page is not really needed because your homepage acts as a blog page. However, if you use a static page for your homepage (like on RapidWPSites.com), then a blog page might be useful for your visitors.

I've added one so you can see how that would look on my site.

I've called the menu item "What's New?", so that visitors intuitively know that the link will take them to a place on the site with new content.

Since my Wordpress page is called "blog", when I added this blog page to the menu, Wordpress automatically labeled the menu item "Blog". However, it is easy to change the "navigation label":

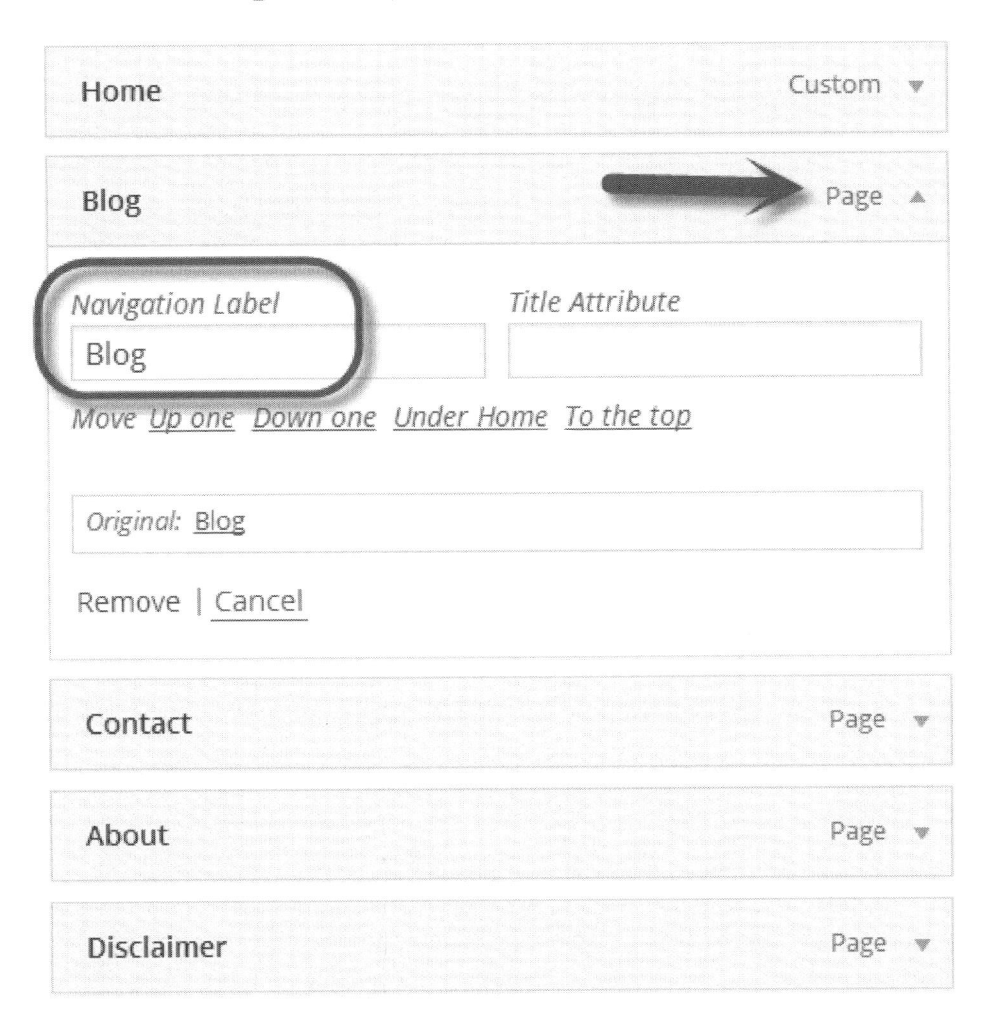

Just open up the settings for that menu item, and rename the **Navigation Label**. Remember to save the menu after making any changes. Here is my top navigation menu now:

Click on the "**What's New?**" link and you'll see the latest posts on the site.

Beginner's Mistakes

There are a number of simple mistakes that beginners make when they build a site with Wordpress. This chapter lists some of those mistakes.

Post & Page Titles

No two posts should have the same title on your site. No two pages should have the same title either. A post should not use the same title as a page, and vice versa. All post and pages must have unique titles.

If you use the same title on two documents, Google will think you have two articles about the same topic, and wonder why. When Google starts wondering about your site, you are at the top of a very slippery slope.

In addition, if you give two posts the same title, the filename automatically generated by Wordpress will mean both filenames are nearly the same. Wordpress handles duplicate filenames by adding numbers to the end. If you created three pages with the title "contact", Wordpress would give them these filenames:

1. Contact
2. Contact-1
3. Contact-2

Tags & Category Names

Never use the same word or phrase for a category name AND a tag. A phrase can be EITHER a category OR a tag, but not both.

Similarly, never use a word or phrase that you have used as a page/post title as either a tag or category.

For example, suppose you had a health site.

If you had a category called diabetes, you could not use the word diabetes as a post/page title, or a tag. You could have a page/post title or tag that included the word diabetes as a longer phrase, like "gestational diabetes", or "pre-diabetes".

Using Tags

Never use more than 4 or 5 tags on a post. Tags should be there to help visitors, so giving visitors long lists of tags will make them useless. Also, indiscriminate use of tags means you'll end up with a lot of tag pages, each listing very few posts.

Remember what I said earlier in the book. No tag should be used if it is only being used on one post (or two, and maybe even three depending on the size of your site).

Privacy Settings

There is a setting in Wordpress that will basically make your site invisible to the search engines.

Go to **Reading** in the **Settings** menu.

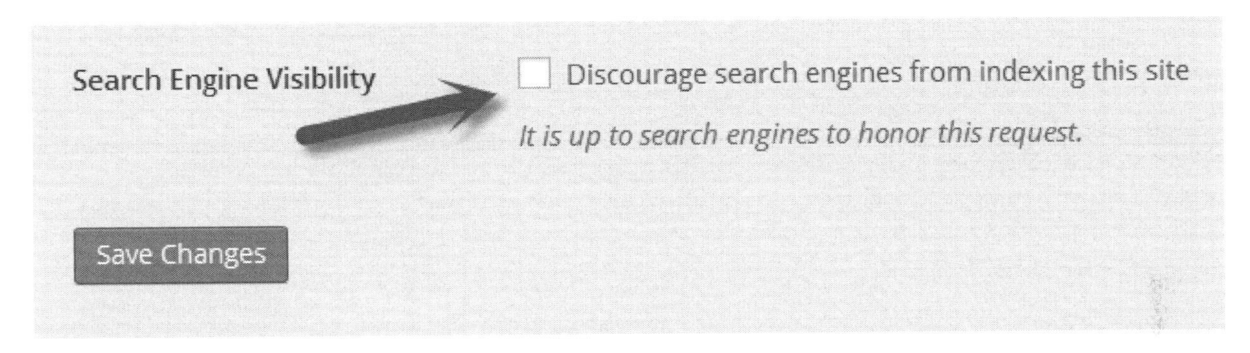

This check box is there to stop search engines finding, spidering and including your site in the search results. Some webmasters use this when they are initially building a site, and then uncheck it when they want to open the site to the public. However, this is not necessary. I'd recommend you leave this unchecked at all times.

If you do find that your site isn't getting indexed and included in Google, do check this setting.

Spam Comments

Over the years, I have seen a number of my students committing this sin. They'll approve a comment on their site, simply because the comment is flattering to them. We've talked about this type of comment before. My advice to you is simple. No matter how few comments you may have, NEVER approve a comment that does not add to the conversation of the post it will appear on.

NEVER!

Plugins for all occasions

We have already installed and used some great Wordpress plugins. However, there are a lot more out there. In this chapter, I'll list the plugins that I have found to be the most useful on my own sites. Some of these plugins are used literally on all of my Wordpress sites, while a couple are only used for more specific projects.

To keep this book shorter, and only teach you on a need-to-know basis, I will list the plugins with a description of what they do. If you want a more detailed tutorial on using one of these plugins, you can find it on the RapidWPSites.com website.

Wordpress SEO

Wordpress SEO is a free plugin that can help you set up your site with the search engines in mind. SEO stands for Search Engine Optimization, and although we have to be a lot more careful when doing SEO on our sites, this plugin is well worth installing. It is an extremely feature-rich plugin that gives you a fine level of control over all posts, pages, tag pages, category pages, etc. I use this on every site I build.

Pretty Link Lite

Pretty Link Lite is a free plugin that allows you to create "prettier" links from longer, "uglier" links.

Why might you want to do this?

In the next chapter we'll talk a little bit about affiliate programs and these have notoriously ugly, long links. Pretty Link Lite is great way to make those links more manageable.

Stop Spammers

Stop Spammers is a free plugin to help stop comment spam. It is a lot more sophisticated than the Growmap plugin we installed earlier and a lot more aggressive in the fight against spam. So much so in fact, that it can also stop legitimate visitors from posting. However, when you get to a certain spam threshold, this is the plugin I recommend.

Formidable Pro

Formidable Pro is a commercial plugin that allows you to create just about any type of web form for your site. While it is overkill for a simple contact form, I use this plugin to allow visitors to submit information to me, like images, guest posts, etc. Formidable Pro gives me total flexibility.

CI Backlinks

CI Backlinks is a commercial plugin that I helped develop, which automates internal site linking in the body of your articles. Internal site links help your visitors find their way around your site, but also help the search engines spider your site, and decide what the web pages on your site are about.

Dynamic Widgets

Dynamic widgets is a free plugin that allows you to choose specific pages, posts, categories etc to display widgets on. I use this on most of my sites so that I can create custom sidebars for different categories on the site. If someone is reading a post on my site about web hosting, I can make sure that they see specific web hosting advertising in the sidebar.

I also usually create a unique sidebar for my homepage.

I believe that Google prefers websites that don't have the exact same sidebars & footers on all web pages. This plugin helps you achieve that, since you can control which widgets appear on which pages, in which widgetized areas of the page.

W3 Total Cache

W3 Total cache is a free plugin to speed up your site. It is a little complicated to set up, but well worth the effort.

Wishlist Member

Wishlist Member is a commercial plugin that allows you to set up a membership site (paid or free) on your website. I use it for the training programs and courses that I create.

SimplePress

Simplepress is a free plugin that allows you to set up a forum on your site. If you want to grow a community on your website, this plugin can create a forum on your site, with a few mouse clicks.

Making Money with your website

There are a lot of different ways you can make money with your website. I won't go into too much detail in this book, but I will briefly discuss the options, and if you want more details, check out the RapidWPSites.com website.

Before we begin, I should add that all of the following forms of site monetization are free to join and do not cost anything to run on your website.

Affiliate programs

An affiliate program (sometimes called a partner program) is a good way to make some money from your site. A lot of great companies run them, and you can apply to join relevant programs.

Amazon has a great affiliate program. When you join, you can link to any product on the Amazon website from your own website, using a link that Amazon gives you. This link is long and ugly, which is where Pretty Link Lite comes in. If someone goes through your link and buys something, you get a commission.

The amount of commission you get with affiliate programs varies enormously. For example, Amazon pays around 4% - 8% of the order value, but they convert customers very well.

Other sites like Clickbank specialize in digital products (eBooks & software). The average commission is probably around 50%, but you can earn 75% commission on some products, sometimes even more than that.

Shareasale and Commission Junction are two affiliate networks I use.

An affiliate network is a company that works with other companies that want to run an affiliate program. You can sign up at Shareasale and/or Commission Junction (often just referred to as CJ), then apply to join any affiliate program on their books. Some affiliate programs will accept you immediately; others require a manual review of your site and application. However, it is typically very easy to join affiliate programs through both of these networks. If you make a commission on a network, the network collects the commissions for you, and then pays you every month or so on cleared balance.

Google Adsense

When you visit Google and search for something, the top few results are typically adverts related to what you searched for. Companies are paying for these adverts.

If you click on one of these adverts in Google, the company that paid for the advert pays Google some money. The amount they have to pay is based on the "cost per click" (or CPC) value of that advert. Adverts in more competitive niches cost more, so the CPC is higher.

Google Adsense is a program that allows you to put similar "Adsense" adverts on your website. When someone clicks on one of these Adsense adverts on your site, Google get paid the CPC by the company that owns the advert. Google then share this money with you.

Chitika

Chitika is very similar to Google Adsense. Chitika will give you code to insert into your web content, and when someone visits your pages, it will display adverts that are relevant to your content. If someone clicks through on these ads, you make a little money.

For more information on these monetization options, plus specific tutorials, see the RapidWPSites.com website.

Where to go for more help

This book covered the basics of getting a website up and running. I know you will love Wordpress, and many of you will want to do more with it than I was able to cover in this book. That is why I created the RapidWPSites.com website.

Not only did it serve as an example as I wrote this book, but it also offers a lot more help, tutorials and reviews related to Wordpress. You can also contact me directly on the site.

I do have a couple of other books you might be interested in as well – Wordpress for Beginners and Wordpress SEO.

Wordpress for Beginners was my first book on Wordpress. It goes into a lot more detail, and covers all of the options, features and screens in the Wordpress dashboard.

Wordpress SEO looks specifically at getting Wordpress sites to rank highly in the search engines.

You can find more details about both of these books at the end of this book.

Did you enjoy this book?

If you liked this book (or even if you didn't), PLEASE add a review on the Amazon website. You can find the book listing by searching Amazon for B00JGWW86W.

All the best

Andy Williams

More Information from Dr. Andy Williams

If you would like more information, tips, tutorials or advice, there are two resources you might like to consider.

The first is my free weekly newsletter over at ezSEONews.com offering tips, tutorials and advice to online marketers and webmasters. Just sign up and my newsletter, plus SEO articles, will be delivered to your inbox. I cannot always promise a weekly schedule, but I try ;)

I also run a course over at CreatingFatContent.com, where I build real websites in front of members in "real-time" using my system of SEO.

My other Kindle books

All of my books are available as Kindle books and paperbacks. You can view them all here:

http://amazon.com/author/drandrewwilliams

Here are a few of my more popular books:

Wordpress for Beginners

Do you want to build a website but scared it's too difficult?

Building a website was once the domain of computer geeks. Not anymore. WordPress makes it possible for anyone to create and run a professional looking website

While WordPress is an amazing tool, the truth is it does have a steep learning curve, even if you have built websites before using different tools. Therefore, the goal of this book is to take anyone, even a complete beginner, and get them building a professional looking website. I'll hold your hand, step-by-step, all the way.

As I was planning this book, I made one decision early on. I wanted to use screenshots of everything so that the reader wasn't left looking for something on their screen that I was describing in text. This book has plenty of screenshots. I haven't counted them all, but it must be close to 300. These images will help you find the things I am talking about. They'll help you check your settings and options against the screenshot of mine. You look, compare, and move on to the next section.

With so many screenshots, you may be concerned that the text might be a little on the skimpy side. No need to worry there. I have described every step of your journey in great detail. In all, this publication has over 35,000 words.

This book will surely cut your learning curve associated with WordPress.

Every chapter of the book ends with a "Tasks to Complete" section. By completing these tasks, you'll not only become proficient at using WordPress, but you'll become confident & enjoy using it too.

Search Amazon for **B009ZVO3H6**

Wordpress SEO

On-Page SEO for your Wordpress Site

Most websites (including blogs) share certain features that can be controlled and used to help (or hinder, especially with Google Panda & Penguin on the loose) with the on-site SEO. These features include things like the page title, headlines, body text, ALT tags and so on. In this respect, most sites can be treated in a similar manner when we consider on-site SEO.

However, different platforms have their own quirks, and WordPress is no exception. Out-of-the-box WordPress doesn't do itself any SEO favours, and can in fact cause you ranking problems, especially with the potentially huge amount of duplicate content it creates. Other problems include static, site-wide sidebars and footers, automatically generated meta tags, page load speeds, SEO issues with Wordpress themes, poorly constructed navigation, badly designed homepages, potential spam from visitors, etc. The list goes on.

This book shows you how to set up an SEO-friendly Wordpress website, highlighting the problems, and working through them with step-by-step instructions on how to fix them.

By the end of this book, your WordPress site should be well optimized, without being 'over-optimized' (which is itself a contributing factor in Google penalties).

Search Amazon for: **B00ECF70HU**

SEO 2013 & Beyond

Search Engine Optimization will never be the same again!

On February 11th, 2011, Google dropped a bombshell on the SEO community when they released the Panda update. Panda was designed to remove low quality content from the search engine results pages. The surprise to many webmasters were some of the big name casualties that got taken out by the update.

On 24th April 2012, Google went in for the kill when they released the Penguin update. Few SEOs that had been in the business for any length of time could believe the carnage that this update caused. If Google's Panda was a 1 on the Richter scale of updates, Penguin was surely a 10. It completely changed the way we needed to think about SEO.

On September 28th 2012, Google released a new algorithm update targeting exact match domains (EMDs). I have updated this book to let you know the consequences of owning EMDs, and added my own advice on choosing domain names. While I have never been a huge fan of exact match domains anyway, many other SEO books and courses teach you to use them. I'll tell you why I think those other courses and books are wrong. The EMD update was sandwiched in between another Panda update (on the 27th September) and another Penguin update (5th October).

Whereas Panda seems to penalize low quality content, Penguin is more concerned about overly aggressive SEO tactics. The stuff that SEOs had been doing for years, not only didn't work anymore, but could now actually cause your site to be penalized and drop out of the rankings. That's right, just about everything you have been taught about Search Engine Optimization in the last 10 years can be thrown out the Window. Google have moved the goal posts.

I have been working in SEO for around 10 years at the time of writing, and have always tried to stay within the guidelines laid down by Google. This has not always been easy because to compete with other sites, it often meant using techniques that Google frowned upon. Now, if you use those techniques, Google is likely to catch up with you and demote your rankings. In this book, I want to share with you the new SEO. **The SEO for 2014 and Beyond.**

Search Amazon for **B0099RKXE8**

An SEO Checklist

A step-by-step plan for fixing SEO problems with your web site

A step-by-step plan for fixing SEO problems with your web site

Pre-Panda and pre-Penguin, Google tolerated certain activities. Post-Panda and post-Penguin, they don't. As a result, they are now enforcing their Webmaster Guidelines which is something that SEOs never really believed Google would do! Essentially, Google have become far less tolerant of activities that they see as rank manipulation.

As webmasters, we have been given a choice. Stick to Google's rules, or lose out on free traffic from the world's biggest search engine.

Those that had abused the rules in the past got a massive shock. Their website(s), which may have been at the top of Google for several years, dropped like a stone. Rankings gone, literally overnight!

To have any chance of recovery, you MUST clean up that site. However, for most people, trying to untangle the SEO mess that was built up over several years is not always easy. Where do you start?

That's why this book was written. It provides a step-by-step plan to fix a broken site. This book contains detailed checklists plus an explanation of why those things are so important.

The checklists in this book are based on the SEO that I use on a daily basis. It's the SEO I teach my students, and it's the SEO that I know works. For those that embrace the recent changes, SEO has actually become easier as we no longer have to battle against other sites whose SEO was done 24/7 by an automated tool or an army of cheap labor. Those sites have largely been removed, and that has leveled the playing field.

If you have a site that lost its rankings, this book gives you a step-by-step plan and checklist to fix problems that are common causes of ranking penalties.

Search Amazon for **B00BXFAULK**

Kindle Publishing

Format, Publish & Promote your books on Kindle

Why Publish on Amazon Kindle?

Kindle publishing has captured the imagination of aspiring writers. Now, more than at any other time in our history, an opportunity is knocking. Getting your books published no longer means sending out hundreds of letters to publishers and agents. It no longer means getting hundreds of rejection letters back. Today, you can write and publish your own books on Amazon Kindle without an agent or publisher.

Is it Really Possible to Make a Good Income as an Indie Author?

The fact that you are reading this book description tells me you are interested in publishing your own material on Kindle. You may have been lured here by promises of quick riches. Well, I have good news and bad. The bad news is that publishing and profiting from Kindle takes work and dedication. Don't just expect to throw up sub-par material and make a killing in sales. You need to produce good stuff to be successful at this. The good news is that you can make a very decent living from writing and publishing on Kindle.

My own success with Kindle Publishing

As I explain at the beginning of this book, I published my first Kindle book in August 2012, yet by December 2012, just 5 months later, I was making what many people consider being a full time income. As part of my own learning experience, I setup a Facebook page in July 2012 to share my Kindle publishing journey (there is a link to the Facebook page inside this book). On that Facebook page, I shared the details of what I did, and problems I needed to overcome. I also shared my growing income reports, and most of all, I offered help to those who asked for it. What I found was a huge and growing audience for this type of education, and ultimately, that's why I wrote this book.

What's in this Book?

This book covers what I have learned on my journey and what has worked for me. I have included sections to answer the questions I myself asked, as well as those questions people asked me. This book is a complete reference manual for successfully formatting, publishing & promoting your books on Amazon Kindle. There is even a section for non-US publishers because there is stuff there you specifically need to know. I see enormous potential in Kindle Publishing, and in 2013 I intend to grow this side of my own business. Kindle publishing has been liberating for me and I am sure it will be for you too.

Search Amazon for **B00BEIX34C**

Self-Publishing on Createspace

Convert & Publish your books on Createspace

Self-publishing your own work is easier than at any time in our history. Amazon's Kindle platform and now Createspace allow us to self-publish our work, with zero costs up front.

Createspace is a fantastic opportunity for writers. You publish your book, and if someone buys it, Createspace print it and send it to the customer. All the author needs to do is wait to be paid. How's that for hands-free and risk-free publishing?

This book takes you step-by-step through my own process for publishing. Topics covered include:

- Basic Text Formatting
- Which Font?
- Links and formatting checks
- Page Numbering in Word
- Adding a new title to Createspace
- Price calculator and deciding on Trim size
- Image DPI requirements
- Paint Shop Pro conversion process
- Common formatting problems
- Book Cover Templates
- Creating the cover with Photoshop Elements
- Creating the cover in Paint Shop Pro
- Submitting the book & cover to Createspace
- Expanded Distribution?

The book also includes links to a number of video tutorials created by the author to help you understand the formatting and submission process.

Search Amazon for **B00HG0GE0C**

CSS for Beginners

Learn CSS with detailed instructions, step-by-step screenshots and video tutorials showing CSS in action on real sites

Most websites and blogs you visit use cascading style sheets (CSS) for everything from fonts selection & formatting, to layout & design. Whether you are building WordPress sites or traditional HTML websites, this book aims to take the complete beginner to a level where they are comfortable digging into the CSS code and making changes to their own site. This book will show you how to make formatting & layout changes to your own projects quickly and easily.

The book covers the following topics:

- Why CSS is important
- Classes, Pseudo Classes, Pseudo Elements & IDs
- The Float property
- Units of Length
- Using DIVs
- Tableless Layouts, including how to create 2-column and 3-column layouts
- The Box Model
- Creating Menus with CSS
- Images & background images

The hands on approach of this book will get YOU building your own Style Sheets from scratch. Also included in this book:

- Over 160 screenshots and 20,000 words detailing ever step you need to take.
- Full source code for all examples shown.
- Video Tutorials.

The video tutorials accompanying this book show you:

- How to investigate the HTML & CSS behind any website.
- How to experiment with your own design in real time, and only make the changes permanent on your site when you are ready.

A basic knowledge of HTML is recommended, although all source code from the book can be downloaded and used as you work through the book.

Search Amazon for **B00AFV44NS**

Migrating to Windows 8.1

For computer users without a touch screen, coming from XP, Vista or Windows 7

Review: "What Microsoft should buy and give away now to drive sales"

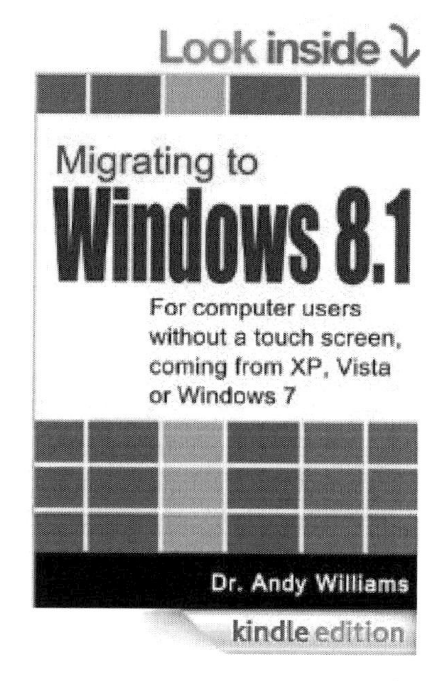

New PCs are coming pre-installed with Windows 8, Microsoft's new incarnation of the popular operating system. The problem is, the PCs it is installed on are not usually equipped with the piece of hardware that Windows 8 revolves around - a touch screen.

Windows 8 is probably the least user-friendly version of the operating system ever released. It's almost like two different operating systems merged together. From the lack of a start menu, to features that only really make sense on a tablet or phone, Windows 8 has a lot of veteran Windows users scratching their heads. If you are one of them, then this book is for you.

After a quick tour of the new user interface, the book digs deeper into the features of Windows 8, showing you what everything does, and more importantly, how to do the things you used to do on older versions of Windows. The comprehensive "How to" section answers a lot of the questions new users have, and there's also a complete keyboard shortcut list for reference.

If you are migrating to Windows 8 from XP, Vista or Windows 7, then this book may just let you keep your hair as you learn how to get the most out of your computer. Who knows, you may even get to like Windows 8.

Search Amazon for **B00CJ8AD9E**